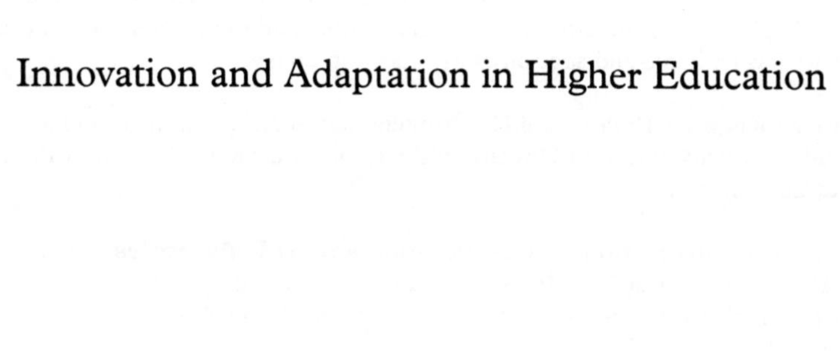

Innovation and Adaptation in Higher Education

Higher Education Policy Series
Edited by Maurice Kogan

Higher education is now the subject of far reaching and rapid policy change. This series will be of value to those who have to manage that change, as well as to consumers and evaluators of higher education in the UK and elsewhere. It offers information and analysis of new developments in a concise and usable form. It also provides reflective accounts of the impacts of higher education policy. Higher education administrators, governors and policy makers will use it, as well as students and specialists in education policy.

Maurice Kogan is Professor of Government and Social Administration at Brunel University and Joint Director of the Centre for the Evaluation of Public Policy and Practice.

Integrating Europe though Co-operation among Universities
The Experiences of theTEMPUS Programme
Barbara M. Kehm, Friedhelm Maiworm, Albert Over, Ronny Reisz, Wolfgang Steube and Ulrich Teichler
ISBN 1 85302 495 3
Higher Education Policy 43

European Dimensions
Education, Training and the European Union
John Field
ISBN 1 85302 432 5
Higher Education Policy 39

Higher Education Policy Series 22

Innovation and Adaptation in Higher Education

The Changing Conditions of Advanced Teaching and Learning in Europe

Edited by Claudius Gellert

Jessica Kingsley Publishers
London and Philadelphia

Sponsored by the Commission of the European Communities and the European University Institute, Florence

---

First published in the United Kingdom in 1999 by
Jessica Kingsley Publishers Ltd
116 Pentonville Road,
London N1 9JB, England
and
325 Chestnut Street,
Philadelphia, PA 19106, USA

www.jkp.com

Library of Congress Cataloging in Publication Data

A CIP catalogue record for this book is available from the Library of Congress

British Library Cataloguing in Publication Data

A CIP catalogue record for this book is available from the British Library

ISBN 1 85302 535 6

Printed and Bound in Great Britain by
Athenaeum Press, Gateshead, Tyne and Wear

Contents

Preface

The present volume brings together a collection of contributions about recent changes in the realm of teaching and learning in European systems of higher education. The 1970s and 1980s can perhaps be seen as periods of major structural reforms and differentiation which were accompanied by fundamental processes of functional change, for instance, by expansion of educational opportunity, increased responsiveness to industrial demands and above all the emergence of new forms of non-university provisions of advanced learning. In recent years, however, the emphasis has shifted towards a closer investigation and assessment of the internal organisation and workings of higher education institutions. Government interference has increased almost everywhere, and the organisation of teaching and learning has received particular attention.

One of the conclusions we can draw from the papers presented here is that the change taking place usually is incremental; it reflects the interplay between internal and external pressures. An aspect all of the papers clearly have in common is the important issue of institutional vulnerability, motivating many of the colleagues to analyse the pressures that have accumulated for university staff and the effects these had on research for example.

In many areas the problems facing continental European higher education are quite similar, and differ considerably from the situation in the United Kingdom. But in one important respect, continental universities share a more favourable fate than their British counterparts. They are, despite their numerous deficiencies, enjoying a large degree of esteem and support by the public as well as their governments. This reflects a general understanding of the vital role of this institution for the economic and socio-political future. For someone working in a British university it seems odd that this academic system, which in comparison with Europe is one of the most successful in preserving high standards of quality and efficiency in its organisation of teaching and learning, is at the same time among the least publicly appreciated. Of those who have, besides the contributors, helped me in preparing this volume, I would in particular like to mention the following: D. Brewis, D. Detring, E. Leitner, R. Morgan, A. Sprokkereef, and A. Lankester-Owen of Jessica Kingsley Publishers.

Claudius Gellert

Introduction

The Changing Conditions of Teaching and Learning in European Higher Education

Claudius Gellert

Differentiation

Perhaps the single most important influence on curricular and other organisational aspects of institutions of higher education in Europe is the fact that the traditional homogeneous university systems have become diversified through the development of alternative sectors in higher education. In many countries more practically oriented tertiary institutions have been created which are cheaper than the conventional universities; more responsive to economic and technological needs of industries and the employment system; and socially more open by offering second chances to mature students and formerly disadvantaged sections of the population, with shorter study periods, higher teaching loads for the professors and less emphasis on fundamental in favour of applied research. In some systems internal processes of differentiation have also taken and are taking place; for instance, in both Spain and Italy recent reforms provide for short courses within universities.

The organisation of teaching and learning has been affected through this development in several ways. First of all, these new alternative sectors in higher education have demonstrated that higher education and academic degrees can be achieved through much more tightly organised curricula, study programmes and examination systems than had been usual at universities. In Germany, for instance, courses at *Fachhochschulen* normally last between three and four years, while an average study period for a first degree at the university now embraces seven years. This has sparked off a lively debate both in the UK and in other countries about the efficiency of traditional university training. It has been argued that in times of financial stringencies and increasing numbers of new entrants in higher education, societies cannot any longer afford the more amorphous educational structures at universities and that they should become more accountable to society and the taxpayer. One of the considerations taken into account by those analysing differing national settings in the following contributions was therefore to determine to what extent individual European countries observe changes within their higher education which can be explained in such a way.

Degree structures

Another determining factor shaping teaching and learning in higher education, exists in the traditional prevalence of specific structures of degree courses and programmes in the respective systems: because the starting point, as it were, of higher education development within respective systems determines to a large extent the amount of change which is necessary under pressures and influences from outside and sometimes from inside. In systems which already possess a well-defined curricular and degree pattern – such as in Britain, where there is a fairly clear distinction between institutional executions of university functions like disciplinary-based personality development on the undergraduate level or research training on the graduate level, or the extramural completion of professional training under the auspices of professional associations – the likelihood for immediate change under the influence of new expectations, say, from the labour market, is much smaller than in systems with a considerably looser structural arrangement. In Germany, for example, with its traditionally largely uncoordinated system of degree programmes and course structures, pressures have been considerably increased over the years for more responsiveness to perceived needs of the economy and the labour market. Thus, the Anglo-American systems in particular have served as paradigms for the reform and innovation debates which have been taking place in Germany and other continental European countries for a long time, and in which many observers have argued that a distinction between undergraduate and graduate studies is needed. As a first step, an initial professional qualification should be achieved, but research-oriented training should only happen on the second level. It remains to be seen, also through the accounts given by the analysts of this volume, to what extent such efforts and suggestions have been put into practice already, or are planned for the near future.

Political reforms

A major determinant of curricular and organisational changes in higher education has, of course, been the influence which national governments have exercised through large-scale reform programmes or single pieces of legislation. Such reforms were visible practically in all European countries over the last ten to fifteen years. In some of the Mediterranean countries these reforms had primarily to do with the attempt to build up diversified provisions of higher education (including more practically oriented training institutions) which would be compatible and competitive with other European systems. In France, primarily in the reform of 1984, this process was concerned with the organisation and vocationalisation of courses of the first cycle. In Germany yet another emphasis was pursued, i.e. a swing to a more deregulated system of higher education (the breaking up of traditional authority structures) in the form of the first Federal Framework Law for Higher Education (HRG) of 1976 and then a return to more strictly and tightly organised decision-making processes in the form of the revised HRG of 1985. At present, political debates centre on the perceived need for a third version of the HRG.

The most interesting case is perhaps the British one, where in the White Paper of 1992 the government had to concede that the assimilation between polytechnics and universities had led to a virtual breakdown of the binary system, and opted for an integrated higher education system similar to that in Australia. The question there is whether the original intentions behind the creation of a diversified dual system with a more practically oriented segment of higher education are not valid any longer, or whether, on the contrary, the needs and expectations from the economy and the labour market have perhaps even increased in that direction. In the latter case this would perhaps lead to a vacuum in the British higher education system which could be filled by the private 'third sector', as the corporate classroom provisions have been called by the OECD. We will return to the case of the integrated British system later.

Secondary education

One of the most important features, but also one of the most neglected ones, in explaining course structures and academic programmes in European higher education is the relationship between secondary and tertiary institutions. There are basically two models of this relationship. The first is perhaps best illustrated by reference to Great Britain, where there is a fairly tight connection between universities and secondary schools. Not only do the higher education institutions require an applicant for a study place to have passed A-levels in the respective subject which he or she intends to study (at least where such a subject exists at A-level), but the universities are also directly involved in the development and definition of what should be required, taught and examined at upper-secondary school levels.

The counter-model used to exist in Germany, but is now probably more prevalent in countries such as Italy, where the relationship between secondary schooling and university training is still extremely loose. In those countries it is assumed that a rather generalist secondary examination in a number of subjects, secures a broad enough education to enable the candidate to study in any area at university. In Germany the situation has changed since 1976, because of an upper-secondary school reform which brought about a reduction of the number of subjects which had to be passed in the *Abitur.* But this specialisation of subjects – and here Germany differs from Britain – does not direct the secondary-school leaver into a certain subject area at university, but he or she is still free to choose among all the available disciplines. Thus, the contributions to this volume also attempt to determine to what extent the European countries in their models of transition from secondary to tertiary education approximate any of these two paradigms, or whether they have developed a significantly different approach.

Expectations from the labour market

In the past there were two main political arguments for higher education expansion: first, the 'social demand approach' (i.e. the wish to increase educational opportunities for larger proportions of the population); and, second, the 'manpower requirement approach' which emphasised the need for more highly qualified personnel in times of rapid economic and technological change. However, with regard to micro-level consequences on course programmes and structures, the latter dimension is more important, as the 'social demand approach', if it is successful, may lead to any kind of higher education enlargement. The 'manpower requirement approach', in contrast, takes into account specific demands and expectations from industry and the labour market, which, in turn, may lead to innovation and reorganisation processes in curricular and degree matters. In this respect, there have been many recent developments on a European level which have to be accounted for, and which are being addressed in many of the analyses presented here.

European integration

While all the above aspects have been important influential determinants of possible changes in the area of the organisation of teaching and learning in European higher education, it is the European integration process itself which will be one of the most consequential determining factors in the near future. Because despite a general lack of formalised legal legitimacy in the area of education, including higher education, the Commission of the European Communities has in recent years managed to influence higher education processes to a considerable extent. This is primarily due to the passing of the Single European Act and the Treaty of Maastricht, as well as to decisions by the European Court which have made higher education a legitimate object of policy making on the European level.

Apart from these legal frameworks, a whole range of initiatives on behalf of the Commission has for several years brought about a gradual and increasingly manifest change in the course structures of the higher education systems in Europe. Although still largely unnoticed by the general public, there exists an increasing pressure towards harmonisation and integration on that level. That pressure stems primarily from a large number of initiatives and voluntary participation schemes which have been brought about by the Commission, such as exchange scholarships for large numbers of students and teaching personnel, interactive schemes between universities and industry and research support programmes. The ERASMUS programme in particular has been putting many European universities and departments under pressure to adjust their course structures and study programmes to the experiences, expectations and quality levels which exist in other systems. This is because the students who participate in the ERASMUS exchange and scholarship scheme can reasonably expect that the courses which they have participated in and the exams which they have passed in another country will be acknowledged and accepted with equivalent credits at their own home university. This in turn forces the departments at home to reorganise, so that credits which have been acquired in another system fit into existing course and examination structures. So far, much has happened 'behind the backs' of governments and the public, but to the extent that such consequences and measures concerning organisational change in higher education will become apparent, the need to reconcile them with national and regional traditions and structures will increase. Comparative analyses of European systems of higher education, therefore, cannot but take a close look at these Community-led developments.

Student learning as a measure of institutional efficiency

Before turning to a short account of the contributions in this volume, there is one essential area of higher education, which in a comparative perspective is often insufficiently dealt with: the problem of institutional quality and efficiency. Since present European higher education is so highly differentiated, as has already been pointed out, it is difficult to compare the advantages and disadvantages of the respective systems, to identify differing modes of defining and forming academic competency among them, and to clarify possible areas in which they can learn from one another.

In order to understand the present one has to look at the past, and here we may identify three major models which have influenced the developments elsewhere. First, for more than three hundred years there existed an ideal of higher education in England which aimed at the formation of a student's character or personality not only through learning, but also through a specific communal lifestyle and extra-curricular activities. This can be termed the 'personal development model', or the ideal of a liberal education, and has in the past been associated with Cardinal Newman and the Oxford movement. In Germany, in contrast, there emerged during the nineteenth century the Humboldtian or 'research model', i.e. a specific understanding of gaining empirical knowledge and the attempt to utilise it directly for teaching purposes. While the English ideal was primarily aimed at the student, the German one concentrated on the discipline. The third major system is the Napoleonic one in France, which can be called the 'professional training model', since it places most emphasis on learning for the professions, leaving research mostly outside the universities (and the *Grandes Ecoles*).

The above models are not exclusive, but still represent a predominant feature within each national structure. Most Mediterranean and Eastern European countries followed the French model; other European states tended towards the German paradigm. The US (on the undergraduate level) and many other English-speaking countries were strongly influenced by the English paradigm.

A close look at German developments demonstrates that the Humboldtian ideals not only led to serious difficulties during the nineteenth and the first half of the twentieth centuries, but also prevented a fundamental reform of the German universities after World War II. In Germany, as elsewhere in Europe, there is open access to the university for all with the required secondary school qualifications. Students can choose and change universities freely; they also determine when they wish to take exams. Professors, also protected by Humboldtian principles such as the 'freedom of teaching and learning', mostly teach whatever they like, and hardly engage in personal tutoring of students. The result is, besides a total overcrowding of the tertiary institutions, a lack of curricular tranparency, weak course management, an average study period of seven years for a first degree, and a high drop-out rate. In other systems with loose organisational arrangements, like Italy, the consequences are similar.

Therefore, if we attempt to compare the relative merits and the efficiency of academic enterprises, we should not only consider the usual parameters of the research paradigm – such as research output, citation indices and the like – as important as they are for the definition of standards within the profession. Rather, the organisation of the learning process of students should receive primary attention. Because so far, it seems, neither universities engaged in student exchange programmes, nor employers trying to recruit in a European labour market, nor governments or other authorities really understand what a specific period of studies in one system in comparison with another implies with regard to the mediation of varying degrees of social and professional competency.

The latter, it can be argued, is primarily influenced by such parameters as workload, intensity of supervision and counselling, input of individual effort, output in the form of papers and exams, as well as extra-curricular activities and a communal lifestyle of teachers and students. The ultimate measure of quality in higher education, it could thus be argued, consists in institutionalised mechanisms for assuring large degrees of individual effort and competency. Indeed, the aims of higher learning are then, not least for purposes of transnational comparisons, more adequately described in terms of *how*, rather than *what* students are made to study.

These aims, however, are not only clearly contained in the function of personality development or liberal education, leading to the formation of social competency or generic skills. This conception, in the Anglo-American tradition, is also closely intertwined with expectations of the labour market for the determination of what counts as high-quality output in higher education. Increasingly, there is evidence that the employment system on the Continent also demands a revision of a too narrowly conceptualised curriculum and is interested in broad social and professional competences, i.e. in disciplined and systematically working graduates with transferable skills such as leadership qualities, who possess the ability to methodologically approach problems and who can be trained in the workplace for specific topical requirements.

It was asked earlier whether quality comparisons can be facilitated, and whether we can learn from one another in the field of higher education. To the extent that it is the organisation of learning (and teaching) which ultimately determines a university's efficiency (while the research paradigm on its own could well be pursued in academies and research institutes), it seems that the heirs of Humboldt are gradually moving in the direction of Newman. In this fundamental respect, therefore, the English ideal of higher education, in comparison with many Continental European models, has perhaps more to be said for it than is often acknowledged.

The contributions to this volume

The following contributions attempt to address some of the problems and considerations which have been referred to above. Obviously they not only differ to some degree in their respective methodological approaches, but are all specific because of the wide historically determined variation in structures and developments. However, this is not only an unavoidable restrictive framework, but by the same token also the very reason for the diversity and distinctiveness of the national conditions which make the European landscape of higher education institutions such a fascinating research field.

Thus, the first account, appropriately, is strongly historically oriented. In his introduction to the paper 'Utilitarianism by Increment: Disciplinary Differences and Higher Education Reform in France',

Guy Neave goes back in time to find the roots of the French education system and especially the role of the *Grandes Ecoles*. In 1775 the *Ecole des Ponts et Chaussées* was established among others to provide a high level of technical and vocational training. This vocational impulse in French higher education found a place outside universities which in fact had been closed down in a series of decrees between 1791 and 1793. Other schools were established and what they had in common was a highly technical orientation, on the one hand, and the purpose of training a technical élite in knowledge intended to apply to defence, administration, diplomacy and schooling, on the other. Today still, the private and public sector *Grandes Ecoles* are highly selective with admission on the basis of competitive entry examinations, and they draw their students from another uniquely French educational institution, the *Classes Preparatoires aux Grandes Ecoles*.

The French education system is involved in a massive expansion. In 1980 20 per cent of the age group cohort went to university; in 1989 this was 38.5 per cent, and the percentage at present is increasing dramatically as a result of the excellent performance of upper secondary education.

Universities have to deal with an increased demand for change from the economy and changing expectations from parents and pupils. The government sets the framework conditions for diplomas and degrees and has central control over state diplomas. Parallel vocational tracks to existing courses and courses over two years have been introduced which can be followed after a one-year certificate of university studies. The paper concludes that steady adjustment may be possible when change is introduced without much public interest or pressure.

Mary Henkel and **Maurice Kogan** in their paper 'Changes in Curriculum and Institutional Structures: Responses to Outside Influences in Higher Education Institutions', discuss the way in which the internal workings and products of higher education institutions in the UK are affected by external pressures, including those of central government and the world of employment.

First, some attention is paid to the political and resource pressures on higher education institutions (HEIs). It is argued that the UK is a strong case of the power of external influence because the role of its central authorities has changed from that of providing a resource and political frame for institutional autonomy, to the sternest forms of governmental prescription. Government pressures on curriculum content and new policies on quality assurance (like the Academic Audit Unit) are discussed. The paper also points at pressures from two forms of market mechanism, both reinforced by reductions in resources for public and university institutions, marketing of courses and the system of funding which requires bidding for each student place. Other recent phenomena are the pressure for managerialism and efficiency placed on the leadership of institutions of higher education and selectivity in the distribution of funds.

The second part of the paper is based on the results of a Brunel University study and discusses changes in the curriculum. As a tool to assess the aims of curricula the paper uses two basic models of curriculum organisation, the individualistic and the directed.

Tony Becher and **Ronald Barnett** address 'The Reshaping of the Academic Curriculum in the United Kingdom'. An attempt is being made to get a sense of the dynamics between society and the higher education curriculum: what are the messages from society, how are they received and what changes take place at the level of the curriculum?

A number of curriculum changes are currently being introduced by higher education institutions, including less specialised undergraduate courses, credit transfer arrangements, access programmes, distance learning, interdisciplinary curricula and modular degree programmes. The take-up of these innovations has been uneven across subjects and between institutions. The incremental nature of the curricular change is in a large part a consequence of decentralisation. In general, institutions lower down the hierarchy of British higher education (polytechnics and post-war universities) have had greater recourse to innovative programmes.

The paper examines changes in four disciplines: economics, engineering, history and physics. In order to shape the discussion the authors adopt a framework to order their material. They adopt categories along one dimension, subject-specific developments and cross-subject developments; and along the other dimension, intrinsic and extrinsic factors. The analysis of the four disciplines shows that they have all fared differently in the context of British higher education. Even when the same general label can be attached to innovative developments in different fields, that label will often have a distinctive meaning. At the micro level, subtle distinctions emerge which are effectively concealed at the macro level. Academic status does perhaps play some part in readiness for innovation. Physics, for example, has so far been able to resist change, while engineering, which in Britain enjoys a lower status, has innovated to preserve its institutional standing.

Whatever the causes, it is clear to the authors of the paper that curricular innovation in British higher education is characterised more by piecemeal, specific, subject-by-subject change than by grand overall design. Campaigns for change by system-wide planners or reformist groups have had only a marginal impact on everyday curricular concerns of staff and students. Higher education remains a bottom-heavy enterprise, and as such is not easily receptive to attempts at bottom-down reformation.

Ewald Berning, in his contribution 'Impacts of Social and Political Changes on Higher Education Curricula: Selected Examples from Germany', attempts to underline structural conditions and backgrounds causing and enabling changes and adaptions in higher education curricula. The first part of the paper briefly addresses the philosophy of German universities, the competence of the *Länder* in the field of education and the double character of German institutions of higher education both as state institutions and corporations under public law. Since 1945, German higher education saw first a period of reconstruction and then, in the 1960s, an expansion. Higher education curricula were influenced most by the decision at the beginning of the 1970s to found a new type of institution, the *Fachhochschule. Fachhochschulen* train their students on the basis of scientific knowledge and methods but very close to practical needs in future professional fields. Physics, economics and engineering are taught at both university and *Fachhochschule* level, while history can be studied at university only. *Fachhochschulen* try to guarantee their practical education by, among others, the following methods:

1. study contents are designed according to practical professional needs
2. professors at *Fachhochschulen* must have worked for at least five years in a position outside *Fachhochschulen* in their field of activity
3. studies at *Fachhochschulen* are organised in a 'sandwich system'
4. the *Diplomarbeit* (thesis) is very often done on the job to solve a practical problem

5. professors at *Fachhochschulen* are assisted in teaching by experts from outside.

There has always been an intensive discussion regarding in what direction and for which aims students should be trained in the various curricula and types of institutions. Universities have traditionally been more vigorous in rejecting the expectation of *Berufsfertigkeit* (vocational skills) of graduates. Gradually, a certain consensus has been achieved that higher education graduates should be *berufsfähig* (vocationally oriented).

An important problem in German universities has been the duration of studies. The first possible degree in Germany is a Master's-level degree and the question has been how to cut back on study time without introducing an intermediate graduation level such as the Anglo-American Bachelor's degree. The main demands coming from the fields of professional and industrial practice are for the 'scientification' of studies and for a more practical orientation in the curricula. Curricula in physics, economics and engineering contain many practical and profession-related elements, such as compulsory professional experience of at least six months, practical semesters, strong relations of professors with industry, close relations between faculties and professional associations and applied research in many *Diplomarbeiten*. The history curriculum, however, is less geared towards practice and profession. Their changes are mainly due to inner changes of the disciplines and conceptions themselves.

On a long-term basis, many changes in higher education curricula are a result of difficulties and opportunities in the labour market, of which this paper gives some examples. As a result of European integration, more courses are being set up in a European perspective and cross-country aspects are being introduced in many curricula.

In general, innovation and adaption in higher education curricula in Germany have proved difficult to achieve. One of the most important steps in study reforms, the founding of *Fachhochschulen*, was not radical enough, because these new institutions are not sufficiently supported in terms of funding, personnel, equipment, and teaching and research facilities. The autonomy of universities and *Fachhochschulen* in forming their curricula and to defend them against public administration and politics does on the other hand not free them from the obligations of accountability, efficiency, evaluation and reforms. It seems that in Germany a precise evaluation of teaching is necessary to find out in what direction innovation and adaptation will be needed.

Following Berning's account of the West German situation, **Einhard Rau**, in his paper 'Radical Restructuration: The Consequences of West German Interventionism for the East German System of Higher Education' deals with some of the consequences of German unification in 1990.

Looking at the Treaty on German Unity (*Einheitsvertrag*) there is no doubt that the standards in higher education of the former FRG, were meant to define the future development of the former GDR. The paper gives an overview of the probems involved in reuniting German higher education. A rough comparison of data provided in the paper shows that the FRG with a population approximately four times bigger than the population of the GDR, had about four or five times more institutions of higher education, about five or six times more graduates, about six or seven times more freshmen and nearly ten times more students. The quantitative situation therefore, does not imply major problems in building one system out of the two.

However, the situation is much more complicated. Higher education, science and research in the GDR were structured and organised quite differently from the FRG. Higher education was totally centralised and rigidly organised. Educational planning strictly followed the manpower approach. Institutions of higher education were places of education and training and not so much research institutions. Research in the GDR was mainly concentrated in the academies of sciences which existed for more or less all fields of science.

The effort to build a unified, modern system of higher education in Germany encountered several problems:

1. the changing of a planned system into a market system would necessarily bring open admission and a forseeable increase in student numbers
2. science and research in East Germany needed to be restored thereby getting rid of its ideologised parts
3. the general situation of higher education in the former GDR, with respect to the condition of buildings and equipment including the necessary machines, books, and elementary resources etc., needed significant investments.

As the two systems to be reunited meet in Berlin, the paper takes the situation there as an example for the description of restructuration of East German education and the consequences of West German interventionism. Following the *Einheitsvertrag,* the German Science Council took the initiative to implement Western standards into the East German system and was commissioned to provide the necessary data and information for the decisions to be made. The reconstruction of democratic and efficient institutions of higher education and the social care for the people working at these institutions were identified as the most urgent problems. The Science Council set up a number of disciplinary oriented evaluation commissions to evaluate institutions, their products and their future perspectives.

Some in the West German system had hoped that unification was a chance to restructure the education system in general. In the beginning of 1990 it became clear that there would not be much room for improvement and reform and that financing the reform was going to be a problem. Rau concludes that doubts must be raised whether the East German higher education system has been worse than the West German one in every respect. There are so many interests involved and so many people directly affected by the changes in the East German education system that it is hardly surprising that the restructuring process was a difficult and ineffective one, hampered by inflexibility and lack of creativity in both East and West.

The Italian system of higher education has also undergone far-reaching changes in recent years, as **Roberto Moscati** demonstrates in his paper on 'Intended and Real Changes in Italy's Higher Education System: The Case of Economics and Engineering'.

In its first section, the paper deals with the changes the Italian educational system has been undergoing in recent years, especially the introduction of the short cycle. In the second section, the study of engineering is examined in more detail, including the changes made with the introduction of the short cycle. These include new procedures for the evaluation of students and an increase of teaching personnel. The main problem that had to be addressed was how to relate the short and long cycle tracks to each other. In the third section, the discipline of economics receives attention.

Traditionally, economics in Italy has been characterised by a strong tendency towards a theoretical approach of the economic reality. In the last few years there have been several proposals for change. Courses in managerial economics are being introduced and there is a trend towards the introduction of courses which combine economics with subjects like engineering. The process of setting up a short cycle degree and the consequences for the rest of the curriculum is difficult and still underway.

Eduardo Marçal Grilo and **Manuel Carmelo Rosa**, in their contribution, deal with 'Evaluation and Organisational Change in Selected Disciplines of Portuguese Higher Education'. They address four issues: the risks of 'high speed' expansion of the private system of higher education in Portugal; modifications of the legal and political framework of the system; new curricular developments resulting from European agreements; and finally, fundamental modifications in engineering training courses.

The rapid growth of the private system of higher education is a result of an increasing number of students who are seeking entrance to public higher education and who come up against a *numerus clausus.* The private institutions attract (part-time) teaching staff from the public sector and charge high fees. The quality of these institutions should be a concern, but there is a 'silent conspiracy' not to address the problem as all participants in the process have good reasons not to criticise it. The government believes that the market will solve the problem, but the author of the paper calls for an evaluation procedure to be set up. Recent laws have granted larger autonomy to the university institutions and polytechnics. In practice this means that these institutions can now:

1. establish administrative and scientific governing bodies as well as appoint their heads
2. define criteria for the selection of students
3. create new training courses
4. plan the development of the institution
5. select and recruit academic and non-academic staff
6. obtain alternative financial resources such as research and consultation and from the student user an increased income in fees.

Difficulties involved in implementing these changes are the financial constraints imposed by central administration and the lack of experience of the staff of the institutions. There has been an intensive debate in Portugal about the mechanisms and the organisational structure of a new financial system, the definition of criteria to allocate funds from the national budget and the role evaluation has to play.

The integration of Portugal into the EEC/EU has brought to the higher education system a closer cooperation with other systems and participation in EU programmes.

Resembling in several respects the recent developments in Italy, an account of recent higher education changes in Spain is given by **Emilio Lamo de Espinosa** and **Inés Alberdi** in their paper 'An Attempt to Diversify University Curricula: The Case of Spain'.

The paper outlines that the 1983 university reform law has changed the university system from a centralised to a more autonomous model. Roughly all higher education in Spain is currently university education, since the 1970 general education law integrated the technical schools into the university system, and within the framework of the 1983 reform the remaining higher studies joined the universities. The paper discusses the organisation of the universities and explains that as a result of the 1983 reform there is a stronger orientation towards research activities. Since 1983 eleven new public universities have been created and three private ones followed. A 1991 decree fixed the requirements and general conditions for the establishment of these universities in order to secure their ability for training and research.

There are two types of degrees in Spain; first, the national degrees, which are official, have a legal national recognition and are homogeneous. The universities are also able to offer university degrees which are unofficial but the study programmes of which enjoy a larger degree of freedom and are able to introduce innovations more easily. The growth of university degrees has been enormous. In the 1980s, reforms were introduced to update and diversify existing programmes and curricula of national degrees and in 1990–91, 96 new degrees were set up and approved.

In general, the Spanish curriculum has the following characteristics:

- the study programme has traditionally been rigid, and even after the introduction of reforms only a maximum of 15 per cent of the curriculum is available for free choice of the students
- only recently some efforts have been made to form stronger connections between education and the labour market

- as a national degree is the legal requirement to exercise most of the professions, professional corporations have had a strong influence on curricula and have sometimes resisted innovations
- since 1983 a three-cycle system has been in operation: the first cycle of two to three years; the second cycle of four, five or six academic years; and the third cycle offering a doctorate (official), a Master's (unofficial), and specialisation studies which do not end in official degrees
- traditionally the Spanish academic year lasts nine months and is not subdivided into semesters. This is under discussion because it is a system less appropriate for more open curricula where students can choose their subjects and do not follow a strict programme
- the duration of the degrees has traditionally been a five-year programme, but has in some instances been reduced to four.

The official degree in physics has been regulated since 1990 by Royal Decree, and is organised in two cycles. Several new engineering degrees were approved in that same year. The curricula in itself has not changed much, but it has been adapted to the cycle system and a number of new technical engineering diplomas have been created which will be part of the first cycle only. Also in 1990, the full degree in economics and the general direction for its curricula was regulated by Royal Decree. Economics is now also regulated in two cycles. Mandatory subjects form 30 per cent of the total of the curriculum and the rest of the curriculum is designed by the university in question. The 1990 Decree establishing the history degree also puts the mandatory subjects for the diploma at 30 per cent of the total.

The fourth Mediterranean account by **Stefanos Pesmazoglou** on 'Patterns of Studies in Greek Universities: A Micro-Level Approach of Four Disciplines' completes the overview of the major systems of the south.

The paper begins with an analysis of the development of the Greek higher education system and its shortcomings. The analysis is structured around three factors that have dominated the system: the politics of populism, the politics of corporatism, and the politics of state patronage. The contradictory forces at work in respect of the specific cases of economics, chemical engineering, physics and history are then examined. Finally, the extent to which the European Community has acted as a catalyst for change in Greece is analysed.

Particularly, the role of the EC in the development of the Greek higher education system is explored. At first, the Education Council in Greece identified external finance with dependence, and international funding was blocked. Only in those departments where things were moving and where there were active individuals, was EC funding obtained. In general, EC funding has benefited the more positive centres of activity within the Greek system. Participation in EC programmes has caused language problems and there are not many in-going students. It was noticed that the Greek example shows how exogenuous factors can affect the university system.

In the following contribution by **Patrick Clancy** on the 'Changing Priorities in Higher Education Programmes in Ireland', the author points out that the major structural changes in the higher education system in Ireland are broadly similar to those which occurred in other western European countries. The last three decades have seen continuous expansion and significant diversification, while at a structural level the main feature was the development of a large non-university sector.

The paper examines changes in the programmes of study in higher education. The first section is dedicated to an analysis of changes in the second level system, which resulted in increased demand for places in higher education. Seventy per cent of the age cohort take the Leaving Certificate Examination, preparation for which now dominates second level education. The normal number of subjects studied for the Leaving Certificate is seven, and the paper discusses the trend evident in recent years in the take-up of these subjects. From 1992, the Leaving Certificate became the sole vehicle for selecting entrance into university; before this there were also separate matriculation examinations, the abolishment of which has been controversial. The decision was accepted when the universities were given guarantees about their continuing representation on the appropriate syllabus and monitoring committees, thus ensuring their ongoing influence on the Leaving Certificate. The paper briefly discusses the 'points system' operated by the universities and changes in terms of entry in various subject areas.

Three levels can be distinguished in programmes of study in higher education: sub-degree level, degree level and postgraduate level.The duration of these programmes vary. Almost all the short cycle sub-degree level programmes are to be found in the technological sector.

The work of the universities is concentrated on offering degree level courses.

The paper then examines changes in the distribution of higher education students by level of study. In general, there is a spectacular growth in the technological sector, a more modest growth in the HEA sector and a reduction of 15 per cent in enrolment in the colleges of higher education. There has been growth of 43 per cent of first degrees and a 125 per cent increase in output of postgraduate degrees. The paper then monitors developments in selected disciplines based on the situation in University College Dublin, the university with the largest enrolment and the most comprehensive range of faculties.

Another trend is the increase of students taking a Master's course and especially the increased popularity of the taught Master's programme. Neither history nor economics have contributed significantly to the increase of PhD students over the past decade. In physics however, there has been a fast rate of postgraduate enrolment. The take-up of physics at degree level has declined but there has been a sharp rise in participation in engineering studies. Most of the new postgraduate programmes have been developed as a result of vocational considerations and are of an applied nature, with the objective of preparing graduates for labour market entry.

Peter A. M. Maassen and **Egbert de Weert**, in their paper on 'Innovations in Dutch Higher Education – Barriers and Challenges', start with the observation that the Dutch higher education system is binary (universities and HBO), and that the two sectors are considered as 'equal but different'. The paper describes methods of enrolment, selection and entrance characteristics, student:staff ratios, length of study programmes, completion and transfer rates and the organisation of first-year courses.

Until the 1980s, the only quality assessment of educational aspects, if any, was internal, such as voluntary assessment of courses or programmes by faculties or individual teachers. Since 1988 the central role in the quality control process has been taken up and tried out in four disciplines by the VSNU. In the HBO sector, there have been plans to set up a similar procedure.

In recent debates on higher education policy, the relationship between higher education and employment has been one of the prevailing themes. After discussing the general context of this issue, the paper examines in more detail trends in the humanities and social sciences, particularly the weak employment situation for graduates in these fields. It is concluded that this is not solely determined by the content of education programmes and that other non-cognitive qualifications and factors have to be taken into consideration as well.

To conceptualise curricula developments in the Netherlands, the paper uses two sets of distinctions: first, the distinction between the traditional disciplinary model and the convergent model; and second, the theory–practice dichotomy. Proponents of the convergent model, the opposite of the traditional model, pursue a broadening of programmes, more flexibility and more differentiation in terms of level of education, educational goals, theoretical or practical focus, duration of studies, de-coupling of resource and education, and a modular course structure. This model has gained wide acceptance in the humanities and social sciences. Three explanations are given in the paper: the large number of students enrolling in the humanities and social sciences who are heterogenuous in motivation, interests and quality; a very uncertain and diffuse job market; and, finally, the internal structures and development of the disciplines.

The second distinction is made between theory and practice, as the convergent model does not necessarily imply that a closer link between education and employment can be achieved than in a traditional, disciplinary model.

Through this scheme, four types of programmes can be generated. First, those which are based upon clear disciplinary approaches. Second, those which are practical or problem oriented. Third, those which offer a broad range of knowledge and experience so that employment chances are enhanced. Fourth, those programmes which select courses from various disciplines and combine these into a new setting with an explicitly vocational perspective.

Finally, the paper addresses the question of how from the point of view of two disciplines (history and economics) the relationship with employment can be conceived, and how responsive the discipline is or can be to external needs. It concludes that despite intrinsic barriers to the externally initiated urge for innovation, Dutch higher education is on the move, resulting in a large number of innovations, which was one of the major goals of the steering strategy towards higher education in the Netherlands.

If practically all contributions so far on recent developments in the organisation of teaching and learning have revealed quite a massive process of transformation all over Europe, **Johan L. Vanderhoeven** shows in his paper 'Change under Exogenous Pressure: Belgian Higher

Education After Thirty Years' that teaching and learning in Belgian higher education in contrast have undergone virtually no dramatic changes over the last thirty years.

An 'epoch-making' law on integrating the higher education system in 1970 was not efficient enough to revitalise the system in relation to its environment. The successful expansion of the system and the demand-led policy sustaining it, ultimately contributed to the replacement of traditional policies by expenditure-driven decisions (at least in the Flemish community; the French-speaking community is expected to follow). The State Reform turning Belgium into a federal state is considered to be another facilitator of political nature.

In Danish higher education there are programmes at three different levels: shorter programmes of one to two years, medium-level programmes of three to four years and long programmes scheduled to take normally five years, leading to the *kandidat* Degree. Higher education institutions can be divided into three main sectors: the university sector, the college sector and the vocational schools. In Denmark, the need for educational reforms in higher education has been stressed in many reports commissioned by the Minister of Education since the late 1970s. Many new higher education courses have been set up in Denmark throughout the 1980s and many of the existing courses have undergone more or less substantial changes. In 'Changes in Danish Higher Education in the 1980s **Poul Bache** from the Ministry of Education in Copenhagen discusses these changes in the long and medium cycle higher education study programmes.

This paper identifies the major actors in the process of change and mentions politicians, the Ministry of Education, the advisers of the Ministry, the labour market and the institutions who enjoy a considerable autonomy.

The extent of the changes also receives attention. During the period in question, two educational changes have been carried through which have led to changes for many of the higher education institutions. One is the introduction of a system of open education which was introduced by statute in 1990. The second was the introduction of the Bachelor's degree which was established by ministerial order in 1988. This degree is awarded after three years of study and all students who complete the first three years of a degree are awarded this degree.

The paper then proceeds to examine the new courses set up in Denmark. By far the majority of the new courses have been set up in the university sector. A large part of the new courses are 'combination' courses; combination with computer science and internationalisation occurred most. Another large group of new combination courses relates to biotechnology and economics. Most of the initiatives for the establishment of new courses came from the institutions. In Denmark there is no systematic evaluation of new courses but some of the courses have been evaluated either on the Ministry's initiative or that of the institution in question. According to Bache, the relatively high number of new courses in the university sector shows the universities' aptness to adapt to requirements from the labour market, the students and the political system. The Ministry has used finance mechanisms as a policy instrument and has allocated special grants to institutions for the development of new education programmes.

In conclusion, new courses in the higher education sector in Denmark have been created in educational areas where institutions enjoyed a relatively high degree of freedom (universities), where institutions were allowed to increase the influx of students (technical and natural science courses) and, finally, in areas that were at risk of losing capacity as a result of ministerial decisions inspired by the labour market situation.

CHAPTER 1

Utilitarianism by Increment

Disciplinary Differences and Higher Education Reform in France

Guy Neave

Introduction

There is in military parlance an old and very wise axiom. This axiom says that 'Intention does not imply capacity'. And there is its counter proposition, namely that 'Capacity does not imply intention'. Now what applies to the precise discipline of Herman Kahn and the Domesday Machine also, by extension, applies to his civilian counterpart, the educational planner and administrator. The latter, as Mark Twain once observed about education and soap, may not be as sudden as a massacre, but both are more deadly in the long run. And this is certainly the case in that most planned of all higher education systems – the French. As few can have failed to note over the course of the past decade, the intent to reform is quite massive. Capacity is quite a different matter. And how far what is placed upon the statute books reflects the reality of practice is again a subject of interest and enquiry. Yet, the one mistake that many students of centralised systems of higher education tend to make – and it is perhaps inevitable – is to believe in legislative reality. As we are coming to realise, the legislative world, that of the grand ministerial plan and the administrator's intent, is very different from what really takes place at the institutional level. And behind the façade of legal homogeneity which is the basic ideology of centralised systems (Neave 1990) and certainly their justification, institutional diversity and difference are no less present but are more covert and less immediately obvious.

In this setting the use of disciplines as the basic unit of analysis is an important intermediate corrective. It is important for three reasons: first, because it enables us to retain a macro perspective on systems; second, because it gives us deeper penetration into the way in which organisations really work as opposed to the way legislators would have us believe they work; finally, because the use of disciplines as an analytic tool gives us a better purchase over the interplay between structures on the one hand and functions performed in and by, them on the other (Gellert 1991b). To be sure, the disciplinary perspective is no substitute for thorough analysis at the institutional level and this is more than ever necessary when systems of higher education which, historically, have rested upon the canons of centralisation seek, at least publicly, to move towards a more flexible and negotiated environment that takes account of an expanding number of partners and interests at regional or local level (Guin 1990). But such a level of disaggregation, whilst it would almost certainly cause us to amend our ways of looking at how institutions work, must remain an undertaking that requires more time than this project has budgeted for. In short, *en attendant* the reconstruction of our ways of looking at the French higher education system from the bottom up, the perspective that disciplines unveil may serve as a reasonable stop-gap device.

Before going into the finer points involved in the four disciplinary areas of engineering, physics, economics and history – disciplines which some of us have already used in another project to examine the paths that take students from the first degree towards the research system (Clark 1993) – it is appropriate to give them a contextual setting. This has two main dimensions: the first historic and structural, the second contemporary and political. In the first, I wish to draw attention to some of the unique features that the development of the French higher education system over time has thrown up. In the second, I want to provide a backdrop to the current *problématique* facing the contemporary higher education system in France; it is only against this setting that we may fully understand the nature of the debate which concentrates on the purpose and structure of first degree studies and thus their articulation with secondary schooling. In short, whatever the points that a functionalist analysis may score against those who espouse a structural approach, both structure and function are embedded in an historical context. Furthermore, though this may appear as special pleading, when the short-term, pragmatic, utilitarian – and frankly opportunist – appear to govern the thoughts of the Prince and his servants, it is as well to remind ourselves that the university *stricto sensu* is one of the last of society's institutions to be built around the concept of historic memory. In this, it is not alone. There have been other social institutions – the legal profession being one, the churches, temples and synagogues being others (Neave and van Vught 1991). But still and for all that, the university retains this function though at diminishing pace and perhaps also influence.

Historical context

The tension between general culture and vocationalism is as perennial in education as the tensions between 'useful' and 'sacred' knowledge in a pre-secular age or between education and schooling at primary or secondary level. To be sure, the debate between fundamental and vocational knowledge, between education and training, stands as a latter day edition of the distinction between knowledge sacred and profane, between values, ethics on the one hand and techniques and their application on the other. Or put another way, the distinction turns around the knowledge the individual was held to need for perpetuating and living in harmony with the spiritual order as opposed to the possession of those techniques which permit him either individually or collectively to master his physical environment. There are, not surprisingly, fields and disciplines that cross these boundaries, and the university was, from the first, closely associated with their development: law, government, public administration, which seek to ally knowledge dealing with the moral order with the techniques of administering and upholding it.

The process of divorce between value disciplines and disciplines of technique has been a protracted one in most European countries. The eighteenth century, in many Western European countries, marked a watershed in the acceleration of this process, beginning with the Cameralist School of Public Administration in Halle and developing in a more fundamental manner with the rise of the Physiocrats in France and with the forging of the field of Political Arithmetic in Scotland.

What the German-American historian, Karl Becker, termed the 'Heavenly City of the Eighteenth Century Philosophers' introduced a fundamental distinction between the spiritual order and the means of its perpetuation and the social order and its upkeep. In Becker's eyes, the eighteenth century ushered in a radical reinterpretation of the purpose of man upon this earth (Becker 1934). No longer was he engaged in preparing himself for the Augustinian vision of the Heavenly City. His task was rather to *build it in* this world. Just as we talk about rationalising government and management in contemporary social life, so then the new social order would equally be built upon reason, not upon revealed knowledge, belief and the social structure which accumulated around society based on a religious world view. The process of rationalism took many forms: attempts to codify the whole range of human knowledge – the French Encyclopedists being one example, to place law upon a natural as opposed to a spiritual order – Montesquieu being typical of this latter drive – or, nearer our immediate concern, the introduction of rational methods for the administration and development of the State which in France may be identified with the Physiocrat school of state administration, gathered around the Minister Turgot. The efficient gathering of taxes, development of what today would be called the economic infrastructure and its administration were the prime concern of this group of state reformers.

The Physiocrats were an important element in the way one section of French intelligentsia responded to the eighteenth century revolution. The Physiocrats were located in what today would anachronistically be termed the 'apparatus of state', in contrast, for example, with the Scottish philosophers – prime among them being Adam Smith – who worked from within the university and, equally important, regarded the rationalisation of human behaviour taking place individually and from below, rather than being imposed collectively and from above.

The creation of the *Ecole des Ponts et Chaussées* in 1775 (Jilek 1984), was a seminal development. In the first place, it may be regarded as the first institute of higher education set up to train a specialised technical corps of state administration outside the army. In the second place, it stood as one of the first formally constituted engineering establishments in Western Europe. In the third place, it may also be seen as one of the first instances of an institution dedicated to high level technical vocational training in the sense that its training was not primarily given over to determining the values of society so much as developing a knowledge base with the applied and highly utilitarian purpose of injecting a new degree of efficiency into the running of the state.

These were not the only points of significance which surround this pioneering establishment, though they show very clearly that the revolution of the eighteenth century philosophers brought forth its institutional response. From the standpoint of our present concern, namely the structure and function of French higher education, it was no less pioneering. What is less commonly recognised is that the *Ecole des Ponts et Chaussées* constituted the first step in a rather broader development, subsequently taken up by the French Revolution as a basic policy of reform. This policy is not simply a matter of interest to specialists of revolutionary history, though clearly it has its part there too. It also lies at the heart of what might be termed the 'dual strategy' of reform which has remained with us ever since. Thus, if we are to grasp not merely the functional stratification and differentiation that lies inside the contemporary French higher education system, we have also to bear in mind the fact that the particular organisational form that has emerged, is not the episodic by-product of occasional ministerial caprice. It is, on the contrary, an enduring and deeply laid characteristic of French higher education development over the past two centuries.

The usual interpretation of the history of French higher education attaches much importance to the creation of the so called 'Imperial University' in 1806–1808 (e.g. Scotford Archer 1978). Without going into detail, the Imperial University was not a university as is commonly understood elsewhere. It was, rather, the educational arm of the state, combining both upper-secondary schools and higher level teacher training as well as the more traditional faculties of law and medicine. Its purpose was to provide 'cadres for the nation' – high level manpower for the service of the state with the implicit notion that the 'value allocating disciplines' (literature, history) had this purpose too. Just how far the idea went that the value allocating disciplines were associated with the task of forging national unity, can be grasped when one recalls, for example, that of all Europe's nations, only France has philosophy studied in upper-secondary school not simply as a subject, but as a core subject.

The monumental and enduring nature of the Napoleonic reforms has tended to overshadow the fact that it was not the first reform, nor the most radical. And, as we shall see, once one analyses present day French higher education from the standpoint of disciplines, it is indeed arguable, from the standpoint of the present-day structure of French higher education, that the Imperial University was less a reform than a consolidation and less one step forward than two steps back. In short, in the upheavals that beset revolutionary France, a pattern of change was established which, if bypassed by Bonaparte's more prudent efforts and certainly outshone by them, is nevertheless central to our present-day understanding and particularly so in the case of the discipline of engineering.

The French Revolution of 1789 was not simply concerned with rebuilding the social order. It was also concerned both with replacing aristocracy with meritocracy and, no less relevant, with developing 'useful knowledge'; useful, that is, to maintaining a new social and political order. 'Useful knowledge' was primarily defined in terms of the defence of the nation; extending its influence abroad and consolidating the new political order at home. The importance from the standpoint of the history of the 'vocational impulse' in French higher education was that this mission was not assigned to the universities, which had been closed down in a series of decrees between 1791 and 1793. It was, on the contrary, assigned to specialist institutes: public works to the Central School of Public Works (later transformed into the *Ecole Polytechnique*); the revival of the *Ecole des Mines*, first created in 1783, and similarly the resuscitation of the *Ecole des Ponts et Chaussées*. The following year, 1794, saw the establishment of the *Ecole Normale Supérieure*, though the latter, amidst scenes of tumult and uproar, closed four months later.

What these schools had in common however, was their highly technical orientation on the one hand and the fact that, just as the Physiocrats earlier, their purpose was the training of a technical élite in knowledge intended to apply to defence, administration, diplomacy and schooling (Neave 1985). In fine, the origins of the present-day French technocracy are earlier than the reforms which put in place the modern French university. Yet, because the Napoleonic reforms were tinged with a certain selectivity in the matter of the *Ecoles*, they left intact those establishments which supplied the technical corps of the state.

This 'residual' group of institutions might not have retained their original form, had the university itself been able to adjust to the changes – intellectual, technical, and disciplinary – which the nineteenth century threw up. And while the reforms of the revolution were brought up short by the reform of the university, so the subsequent difficulty of the Napoleonic university to adapt gave considerable impetus to that strategy which had first been launched by the educational enthusiasts of the revolution, namely, the development of specialised institutes outside the university. In short, to an increasing extent, as the nineteenth and early twentieth centuries passed so French higher education came to resemble a pattern which analysts have detected in the nation's politics. Broadly speaking it divided into two tendencies: the Party of Order, represented by the University *stricto sensu*, and the Party of Movement, represented by what came to be the *Grandes Ecoles* (Goguel 1946).

This division between the university and the élite non-university sector was not simply legal, administrative and organisational. It was also functional as well. For if some specialised élite establishments were brought into the university ambit and thus the administrative responsibility of the Ministry of Education – the outstanding characteristic of the *Grandes Ecoles* remained and is still today, their relatively specialised nature, their smaller size, and, for the public sector at least, a considerable diversity in the ministries under whose responsibility they fall – Defence, Telecommunications, Agriculture, etc. There is, however, a further distinction to be drawn which is particularly germane to the issues posed by the vocationalisation of higher education as well as to the rather broader *problématique* of mechanisms of reform and what has been termed 'policy styles'.

Broadly speaking, the method employed by French higher education to take aboard new disciplines or, alternatively, a heightened demand for new subject areas beyond those traditionally present in the university, was to create specialised institutes – the *Ecole Pratique des Hautes Etudes* and the *Institut d'Etudes Politiques* founded respectively in 1868 and 1872 are good examples of this gathering process, for such new fields as diplomacy, colonial studies, economics and finance. Such a tactic constituted at one and the same time a species of high level vocationalism, being largely in response to changes in the specialised knowledge required by an expanding civil service as well as a policy of institutional incrementalism (Prinborgne 1992). Increased demands for engineers following World War I were met in a similar manner through the passing in 1924 of the *Loi Astier*, which set in place the *Ecoles Nationales des Sciences de l'Ingénieur.* If, arguably, this procedure was forced upon authorities often as a result of resistance from the university, it shows, nevertheless, that French higher education policy is by no means as monolithic nor as radical as some recent analysts have claimed (for example, the typology developed by Rune Premfors; Premfors 1980). Radical solutions, and system-wide upheavals have certainly been the lot of the university sector, under pressure from social demand on the one hand, and from the demands of a developing economy on the other. But alongside this sector of Order where radical policies were introduced largely as a desperate last recourse, there ran, as we have suggested, a sector of Movement, where institutional incrementalism and a strong sense of vocational adaptability, reigned.

It is significant that, in the midst of the upheaval which broke upon the heads of the authorities in 1968, very little was heard of the non–university sector for the reforms which split the Sorbonne asunder did not extend to the *Grandes Ecoles.* And it is perhaps on account of this unwanted tranquillity, plus the fact that the *Grandes Ecoles* are only with difficulty comparable with other European systems of higher education, that we have tended to focus on the university. In so doing, the 'quiet strength' and the historical development of this second sector have perhaps been underplayed. They are, however, highly important since, in our interpretation, they represent a sustained and incremental drive towards a high level version of vocationalism. The drawing up of vocational policies designed for the university should be seen against this wider institutional and historical backdrop.

Structures

The structure of French higher education is usually analysed along two dimensions: the duration of its initial degrees – short cycle or long cycle – and its admissions policy – open or selective (Furth 1973). Like any schema it is not perfect, but it has the virtue of clarity since it brings out the segmented nature of the enterprise. It is on this matrix that the disciplinary dimension is overlaid and for this reason the structural dimension is vital to our understanding of the relationship between structure, function and discipline. Restricted admission long cycle higher education with two disciplinary exceptions, medicine and pharmacy, lies outside the university in the 200-odd *Grandes Ecoles* which, as we have seen, range from the apex of the French engineering technocracy trained in the *Ecole Polytechnique* down to the more technical aspects of engineering represented, for example, in the *Ecole Supérieure de la Ceramique* at Sévres. Alongside these state sector *Grandes Ecoles* – or even *Petites Grandes Ecoles* – runs another privately run system of which the best example is the *Ecole des Hautes Etudes Commerciales*, controlled by the Paris Chamber of Commerce and specialising in business studies, the economics of the firm. Many of these establishments, which, in contrast to the public sector, often demand substantial fees and tuition charges, have a very different historical origin from their public counterparts. In the nineteenth century, their forerunners were part of a network of '*Ecoles Consulaires*',[1] dispensing commercial studies and run by local chambers of commerce out of levies imposed on their members.

1 I owe this point to Mr Richard Edelstein, Director of International Relations for the American Association of Collegiate Schools of Business, St Louis, Missouri.

Not only are both private and public sector *Grandes Ecoles* highly selective, with admission on the basis of competitive entry examinations, they also draw their students from another uniquely French educational institution. This institution comes in the form of the *Classes Préparatoires aux Grandes Ecoles.* Organisationally the CPGE, of which there are some 230, sit atop the nation's most prestigious lycées. They are divided into two streams known in the inimitable jargon of both teachers and students as '*taupe*' and '*hyper taupe*' for the advanced mathematics stream and '*khâgne*' and '*hyper khâgne*' for the advanced literary stream. As their name implies, they prepare the more brilliant products of the upper-secondary school system for the rigorous and competitive selection for entry to the *Grandes Ecoles.*

Three features set the *Classes Préparatoires* aside from the rest of the secondary school system. First, like the establishments for which they prepare, they too are ferociously selective. Places are limited and those doing the selection are by no means obliged to fill all the places if performance does not warrant it (Neave 1985). Second, they are subsequent to the passing of the Baccalaureat. Since from a legal standpoint the Baccalaureat – the upper-secondary school leaving examination – is deemed to be the first stage of higher education, technically, the level of study undertaken in the CPGE is well up to – some would say beyond – that dispensed in the two years of the university first cycle. Third, their curriculum is markedly different from both the school which precedes them and the university which runs in parallel with them. The CPGE course lasts two years after the Baccalaureat which, when added to the usual three-year study structure found in the *Grandes Ecoles*, amounts to a total of five years post-Baccalaureat work compared to the two required to complete the university first cycle.

From a structural perspective, not only are the CPGE set aside by the three features just mentioned, functionally they mark the boundaries in that basic duality which has been an outstanding and growing feature of French education since the advent of mass higher education in the late 1960s – namely, a separation between those institutions associated with grooming for the top positions in public service, in the state technical corps and, to an increasing extent, in the leading posts of private sector industry. To this extent, the model, first developed for state service, has subsequently been taken over by the private sector, though clearly the latter does not necessarily emphasise the same disciplinary profiles, as we shall see. And finally, because the CPGE form part of the closed sector of French post-secondary education, their suc-

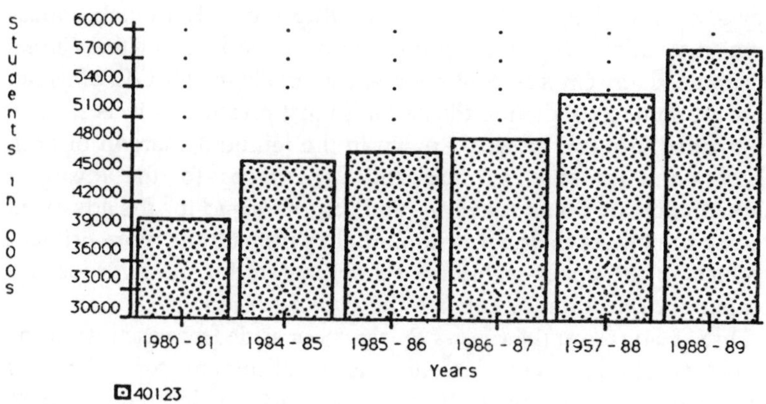

Figure 1.1 Enrolments in CPGE 1980–1989

cess, like that of any club, depends not on who they bring in, but whom they keep out. Even so, the numbers of students admitted has increased substantially over the past decade, partly in response to social demand, partly as a result of a sustained policy to increase the size of the pool from which the nation's high level manpower is drawn. Enrolments in the CPGE are set out in Figure 1.1.

If we turn our attention to the short cycle selective sector, we see certain similarities with its longer counterpart. The first of these is once again structural and relates to the presence of Higher Technicians' Sections (*Sections de Techniciens Supérieurs*, STSs) which, like the CPGE, are post-secondary establishments atop technical *lycees*. Together with the University Institutes of Technology which were founded in 1966, partly to replace the STS, they form a selective, post-Baccalaureat segment running once again in parallel to the university *stricto sensu*. Both may be seen as symbolic of a second dimension in the 'vocationalisation' of French higher education, the first being the very specific and specialised training dispensed in the *Grandes Ecoles* for the social and future political élite.

The drive towards mass higher education went in parallel with the intention of government to attempt on the one hand to deflect part of the student flood away from the universities by channelling it into short

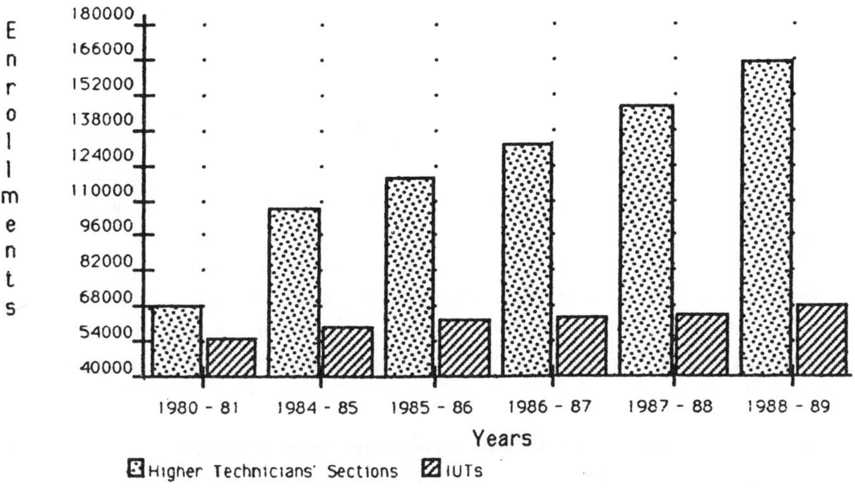

Figure 1.2 Enrolments – short cycle higher education

course higher education directly aligned upon the skills requirements of the secondary and tertiary sectors of the economy. On the other, such a tactic, like its counterparts in Britain of the day and somewhat later in the Federal Republic of Germany, sought to give greater drawing power to technician education by affording it higher education status. The two-year University Institutes of Technology were then intended both to accommodate rising social demand for higher education and, at the same time, to link it firmly to the economy by a very specific curricular provision aligned not on the classical 'university disciplines' so much as on a combination of techniques and skills held to be both highly applied and in short supply: mechanical engineering, applied biology, computing, management of the firm, accounting publicity and communication, applied economics, etc (Doumenc and Gilly 1977). Those graduating from the IUTs were awarded the *Diplôme Universitaire de Technologie*, those from the STS the *Brevet de Technicien Supérieur*. Just how the short cycle sector has evolved is set out in Figure 1.2.

Growth in enrolment rates, above all in the Higher Technicians Sections, are noteworthy and reflect in part the long-term policy, supported by both left and right, with minor quibblings, since 1984, to bring approximately 80 per cent of the age group up to a level equivalent of the Baccalaureat. Since this particular priority has immense implications both for the articulation between secondary and higher education and for the subsequent adjustments that higher education is being obliged to assume to meet a second wave of expansion every bit as massive as that which took place in the heroic age of the 1960s, it is as well to pay a little attention to the less visible changes hidden by this graph.

The expansion of short cycle higher education stands as part of a rather broad process of curricular modification which began in 1969 with the establishment of the Technician Baccalaureat, and the development in 1987 of the so-called 'Vocational Baccalaureat' (*Baccalau-*

Table 1.1 Students passing the Baccalaureat by subject track and orientation

Option	*1980*	*1985*	*1987*	*1988*	*1989*	*1990a*	*1991a*
Humanities A	40391	46704	48627	55441	58057	63661	70006
Economics B	31521	40381	46261	52971	59057	60023	64976
Math. + Physics C	32658	33516	36259	41645	48173	56802	61402
Math. + Nat. Sci. D	48545	44536	48970	51443	54769	58513	61335
Sci. + Techn. E.	5823	5427	5465	6116	6845	7883	8592
Gen. Bacc.	158938	170564	185582	207616	226901	246882	266311
Techno. Bacc. F,G,H	62660	82486	91762	98762	106554	112517	113993
Vocat. Bacc.			880	6529	14315	23649	33124
Total	221598	253050	278224	312907	347770	383048	413428

Source: *Repères et Références* statistiques 1990, Table 12.3 Examens et sorties p.227 a. 'Les résultats du baccalauréat général, technologique et professionnel, session normale de juin 1991' *Note d'Information 91–33,* Paris, Ministère de I'Education Nationale, pp.1–4.

reat Professionnel). The intervening period may be interpreted from a number of different perspectives. It may be regarded as diversifying the 'curricular pathways' leading from secondary school to higher education, a development which, given the overwhelmingly academic bias in that examination, was perhaps not before its time. It may also be seen as cutting new qualification routes from secondary to post-secondary education and as such, a continuation by other means of the policy of deflection which we have identified as part of the basic considerations prompting the creation of the IUTs.

Certainly, one contextual variable which has considerable bearing upon current reforms, just as it is having upon the curricular pathways in higher education as well as their content and control, is the unfurling wave of youngsters reaching the portals of higher education. Table 1.1 sets out the numbers of young people passing the various forms of Baccalaureat over the past decade.

Clearly, not all who pass the Baccalaureat go on to higher education, but general changes in the basic 'pool' from which entrants to higher education are drawn affects radically the whole nature of the enterprise (Trow 1973; Fulton 1992). In 1970, approximately 20 per cent of the age group obtained the Baccalaureat that gives the formal right to a place in the 'open sector' of higher education which, historically, has

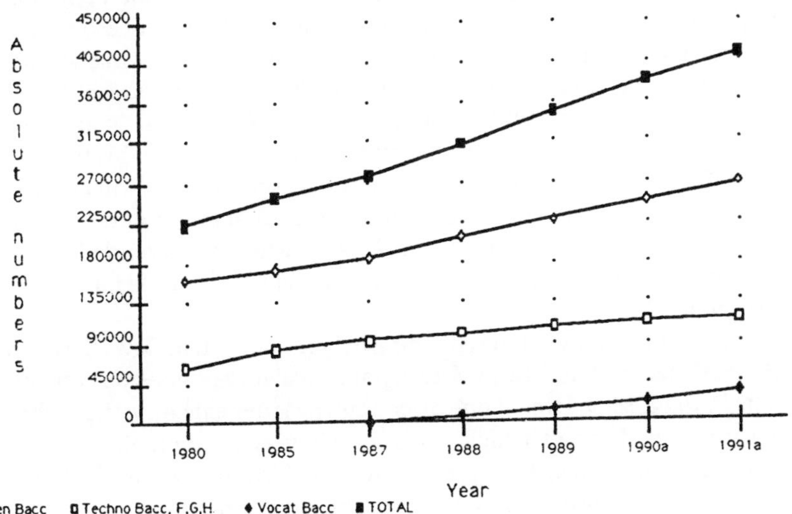

Figure 1.3 Students passing Baccalaureat 1980–1989

been the university. In 1989, the corresponding statistic, which takes no account of the recently established 'Vocational Baccalaureat', was 38.5 per cent. This latter figure, spectacular in itself, is to some extent an artefact inasmuch as the size of the age groups 18–19 has been falling since 1984 (Neave 1984a). Nevertheless, Table 1.1 is a dramatic statement of the potential pressures under which French higher education in general and its 'open sector' – the university – in particular are now labouring. In the course of the ten years from 1980 to 1991, the numbers of those standing on the threshold of higher education have risen by more than 70 per cent. More to the point, it appears that the numbers of those qualified are themselves accelerating throughout the decade.

The bald statistic hides, however, a number of important developments, prime among which is another form of 'vocational impulse'. This impulse emerges in the numbers of students opting for what are termed the 'specialised Baccalaureats'. In contrast to the 'General Baccalaureat' options – literature, economics, mathematics and natural sciences, etc., which were aligned on a model of general culture on the one hand and the structure of university disciplines on the other – the curricular emphasis of 'specialised Baccalaureats' is aligned, broadly speaking, on occupational outlets in the secondary and tertiary sectors of the economy – industry and services. Baccalaureat option H, for example, is built around Computer techniques. The balance between general Baccalaureats and their specialised counterparts has shifted radically in the course of the decade. The latter accounted for 28 per cent of all passing in 1980 and 45 per cent in 1991. As the 'vocational track' begins to draw in increasing numbers of students, so this trend to specialisation and vocationalisation at the secondary level will accelerate, and more particularly since it draws upon that sector of the secondary school system – the Technical *Lycées* – which are intended to absorb the greater bulk of students who, in earlier times, would have left at age 16 or 17.

The overall picture of the changing balance of student flows between General, Technological and Vocational Baccalaureats is set out graphically in Figure 1.3. Even if one discounts the latter category, the potential growth in demand in higher education is very substantial. Indeed, it is not misplaced to see this development as forming a second wave of expansion a generation on from the explosion of the 1960s.

The 'vocationalisation' within the option choice of the Baccalaureat is, of course, a species of induced demand created by direct gov-

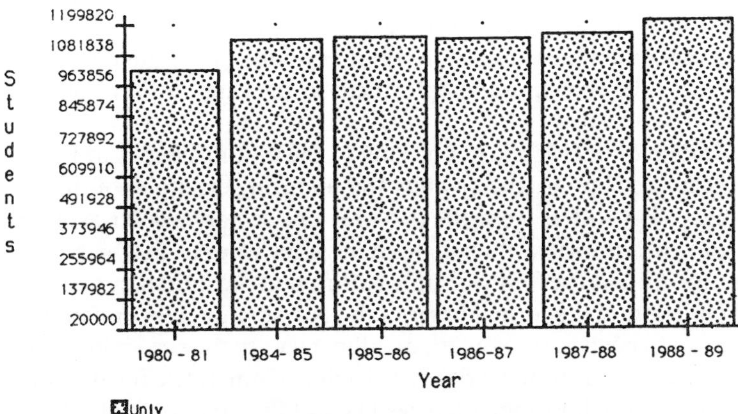

Figure 1.4 University enrolments 1980–1989
Source: Repères et statistiques 1990, Table 10.1 p.185

Note: This does not include CPGE, STS or IVT enrolments

ernment intervention. There is, however, another form of vocationalisation which is the product of the social demand of individuals. It emerges most strongly in the numbers of students opting for that élite track, Baccalaureat C – mathematics and physical sciences – which forms the royal road to the *Classes Préparatoires aux Grandes Ecoles* or, for those who do not make the grade, the élite tracks inside university, medicine and the exact sciences.

So far we have looked at the selective sectors of French higher education, the *Classes Préparatoires*, the University Institutes of Technology and the Higher Technicians Sections which attract some 39 per cent of all Baccalaureat holders, though the intention of the Ministry of Education has been to raise this to 50 per cent and to increase the number of places in the IUTs by a further 50,000.[2] By the same token, the Ministry's aim has been to cut back on the proportion of Baccalaureat holders embarking on first cycle studies at university from 50 to 40 per cent.[3] What is characteristic of these two sectors is, formally at least, the

2 Jospin, L. (1991) 'Une ambition pour l'Université.' *Le Monde*, 27 June 1991.

3 'Simplification des filières, renforcement de l'orientation et modules capitalisables en premier cycle.' *Le Monde*, 27 June 1991.

relative clarity of the career paths to which their qualifications are held to lead and the fact that their programmes are essentially training for those careers, in administration whether public or private for the first and at mid-level technical employment in the case of the second and third.

Vocational precision is not lacking in the 73 universities in France. Medicine and law are the obvious and enduring examples of this. But the university differs from the two previous sectors insofar as it does not control admission. It regulates it in various ways – to which ministers turn a blind eye for the simple reason that the imitation of Nelson and violation of the formal letter of the law are infinitely preferable to losing one's head as the student mobility takes to the streets in defence of its formal constitutional rights. Selection assumes two forms: formal selection through examination results and informal self-selection by which students drop their original choice of course and embark on another one. Whatever the motives, the wastage rate – though improving – is considerable and the productivity of the university in terms of students qualified within the minimum period permissible in the order of 40 per cent of those who embarked on a course. Thus, in 1986, of 100 students entering university, 75 continued the following year and 58 re-enrolled in 1988 – an improvement on previous indications which showed that of those who entered in 1983, 70 continued one year on and 51 were still in place in 1985 (Repères, see Figure 1.4, p.305 and Table 1.1).

Efficient or not in terms of qualified student output, the university *stricto sensu* dominates the French higher education by its sheer size if not by the dynamism of its enrolments which, if they have picked up substantially from 1987 onwards, remained in a state of relative stagnation during the middle of the decade. Even so, pressure of demand is building up from below, as our analysis has shown. The number of first time entrants at the start of the academic year 1988 rose by some 47,000 compared to the entry of 1987 (Repères, see Figure 1.4, p.305 and Table 1.1). Large though it is, the university suffers from the disproportionate power of attraction exercised by the selective sector which has the effect of depriving it of some of the liveliest minds coming out of secondary education. Thus, the time honoured practice of open access to Baccalaureat holders results in certain notable perverse effects, prime amongst them that university entrants are often those unsuccessful in seeking places in the selective sector. Or, more serious by far, that those coming up through the Technical Baccalaureats and aiming for a place in either the STS or the IUTs, through failure to gain a place in that sector, find themselves committed into the *Diplôme d'Etudes Universitaires Générales* in the university – a curriculum for which their secondary school education has not fitted them (Garin 1989).

If we analyse the position of the French university from the standpoint of its functions over and above those basics of generating new knowledge through research (though this is again an example of a segmented function as we have noted elsewhere: Neave 1993), its transmission through teaching and its reception through student learning, it is evident that as part of the overall provision of higher education the university assumed functions slightly different from many of its counterparts elsewhere. In the first place, expansion of the nation's system of higher education was purchased by the expansion of the university. The development of vocational higher education geared towards the industrial and services sector of the economy took place in parallel to the classic university. But it did not, as in Britain, for example, serve as a shock absorber, taking in new students and, to some degree, preserving the role of the university as an instrument for long-term economic and social change. In the second place, the massive expansion of the 1960s and early 1970s did not affect the true élite but equally vocational sector – that of the *Grandes Ecoles*. On the contrary, if anything it made them more desirable.

But however desirable as the royal road to high prestige, great power and high pay, the élite sector remained protected and girt about by two layers of selection – competition to enter the CPGE and competition to enter the *Grandes Ecoles*. The price of maintaining 'a thin stream of excellence' closely tied to state service, to what are termed the *Grands Corps de l'Etat* (Kessler 1978) and, by extension, to nationalised industry, was paid by the French university which, because of the constitutional provision of 'open access', became itself the shock absorber for the transition from élite to mass status. Social demand for higher education, limited, controlled and selected as much by the cost involved of creating new provision as by the principle of selection itself, was channelled onwards and upwards to the university. Thus, the transition from an élite to a mass university was accomplished with a speed equalled only by Italy (Neave and Rhoades 1987). By the end of the 1960s, the transition was complete, though here again the price paid by both university and government was excessively high in terms of social unrest, hasty reforms, and deteriorating material conditions.

Dilemmas of reform

The dilemma that successive French governments have faced over the past two decades or more has in essence turned around the redefinition of the role of the university to meet these new conditions. Or, put another way, how to ensure that the university – highly inefficient in its capacity to transform qualified entrants into qualified graduates – kept pace, first with the changes apparent in the national economy on the one hand and, on the other, with the quite remarkable efficiency of upper-secondary education to qualify ever increasing numbers of young people to the point where parental ambition and social expectation saw higher education as the only honourable course.

There is, of course, another interpretation which has to do precisely with the inability of the short cycle selective IUTs to attract the number – though not the quality – of students for which the government had hoped and planned. Sheer numbers on the one hand, and increasing diversity in the ability and motivation of students on the other meant that the prime task of the university could no longer exclusively be that of scholarship and learning. Though the French university could make claims as strong as any in this direction, it worked under the not inconsiderable handicap of the segmented organisation between the university and the research structure in one sector and the training of the political and administrative élite taking place in another sector. What it did enjoy – and it was very much a two-edged sword – was the conviction among students and junior staff that culture and scholarship were indeed its prime purpose, though who should define that was, not surprisingly, hotly contested (Neave and Rhoades 1987).

Yet governments had limited areas of manoeuvre. These can be classified as falling into two areas: those related to ideology and those related to opportunity, though obviously they were often bundled together. Among the ideological issues which largely blocked university reform up to the mid-1970s was whether the university should set its prime purpose as being education, culture and self-development or whether, in contrast, it should identify its task as training, preparing for work and creating specific skills. Among the issues of a more enduring kind associated with opportunity has remained the issue of selective entry to the university and the preservation of National Diplomas. To both the student estate remains inordinately attached. Even if the heat of the student revolution had drained away by the late 1970s and, with its evaporation, removed much of the opposition to strengthening the university's vocational mission, selection is not an option that political realists will even today contemplate publicly as an across-the-board solution.

For these reasons, the 'revocationalisation' of the university was an exceedingly delicate issue in France. Three factors combined to make this the enduring strategy of successive governments, both right-wing and left-wing. The first emerged in the form of graduate unemployment. This, combined with the halt on teacher recruitment for secondary schools which closed out the major public sector outlet for university graduates, in 1976 forced the government to grasp the nettle and to proceed to 'vocationalising' the second cycle – effectively years three through five after the Baccalaureat. Such a policy, decreed from above in the face of considerable student opposition, imposed the formal requirement that courses be planned with reference to their future occupational outlets. Validation by government of individual courses were made conditional upon this modification (Fragniere 1978).

The second step in the process took the form of high legislative symbolism incorporated in the Higher Education Guideline Law of 1984. The Guideline Law redefined the official status of the 73 universities as 'public establishments' of a scientific, cultural and vocational nature. And, as if to underline the latter element, the mid-layer units, bringing together departments of a certain cognitive similarity known under the 1968 Higher Education Guideline Law as 'Units of Learning and Research', were designated as 'Units of Training and Research' (*Unites de Formation et de Recherché UFR*). If today the vocational mission of the university is not its only purpose, the utilitarian aspect appears for all that to occupy parity of esteem in the official mind.

It must be one of the more outstanding paradoxes in French higher education policy that the development of the enterprise university – a notion first mooted during the government of Charles de Gaulle and rejected by the university world with fervour and opprobrium – should be finally set firmly in place by a Socialist administration under the presidency of François Mitterrand, one of the General's ardent critics. Yet, even the apparently inexplicable can be reconciled once one considers that the vision both Mr Mitterrand and the General entertained for the role of France in Europe, if not in the world, passed by its economic, industrial and technological capabilities. And in these, the higher education system is clearly central. From having been an establishment largely in opposition to government, the university has reverted to its historic role of being an instrument of government policy.

Riding the two horses of increasing opportunity at the same time as increasing competition, French higher education policy is currently committed to major reforms in the structure of both institutions and curriculum. The aim of these reforms is first, to reduce the high 'wastage' rate in the first cycle studies and, second, to introduce greater differentiation and flexibility to take account of a student estate whose talents, if not varied already, are certain to become more so as French higher education presses forward to quasi universal status.

The notion of differentiation has two sub-elements that are essentially legal on the one hand and pedagogical on the other. Both are deeply embedded in a long established ideological set which is now under challenge. This ideological set is extremely important not simply because it informed the basic relationship between university and state. It also informed certain pedagogical assumptions about students, about evaluation and about certification. And, precisely for the reason that it is at present under sustained challenge – paradoxically by government – it is central to our understanding not just of reform but also certain fundamental aspects of the way disciplines are controlled.

The French university from the time of Napoleon onwards has rested on a concept of legal homogeneity. Legal enactment and the creation of formally similar provision for degrees, for conditions of employment and promotion was conceived as a means of ensuring access to a system of higher education that was similar irrespective of geographical location. Legal instruments were not held to be an expression of the heavy hand of the state. That is a very contemporary and Anglo-American Saxon perspective on the matter. On the contrary, they were primarily conceived as a vehicle for equality of opportunity. Or, to put a different gloss on the matter, central control via legal fiat was intended to create a species of juridical space within which the university, acting as a 'supremacy parochial' entity, was identified with the state rather than either the nation or the region (Neave 1990). Legal homogeneity took little account of essential differences of status or performance between individual universities. And the setting down of framework conditions for National Diplomas and degrees stood as part of the state's obligation not just to provide facilities for talent to develop, but to ensure that quality was maintained and that talent developed as far as possible under similar conditions. Such an obligation did not infringe the right of individual universities to develop their own diplomas and degree courses, termed '*Diplômes d'Université*' in contrast to '*Diplômes d'Etat*'. But it did not recognise university diplomas as valid qualifications to apply for a post in public service. And the absence of this right did little to improve the attractiveness of university degrees as opposed to state degrees.

Central control over state diplomas was close and involved, at least until the early 1970s, Paris drawing up national curricula which most establishments were obliged to follow (Guin 1990). In the course of the 1970s, some degree of relative flexibility was injected in the form of what were termed 'national templates or profiles' (*Maquettes Nationales*). Under the system of national templates, the Ministry set out a series of frame factors defining minimum standards. These turned around such aspects as duration of study, the number of hours of teaching to be attached to a particular degree, the system of student assessment and a short list of subject areas to be taught. Within this general frame, individual universities negotiated with the Ministry for national recognition (Guin 1990). The system of 'national templates' introduced the principle, though minimal in form, of variation of course contents between establishments within nominally similar national degrees. It also introduced an amazing complexity of guidelines which some have estimated in the region of 250 for second cycle study alone.

Differentiation in its legal dimension has emerged indirectly in the curricular domain: first in the reduction in the number of curricular templates to around 50 for the second cycle – a welcome development which took place in 1989; second, in the reversal of the procedures for recognition of National Diplomas. A similar proposal for first cycle study has recently been unveiled by the Minister of Education. It involves reducing the 30 or so programmes at the level of the *Diplôme d'Etudes Universitaires Générales* to seven broad subject areas: science; technology; law; economics-management-social sciences; humanities, languages and culture; human sciences cum plastic and pictorial arts; life and health sciences (Courtois 1991). Implicit in the reduction of the number of templates is greater room for individual universities to develop their own specific courses within a frame made less rigid. And the recognition of this is pushed further via a policy designed to blur the lines between state and university diplomas. Essentially, this involves central government according, to all intents and purposes, national recognition to degree courses drawn up and conceived by individual universities in keeping with the specific economic and training requirements of their region (Prinborgne 1992). Thus what are in reality university degrees will receive the vital label of ministerial recognition without which little value is attached to them by students, parents or, for that matter, by employers.

Such diversification has both a political and a pedagogic justification. As regards the former, it corresponds to a shift away from the omnipotent central state and an increase in the role to be played in university life by regional authorities and local industry. Clearly, universities and their courses that are wholly controlled from the centre are incompatible with this long-term objective. The pedagogic justification is governed primarily by the prospect of a further diversification in ability and aptitude of students. Here again, this stands as a departure from the underlying assumptions about the role of the Baccalaureat. Just as the Napoleonic university symbolised homogeneity of quality, so the Baccalaureat represented homogeneity of attainment across the nation. As a nation-wide examination, its purpose was to identify those students who had reached a similar level of ability. This ability was not cognitive alone; it was held also to entertain a considerable measure of maturity – of the ability for self-direction and to plot one's path unaided through the cursus of higher education.

That it has been a singularly powerful, if unspoken, ideology is evident from the remarkable absence of guidance and counselling services in the French university. That it is an ideology increasingly dysfunctional is equally evident from the tendency for student re-enrolments in courses other than those they first embarked upon to rise over the course of the 1980s. The average number of enrolments per student over a three-year period rose from 2.21 in 1983 to 2.32 in 1986 (Repères, see Table 1.1 p.305). An indicator of persistence such a statistic might be. But it is also an indicator of considerable individual time wasted.

To remedy this situation, a number of measures have been taken, the first of which saw the creation of a *Diplôme d'Etudes Universitaires Scientifiques et Techniques (DEUST)* in 1986. This new diploma stands as an alternative track to the DEUG. A terminal qualification, vocational in bias and lasting two years, it is intended for those students unable to keep up with the rigour of the DEUG. In effect, it creates two parallel 'streams' or 'tracks' in the structure of the first degree. Further differentiation is also intended in the reform which was due to be operative in October 1992. The time, however, streaming was to take place inside the DEUG, to be based on a system of transferable credit units (*unites capitalisables*). Instead of being based on a two-year cycle, the DEUG is split into two levels, each comprising six modules. Students collect the

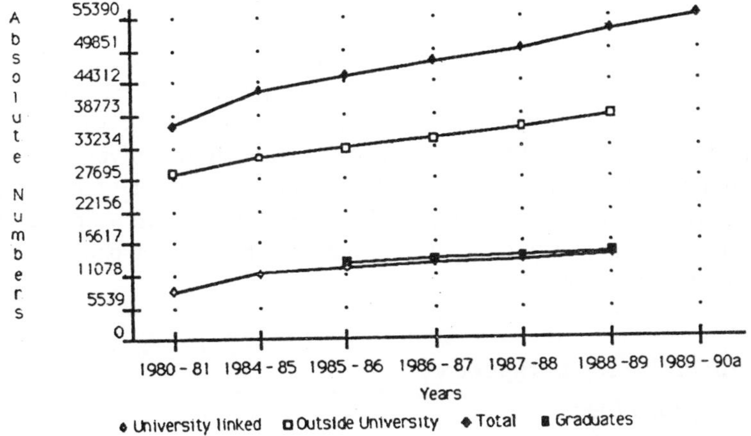

Figure 1.5 Engineering enrolments

Source: Repères et Statistiques 1990, p.185. 'Les Ecoles d'Ingénieurs publiques et privées: année 1989–90' *Note d'Information 90–08,* Direction del'Evaluation et de la Prospective, p.1.

modules according to their own rhythm and at the end of first level gain a 'Certificate of University Studies'. At this point, the individual will, it is hoped, be able to choose between entering employment with a diploma higher than the Baccalaureat, to opt for short cycle higher education given in the University Institutes of Technology or to move over to the long cycle. This latter, to be based on Professionalised University Institutes (*Instituts Universitaires Professionnalisés*) are meant to be closely linked to different sectors of the economy. Studies at second level are more specialised and lead on to the DEUG in a single or in a dual disciplinary format.

Suffice it to say that this reform in effect puts an end to the two-year first cycle which is being split into two – and progressively hives off the majority from those parts of the DEUG that lead on to long course study. The upshot of this is the completion of the missing fourth cell in the matrix traditionally used to present French higher education, namely the 'open short cycle' sector. In short, the drive beyond mass higher education towards the 'universalisation' of the French university accelerate differentiation between institutions on the one hand and accentuate intra-institutional differentiation by the setting up of two if not three streams or tracks in each university at the level prior to the first degree. It remains to be seen whether these developments do not foreshadow the establishment of a *de facto* equivalent of the American Junior College under another name. What is, however, very certain is the demise of the last vestiges not of the Napoleonic university – for that died in 1968 – but a more subtle and enduring version of the same, namely the university regulated and controlled in its most intimate details by central administration. It means, in fine, the departure of the Jacobin university.

A disciplinary perspective

1. Engineering

It is by now evident that the tripartite structure of French higher education imposes a highly complex frame on the sectoral location of our four disciplines of engineering, physics, economics and history. As one breaks out, for instance, engineering as a subject, one brings with it all three sectors – *Grandes Ecoles*, university and University Institutes of Technology. Nor are the majority of engineering students enrolled in the university *stricto sensu*. As Figure 1.5 shows, the majority of students are in establishments outside the university sector.

Such complexity is not rendered any the less when one seeks a narrower definition of what engineering really is. One solution is to take refuge in official definitions. In France, the title or degree of 'engineer' is a 'protected title'. Only those establishments recognised by the Commission for Engineering Degrees (*Commission des titres d'ingénieur*) may award degrees carrying this designation. There are some 183 recognised by the Commission to do this. Even so, what is less clear is the level of study or, for that matter, the way studies are organised. In some instances, three years after the Baccalaureat are required; in others, up to five. More than any other disciplinary field, engineering is split across *Grandes Ecoles*, three *Instituts Polytechniques Nationaux* and the university, establishments which come under the authority of nine separate ministries. This tells us two things about the discipline – first, its origin in France as an outgrowth of military science, an attachment it still retains with pomp and circumstance each 14 July as the students of *Polytechnique* head the parade down the *Champs-Elysées*. Second, that engineering is the heartland of French technocracy since each ministry that has cause to employ engineers has its own school dealing with its own specific version of the discipline. It follows from this that the conditions under which the future engineer administrator at – say – *Polytechnique* studies vary considerably from those available to his counterpart in one of the mass universities of the Paris basin. The former has a pre-salary and, after his first year, a full-time salary. The latter may count on conditions of learning better than his fellows in the humanities and social sciences. What both have in common is a remarkably similar educational background.

Top engineering schools draw their students overwhelmingly from those who passed Baccalaureat C – that is mathematics and physical sciences, an option which remains the most demanding and the most selective of all. In 1989, for example, seven entrants to engineering schools out of ten came through this route.[4] And though attendance at a *Classe préparatoire aux Grandes Ecoles* is becoming less of a *conditio sine qua non* – only one student out of two has been through this route – there remain certain sectors within the world of French engineering education which still impose this requirement. These tend to be the Higher National Engineering Schools (*Ecoles Nationales Supérieures d'Ingénieurs*) and those public sector schools coming under the aegis of ministries other than National Education.

This symbiotic linkage between Bac C, the *Classes préparatoires* and the top drawer engineering schools may be a way of ensuring that the most brilliant minds, sharpened in a diet of extremely specialised mathematics, are attracted to the discipline of engineering. But there are also drawbacks, most particularly when France is seeking to increase the output of graduate engineers. As Figure 1.5 shows, approximately 14,000 engineers are produced each year. Current estimates show this to be around half of what the nation requires. Excellent though the stream undoubtedly is, it is, for all that, too thin. The engineering corps as constituted at present may well be sufficient to move France into the high technology of the twenty-first century. But it is insufficient to sustain and consolidate the brilliant initiative.

4 'Les écoles d'ingenieurs publiques et privées: année 1989–90', *Note d'Information 90–08*, Paris: Direction de l'Evaluation et de la Prospective, 2.

For a number of years, national science policy has sought to increase the supply of engineers (OECD 1986). The principle vehicle for this is to expand provision for engineering education in the university sector and to draw on other curricular pathways. This is already visible. University engineering schools recruit from a very different curricular pool. Seven out of ten of their students are holders either of the *Diplôme d'Etudes Universitaires Générales*, a *Brevet de Technicien Supérieur* or a *Diplôme Universitaire de Technologie*. And, if we go further back into the educational profile of university engineering school students, we find that in 1989, for example, almost half – 45 per cent – had passed through Baccalaureat options other than the prestigious track C.[5] Obviously if French science policy is to attain its ends it will have, to an increasing extent, to draw more broadly on the options streams which, like the technological option of the Baccalaureat, are currently under going massive growth. Or, as an alternative, which is already implemented under the title of the Descomps scheme, to open up opportunities for those who qualified earlier as mid-level technicians to retrain as fully fledged engineers in a species of sandwich (alternance) course.

Nevertheless, engineering along with medicine has one remarkable feature in France and one which over the past years has become more pronounced. Engineering students are predominantly from the upper-middle class, the children of industrial executives (*cadres*). In 1989, approximately 47 per cent of *Grandes Ecoles* engineering students were from this social category, an increase of almost four per cent since 1985.[6] This, perhaps more than any other aspect, is a sure pointer to the fact that this field constitutes an intellectual as well as a social élite. And, more to the point, that the intellectual and social élite, at a time of major economic change, appears to be consolidating its hold on these establishments.

What emerges from this vignette of the engineering field in France is that it has developed out of a very specific organisational base radically different from what one finds elsewhere in the European Community. This, as we suggested in the introduction to this analysis, is deeply embedded in the nation's intellectual and administrative history. Engineering in France is a permeative discipline. It is not located in one type of institution or one segment of the higher education system. But each

5 *Note d'Information* 90–08, op. cit., 2.

6 *Note d'Information*, op. cit., 3.

segment, *Grande Ecole* or university, imprints its particular interpretation and intellectual profile upon the field. It is permeative in another sense as well.

In other European countries, engineering has developed from beneath, formed its own specialised institutions – whether technological universities, *Technische Hochschulen*, etc – which were gradually, and often with considerable misgiving on the part of established disciplines, assimilated into the university. The university retained the commanding heights of prestige. In France, this pattern of institutional assimilation did not pertain. Indeed, only today does one see a gradual assimilation of engineering into the university as part of the 'democratisation' of that discipline. Engineering stood as one of the technical and vehicular disciplines of state service. It stood apart from the university and was often administered by ministries outside Education. Rather than being assimilated into the university, what one can see with remarkable clarity is the university often assimilating some of the practices which identified the engineering *Grandes Ecoles* – the introduction of selective tracks and the linkage with a specific vocational purpose being but two. It is then not a question of assimilating engineering into university to give it, its adepts and its practitioners a respectability they thought they needed. One of the central contemporary issues facing the discipline in

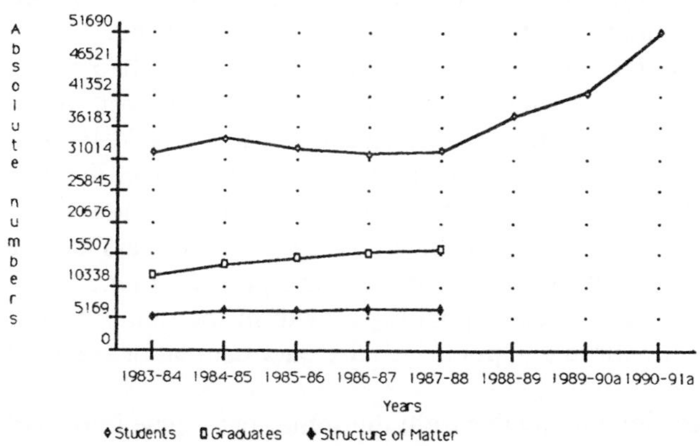

Figure 1.6 Science enrolments 1983–1990

Source: 'Premières inscriptions à l'Université par filière *Repères et Statistiques, 1990,* Tables 10.8, 10.10, pp.199, 203. a. recalculated from 'Les étudiants inscrits à l'Université en 1990–1991', *Note d'information 91–22,* Paris, 1991, Direction de l'Evaluation at de la Prospective, tableau IV p.2.

France today is how to give broader access to a field of knowledge which over the past century has progressively been identified with the apex of French public education. In short, how can the university gain some of the prestige that attaches to the heartland of engineering in the *Grandes Ecoles*.

2. Physics

The structure of first cycle studies in the French university does not, strictly speaking, break out physics as a separate self-standing subject area. It is an important element, to be sure. But the start of the future research physicist's career lies in the *Diplôme d'Etudes Universitaires Générales* and more particularly in the track termed 'sciences' and structure of matter or sciences DEUG A. This track combines a broad subject range embracing mathematics and chemistry as well as physics (Université d'Avignon 1991). Time budgeting – whether lectures, 'directed work' or 'practicals' – is nationally set at approximately 1200 hours over the two-year cycle of the degree. First-year students enrolled on the DEUG A sciences of the structure of matter at Joseph Fournier University (Grenoble I) are, on official estimates, faced with between 24 and 27 hours work per week (Université Grenoble I 1988).

The A track of the science DEUG, as befits that field containing the queen of sciences, draws its students very heavily from Baccalaureats C, D and E; almost half those entering university with Bac C (maths and physics) opt for this track. For holders of Bac D (mathematics and natural science), physical sciences is one of the three most attractive fields along with mathematics and natural science (ONISEP 1991).

As Figure 1.6 makes plain, the past few years have seen substantial growth in the number of students emerging from secondary school qualified for this area of study. Indeed, the past three years have seen the sciences emerging as the fastest growing area in the French university, largely due to the corresponding growth in the numbers of students qualifying through Option C in the Baccalaureat between 1988 and 1990.[7]

The impression one retains from the somewhat sparse information presented in student manuals culled from three universities, is the con-

7 'Les étudiants inscrits a l'université en 1990–1991', *Note d'Information 91–22*, 1991. Paris: Direction de l'Evaluation et de la Prospective, 2.

siderable emphasis placed upon formal lectures and classroom work. First year students at Grenoble, for instance, grapple with ten hours mathematics, eight hours of physics, five of chemistry and two of computing per week. In the second year, the DEUG A divides into specialist sections; physics and mathematics, physics and mechanical engineering, mathematics and physics and a fourth which combines chemistry with physics. The stakhanovite pace of the first year seems less marked. Each track appears to involve around ten hours formal class contact and, most interesting in view of the international nature of physics, an additional compulsory two hours per week are set aside for English to bring students up to a level sufficient to make an oral presentation. In Grenoble, evaluation is based on continuous assessment throughout the year plus end of year examinations. According to official estimates for the year 1987–8, some 75 per cent of those who sat the final examination, passed (Université Grenbole I 1988). What this does not say, however, is what proportion of the original entrants at the start of the course turned up for the final examination!

Only at the level of the Licence (that is, three years after the Bac) does physics break out as a separate and self-standing field. Though doubtless other universities will by now have developed their own

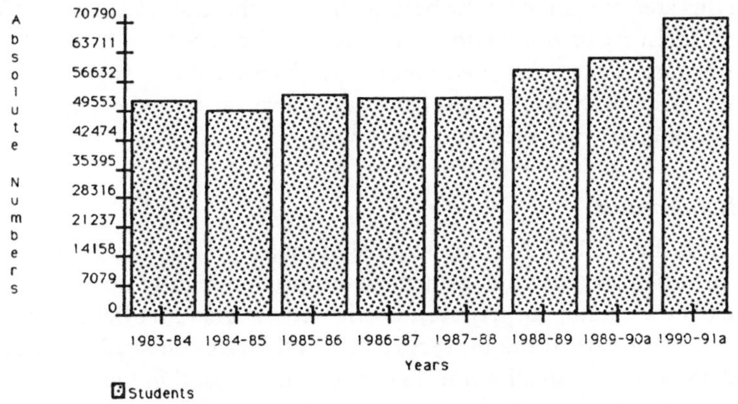

Figure 1.7 Economics and law enrolments

Source: 'Premières inscriptions à l'Université par filière' *Repères et Statistiques op. cit.,* Tables 10.8, p.199. a. recalculated from 'les étudiants inscrits à l'Université en 1990–1991', Note d'information 91–22, Paris, 1991, Direction de l'Evaluation et de la Prospective, tableau IV p.2.

strategy for dealing with the transition from DEUG to Licence, nevertheless the experience of Grenoble I may be revealing. Sixty places are available each year. These are assigned on the basis of previous performance, the individual's record sheet and an evaluation. The successful sixty are faced once again with a substantial workload – 661 hours over one year, of which 229 are formal lectures, 244 directed work and 188 set aside for practicals. Some of the more outstanding may in the course of the year be offered the possibility of entering on a fast track designed to bring students forward to research via the *Magistère* degree. But this requires an average performance of 12/20 in the Licence. The *Magistère*, a second cycle qualification introduced in 1986, is an attempt to strengthen links with research and is yet another example of the tendency towards greater internal differentiation upon which we remarked earlier.

One may derive only a limited amount of information from student manuals. But this, when placed against previous work in advanced student training in France (Neave 1993), leaves some impressions, though how accurate they are at first degree level is a different matter. The considerable emphasis placed on the formally didactical aspect, especially during the first year of the DEUG, appears to prolong the type of teaching found in upper-secondary schools. And though the students entering this area are amongst the best qualified in the university sector, the sheer intensity of work with which they are faced redounds. Whether this is part of the French edition of the physics culture or simply another form of central control bearing down on national degrees is something one may well wonder about.

3. Economics

As with the DEUG A in the science of matter so the DEUG in economic sciences and management draws predominantly upon Option track B which, not surprisingly, is oriented towards that field. Almost half the students in the university first cycle have followed this track (ONISEP 1991). In all, some 25 per cent of all Bac B holders go on to study either economics and management or the slightly less demanding combination known as the administrative, economic and social track (*filière AES*). There is also some cross-flow from students leaving secondary school with Bac C – in 1990 some 7 per cent of this group subsequently moved into economics, largely as a result of the considerable mathematical orientation contained in this option and, in all probability, because they were not successful in their other choices.

Although economics and management (*Sciences Economiques et de Gestion*) breaks out earlier than physics, the way national statistics are put together does not allow us to distinguish between those students enrolled in economics and those following law. We may only obtain an approximate idea of the general trend rather than a precise idea of the dynamic underlying the demand for this field. Though the number of first time university enrolments has grown markedly over the past three years, the increase in law and economics combined has not greatly outpaced the rate of increase for other domains (see Figure 1.7).

Generally speaking, the DEUG in economics is a general course concerned with the introduction of the basic principles of the field. There are two main orientations – economic theory and more applied aspects which later lead on to management specialisations. Like the DEUG A of sciences of matter, economics is a course of some 1200 hours over two years. If we take the course outline of the University of Grenoble II, which specialises in social sciences, we find that the first year is structured around three fundamental courses – economic analysis, quantitative approaches to the economy, and mathematics. Two other compulsory credit units are added to this – the history of economic and social events, and languages, either English or German. Students are expected to follow 20 hours of teaching (course) and lecturing per week and a further seven in directed work (Université des Sciences Sociales Grenbole II 1989). Directed work sessions present students with concrete problems designed to ascertain how far they have mastered what is taught in lectures.

Attendance is compulsory and in one establishment – the University of Nancy II – each directed work session is preceded by a roll call. Those absent more than five times in less than three months without just cause will find themselves excluded from end of term examinations! (Université de Nancy II 1986)

Essentially, the DEUG in economics is an initiatory course to training as an economist at the end of which students may go on to the Licence, sit a category B (British Executive grade) in the civil service or take up work (Université de Sciences Sociales Grenoble II 1989). The Licence (Bac +3) is considered as an intermediary step between general initiation and the fully trained professional economist who emerges from the *Maîtrise* (Bac +4). In effect, specialisation begins only at the Licence. Equally evident are the grafting on of vocational tracks often highly selective, after the DEUG. The *Maîtrise de Sciences et Techniques*, the *Maîtrise de Sciences de Gestion* and the *Maîtrise d'Informatique appliquée à la Gestion* are examples of this. Many of them are highly selective, requiring additional tests, interviews plus an excellent record card (ONISEP 1991).

The field of economics is a particularly good illustration of the vocationalisation of the university, with the plethora of highly specialised degrees often aimed at very specific types of employment; management level accountants and specialist cadres in the private sector. It is also an interesting example at the level of the *Maîtrise* of the university beginning to assimilate some of the selective features which, hitherto have characterised the *Grandes Ecoles* specialising in business studies.

4. History

The career of a future historian is fraught with all manner of obstacles, not least of which is the uniquely French characteristic of combining history at university level with geography. The subsequent development of this latter field from a human to an often highly technical and mathematically based science, plus the fact that over half the students enrolled in a DEUG in history have taken the literary track in the Bac, is no small pitfall even at the start (ONISEP 1991). In addition, some 20 per cent of history enrolments at first cycle level are drawn from the economics option of the Bac. Yet, by all accounts, students opting for history are persistent and the percentage of those repeating a year is relatively low.

In contrast to either physics or economics – which also dwell under various forms in both the non-university sectors, *Grandes Ecoles* and University Institutes of Technology – history, with the exception of the *Ecole Normale Supérieure*, is a university-based discipline at the first degree level. As a general rule, a DEUG in history is made up of a number of compulsory modules which in addition extend out into such disciplines as geography, statistics, sociology, anthropology and economics plus languages ancient and modern. The study of history at this stage is then a pluridisciplinary undertaking. Put another way, it is not a complete programme in the same sense as economics. The 600 hours of class contact which the DEUG each year levies from its victims are not wholly given over to history. At the University of Avignon, the weekly workload in both years one and two is reckoned at around thirteen and a half hours – that is, exactly half the work load in either physics or economics (Université d'Avignon 1991).

At this level, the history course is not regarded as leading towards any specific careers. Indeed, it is seen more as a general training that later will lead on to other fields. In fine, just as the student in the science of matter has to persist through to the Licence to take up a single track physics course, so in history the path is strewn with links to other courses, which themselves are thought to have a certain career value. At the University of Paris VII, for example, openings other than history are placed before the student graduating from the history DEUG, planning (*amenagement*) for developing countries is one; tracks leading eventually to training in journalism is another possibility. As one career guidance magazine warned its readers, 'outside of teaching and the competitive examination for entry to public service, a Master's degree in history has little chance of attracting the interest of a possible employer' (ONISEP 1991). Yet, in the present situation, where history posts in school are few and far between and what expansion there is places special emphasis on mathematics, information technology and sciences, even this grim statement appears to veer towards the optimistic. Perhaps precisely because of the lack of obvious career paths that follow on from history, it is this field of the four which we have examined that seems the least influenced by the drive towards the vocational. As we have seen in the case of physics and economics, clear indications, if only of a general nature, are laid before students about the future type of employment they may expect. And, as we have argued throughout this exposé, the vocational engagement and close alignment with state service has long been the explicit rationale behind engineering. It may well be that as the French university sets its sights upon catering for more and more students that history will remain as the last vestige of a world that higher education has lost, one in which learning for itself was not incompatible with the application of the knowledge one gained from that process.

Conclusion

One can, if one looks hard enough, find elements of exceptionalism in every system of higher education. Sometimes these elements express the very essence of a particular system. In others, they seem merely to be interesting examples that reaffirm a basic commonality across systems. By the extreme complexity of its structure, its organisational stratification and its differentiation, the French higher education system is remarkable in Western Europe. French exceptionalism, as I have attempted to argue, emerges in the form of that profound duality between specialised schools, given over to the preparation of state service on the one hand and the university on the other. Such a duality is not a passing thing and has, rather, been a deeply embedded feature of higher education over the past two centuries. Whereas in most other systems of higher education in Western Europe the vocational domain has largely been subordinate to the domain of learning, in France the situation was inversed. To be sure the university was never subordinated to the *Grandes Ecoles*, neither legally nor organisationally. But the basic vocational clarity of commitment to supply the highest posts in state service afforded a social superiority and as we have seen from some of the characteristics of student flows, an intellectual superiority as well to the non-university domain.

At a time when the university faces a second rush into the lecture theatres which promises to be every bit as spectacular in a quantitative manner as its predecessor in the 1960s, selection on the one hand and vocational clarity on the other – the hallmarks of the élite sector – begin to exercise great influence in the university itself. Thus, we see an acceleration in the commitment of the university, less to 'education' (*enseignment*) and more to 'training' (*formation*).

Another feature which reinforces the French claim to exceptionalism has emerged when we turned our attention to the four disciplines of engineering, physics, economics and history. Each holds a different balance in what may be termed its 'institutional location', with the two extremes being represented by long course Engineering located mainly outside the university *stricto sensu* and, on the other, history, which can only find a niche inside it at first degree level. Physics and economics can be regarded as having a 'dual institutional location' being found both in university and in the engineering *Grandes Ecoles*. But the former, at least at the level of the first university diploma, is still part of a combined general course. Economics too has its dual status for if it exists as a self-standing field in the university from the first, it is also present in the highly selective, private sector business studies *Grandes Ecoles*. Looked at from a wholly disciplinary perspective we find each discipline – save history – stratified across two – sometimes more – institutional locations in which the non-university sector seems to draw off the most able students.

And finally, as we have noted at various points in this analysis, there has been an enduring dualism in what has been termed 'reform styles'. Steady adjustment to change has been the feature of the *Grandes Ecoles*, in all probability because, having no single coordinating ministry, each ministry could introduce change without massive public intervention. This has been the case with the university. Central government intervention has been radical, secretive and not always happy in its outcome. But here again, we may detect certain pointers towards a more incremental style that has characterised the *Grandes Ecoles*. Greater financial autonomy, the loosening up of the definition and controlling power of central administration over course content and validation are feathers in this particular wind. On paper at least, each establishment now sets its own objectives. Whether this means that in the near future, reform in both university and non-university higher education will converge towards a similar incrementalism is something that only time will tell, whether or not ministerial intention is matched by institutional capacity.

CHAPTER 2

Changes in Curriculum and Institutional Structures

Responses to Outside Influences in Higher Education Institutions

Mary Henkel and Maurice Kogan

Introduction

This paper discusses the ways in which the internal working and products of IHEs (Institutions of Higher Education) are affected by external pressures, including those of central government and the world of employment. We begin by rehearsing the influences which became evident in the 1980s. The main areas subjected to change have been the undergraduate and graduate curricula, the research agenda, and the internal decision and policy making structures of IHEs.

Political and resource pressures on IHEs

The UK is a strong case of the power of external influence because the role of its central authorities has changed most radically from that of providing a resource and political frame for institutional autonomy, particularly in the universities, to the sternest forms of governmental prescription.

Pressures on curriculum content

The government declared its intention to promote certain highly instrumental policies and establish them through new mechanisms. Those for curriculum content emerged in such statements as:

> meeting the needs of the economy is not the sole purpose of higher education ... But this aim must be vigorously pursued ... The Government and its central funding agencies will do all they can to encourage and reward approaches by higher education institu-

> tions which bring them closer to the world of business. (Department of Education and Science 1987).

In the same year then, the Manpower Services Commission (now TEED, The Training, Enterprise and Education Directorate) announced at the initial cost of £100m the Enterprise in Higher Education Initiative which would 'enable higher education institutions to … embed activities that promote enterprise into the work of the institutions'. We will return to this later.

The pressures put on higher education do not amount to direct prescription of the curriculum, but constitute part of the new normative environment in which higher education moves.

Quality assurance

Recent policies have insisted on quality assurance of both teaching and research. In the past the curriculum and assessment patterns of the public sector IHEs (led by the 30 polytechnics) were rigorously monitored by the Council for National Academic Awards (CNAA); the universities were almost completely free to determine their own standards, although almost always external examiners were party to the award of degrees. But they were first impelled – reputedly by the threat of the introduction of inspectors (HMI) into the assessment of their teaching – to create an Academic Audit Unit which would evaluate universities' own procedures for the assessment of teaching and assessment.

Then came proposals (Department of Employment 1991) to end the binary system, to allow public sector institutions to call themselves universities, to place all IHEs under single funding councils (one each for England, Wales and Scotland), and to create three types of assessment of teaching. There would be: Quality Control, 'mechanisms within institutions for maintaining and enhancing the quality of their provision'; Quality Audit, 'external scrutiny aimed at providing guarantees that institutions have suitable quality control mechanisms in place'; and Quality Assessment, 'external review of, and judgements about, the quality of teaching and learning in institutions'. Institutions are to have the major stake in a Quality Audit Unit alongside industry and the professions, and funding council assessors. On the face of it, these assurance devices will not affect curriculum content, but they do represent a strong move to place university autonomy over maintaining teaching standards within public scrutiny.

Market pressures

Yet more pressures derive from two forms of market mechanism, both reinforced by reductions in resources for public and university institutions. To make up the shortfall from what had previously been deficiency funding, institutions have been compelled to market their products, including courses to which overseas students are recruited at high fees, graduate 'taught' and short courses in subjects for which there is a demand, and for which institutions may set their own fee levels, and research and consultancy in which objectives are set more by the purchaser than the academics.

A second set of mechanisms has altered radically the funding of teaching. In place of block grants which enabled universities to appoint teachers who were also researchers, and to establish degree courses almost at will, (the public institutions were more constrained), institutions must now 'bid' for each student place, by the course, at a price that they think will be acceptable to the funding council. The University Funding Council (UFC) set 'guide prices' based on historic costs for each subject area, minus 10 per cent, and waited for the universities to submit their offers. Ninety-three per cent of the bids came in at the guide price, but according to the minister of the time this was the universities acting as a cartel. (In fact, entries at the guide price would have required serious reductions in staffing levels at most universities). This pseudo-market will force some institutions to close courses which cannot yield enough money and to introduce serious differences in staffing and other levels between neighbouring disciplines. There will be pressure on the classic British model of personal tutoring and small group teaching.

The assumed link, too, between good level teaching and research is to be broken. Whereas university (unlike polytechnic and college) teachers were also appointed, and funded, to conduct research, funding for student places will progressively omit the research element (assumed to be about 30%). Increasingly, they will have to seek funding *ad hoc* from research councils and other research commissioning bodies.

Pressures for managerialism and efficiency

From the time of the first cuts in the early 1980s, policy pronouncements emphasised that the institution, rather than the departments and the individual academics, should generate and control educational practice. The reductions in public funding placed new burdens on, and elicited new responses from, the institution and its leadership. The Jarratt Report (1985) placed upon vice-chancellors of universities the explicit role of Chief Executive rather than that of *primus inter pares* within a collegium of scholars. It also advocated strong corporate planning within which the mainly lay councils would take a leading role in policy making. It proposed a managerial in place of a collegial model of working which has been the accepted legend, if not the reality, of academic life. Committee structures were to be streamlined and small central planning committees established. The report also advocated such management notions as the devolution of financial accountability to 'cost centres' and the use of performance indicators. The Croham Report (1987), which reviewed the future of the University Grants Committee (UGC) and the government's White Paper, *Higher Education: Meeting the Challenge* (DES 1987), made it plain that: 'The Government has a role in seeking to ensure that suitable arrangements to promote and monitor efficiency are in place for institutions'.

References to basic units and individuals are thin on the ground in these official documents and the power of the department as against that of the institutions is described with hostility (Jarratt Report 1985). They are treated as sub-units of their institutions (Scott 1986). None of these statements begins with an analysis of the academic task upon which organisation might be premised. They rather take it as axiomatic that reform towards efficiency will entail a shift from the setting of objectives by individuals and by disciplinary groups and they will be set by the institutions within the normative frames set by government.

Similar assumptions have been made about the government and management of public sector institutions. The National Advisory Board's report of its Good Management Practice Group, *Management for a Purpose* (NAB 1987), was in part concerned with improving managerial efficiency. The newly created Polytechnics and Colleges Funding Council (PCFC) contracts with institutions for the provision of higher education 'will provide a much improved setting within which (they) can pursue educational effectiveness and efficiency, can develop entrepreneurial skills and attitudes and can respond to national needs' (DES 1987).

Pressures for selectivity

The government has insisted that funds will be distributed selectively. This affects research funding most, although judgements of quality also enter into the funding councils' response to bids for student places. University research has been graded twice and the differentials in core funding have widened progressively since the first grading exercises were announced in 1986.

Government has also aimed to channel research into 'useful' areas including the promotion of 'strategic research' which will be fundamental in its nature but directed towards economic and social ends. IHEs must develop research plans which tend to assume coordination and team rather than individualistic work. Some of the most esteemed teams in natural science are under pressure, because of restricted research council funds, to take on mission oriented work specified by industry or government in place of 'blue skies' work addressing the development of theory. That pressure is more likely to affect the less well esteemed universities, although all feel constrained.

In all of these aspects, the government was the principal source of external influence. Recurrent studies in many countries (Ushiogi 1977; Roizen and Jepson 1983; Boys *et al.* 1988) have shown that whilst employers may be not wholly satisfied with the products of higher education, they cannot articulate demands for IHEs to read off. Government attempts to make higher education responsive to employment needs are often regarded by employers as not capable of developing the personal and working skills that the best of more traditional education can provide (CIHE 1987). Whilst first destinations statistics for the 1980s 'suggest a better market situation for university graduates' they also show 'more complete employment preparation for polytechnic graduates' (Brennan 1991), and it is the polytechnics that have put the premium on employability.

Curriculum organisation and change

We now turn to the main activity variable by which the significance of external pressure can be judged: changes in the curriculum, which, together with work experience, are the principal means by which undergraduates are prepared for employment.

1 Much of what follows in the next sections derives from our study published in 1988 (Boys *et al.*). The authors of the relevant chapters were John Brennan, Maurice Kogan and Penny Youll.

The aims of curriculum and its organisation

Undergraduate programmes may be framed to meet essentially academic objectives or to produce graduates able to apply knowledge and skills in specific areas.

The academic programme aims to prepare graduates who are well grounded in their subject and credible exponents of their discipline. Such courses attempt to introduce the students to the fundamental knowledge and principles of their disciplines and to socialise them into an academic community. Vocational programmes seek to produce graduates able to apply relevant knowledge and skills to particular ends and specific areas of practice.

These two models of curriculum organisation apply the distinction made by Bernstein (1971) between the collection and integrated codes. The collection code emphasises the separateness of the disciplines, their logic and concerns; the integrated code describes the selection of knowledge around some organising theme. For the teacher and student the collection code gives considerable control over what is taught or learned – the individualistic curriculum. In an integrated code teaching and learning are 'directed' by the programme's organising themes – hence the directed curriculum.

In the individualistic curriculum, the exercise of freedom is taken to be a fundamental part of scholarship and, for the student, the experience of making choices is itself educative. Students can influence the direction and content of courses through choice: options which are undersubscribed are unlikely to survive. Equally, staff are free to offer options whether or not they link with other elements of the curriculum: these will typically follow research interests. Curriculum development is likely, therefore, to be discipline-led, incremental, strongly influenced by student demand and staff preference and to show no consistent relationship with employment objectives. Staff may provide opportunities for students to pursue studies which are relevant to work but these will not be compulsory. This model frequently describes the academic, mono-disciplinary degree programme where work orientation is seen as primarily the responsibility of the careers service rather than of the taught curriculum. It is equally applicable to some of the modular degree programmes increasingly common in public sector institutions.

The directed curriculum, in contrast, approximates to the integrated code. The emphasis is on course design, progression, and coherence of separate elements around agreed objectives. Such courses will have a tightly organised curriculum in which required elements and sequences predominate. The programme is designed to meet specific ends in which individual choice is limited. The teachers take collective responsibility for the courses. The student has relatively little influence except through complaint or deciding against entry. Similarly, teachers' freedom is limited since courses must link in a coherent way. Curriculum development will tend, therefore, to be course-led, systematic and less influenced by individual objectives.

Vocational, applied, training and professional courses tend to have a directed curriculum. They have a pre-defined outcome, in many cases strongly influenced by professional or accreditation bodies or the employment market. However, the Brunel study showed that academic degree programmes, based on a belief that students should master the essentials of a discipline, may also be strongly framed by their architects. There are, of course, intermediate positions: the individualistic and the directed curricula are best seen as at two ends of a continuum. Some courses in the Brunel study displayed characteristics of both models. Some discipline-based courses were highly structured: students were required to advance systematically in order to grasp the essentials of the discipline. By contrast some programmes geared to preparation for the labour market placed high value on the promotion of personal development, responsibility for students' own learning and initiative through the exercise of choice. Examples in the study were modular degree structures and project-based learning.

Curriculum content

Course aims reveal themselves primarily through curriculum content and in the balance struck between knowledge, skills, practical experience and socialisation. The complexity of these mixes makes it difficult for systems managers to get purchase over the curriculum. Some disciplines require a sequential build-up of knowledge while some may be treated on a thematic or chronological basis. The balance between immersion in substance and mastery of theory and method varies. There is pressure on curriculum content from the expansion of knowledge, from technological developments and applications, from changes in the preparation of students for tertiary study as well as from concern about graduate employment. Such pressures may result in major course reviews.

Common issues in curriculum debates, irrespective of discipline, course type or institution are: how to maintain high academic standards; how to achieve a balance between academic and more instrumental objectives; the desirability of including skills, particularly if they were deemed transferable; the need to improve graduate employment record; and effective use of staff time especially where there were competing demands of research and teaching.

Patterns of curriculum change

Curriculum development is predominantly incremental and continuous, although there are cases of substantial restructuring or innovation. There is growth in multidisciplinary, interdisciplinary, combined and modular courses and undergraduate programmes which link across traditional discipline boundaries. Physics provides several such links; for example, with biological, geological and medical sciences to offer courses in biophysics, geophysics and medical physics. The development of such courses reflects a demand for technologists who can work together on problems which cannot be tackled within one discipline. A different pattern can be found when several disciplines are focused on a field of activity: the development of a money, banking and finance course at a university offers an example.

An extensive example of multidisciplinarity is a polytechnic modular degree which can respond both to student demand and to external requirements. Such programmes can include marketable studies either as whole subject offerings or as modules. Developments at one college involved a comprehensive recasting of traditional disciplines into cross-disciplinary courses to serve industrial and commercial requirements. There are thus reorderings of the boundaries and 'kinships' between traditional subjects involving regrouping of departments according to vocational or disciplinary links. Some such redefinitions reflect developments in the 'real world': they may respond to newly defined needs for trained manpower. As institutions seek to earn money and to win new students, and as new areas of activity open up (for example, in tourism and other service industries), so it becomes attractive for IHEs to foster interdisciplinary links in order to respond. Those institutions which most need external earnings or more students are perhaps more likely to pursue this path but the objective of relevance appears to gain strength as economic pressures mount, even in high status and long established academic departments.

Course-led development

In noting attempts by IHEs to meet such needs we should be aware that they do not always succeed. A recent study (Brennan 1991) speaks of 'subject and institutional differences in the extent to which, with hindsight, graduates would choose to do the same degree courses again ... the latter relate neither to labour market success nor completely to job preparation. They remind us, perhaps, that some courses at some institutions are just a lot more interesting than others'. Even more sharply, of the groups following the most employment related courses, Brennan writes, 'engineers – from whatever type of institution – are less likely to wish to repeat their choice of degree course than other groups of students, the only exception being university accountants'.

The efficient curriculum

Many changes increasingly concern the efficient use of resources, and decisions to increase the size of tutorial classes or to cut down teaching. This might lead, (Boys *et al.* 1988) to criticism of over-teaching and the resolution to release staff time for research and consultancy by allowing students more individual study time.

Resource reduction not only impels departments to increase external earnings through research and consultancy but, in both the public sector and universities, to increase research output. Some academics, in consequence, expect to reduce teaching in favour of more research, although the most recent resource constraints make this unlikely. Others, while recognising a tension between research and teaching, affirm that commitment to undergraduates should always come first. Success is measured both by what is marketable and by what can be put together economically; any course that can be mounted without major resource requirements is a 'winner'. Effective teaching is also linked with obtaining good undergraduate results, ensuring a thorough understanding of basic principles and reducing drop-out. The notion of efficient pedagogy emerges even in university research-based departments in physics.

Student needs and demands

In most departments, the recruitment of well-qualified students is essential to maintain status within the institution and beyond. Applications for places affect the extent to which departments review critically the appeal of their courses. This may not mean much more than packaging courses in a way that potential students and their advisers can readily understand; for example, degree titles which do not correspond to school subjects may deter candidates. Staff might become more aware of students as potential customers: not only the courses but the environment, the friendliness of the department, the services and support available to undergraduates, are all likely to come under scrutiny.

However, student preferences do not tend to push the curriculum either to more academic or to more vocational treatments. Our student survey (Boys *et al.* 1988) suggested that students are motivated primarily by personal interest and that employment considerations vary in importance according to the subject.

The place of skills teaching

Government and employer concern about developing skills is reflected in many courses but the extent of specific skills teaching varies among the subjects. The spectrum of skills that academics are concerned to promote is: generic study skills, intellectual skills, experimental and technical skills, general and specific work skills. Within this range there is increasing interest in identifying and promoting transferable skills. Institutions also recognise the demand for the literate scientist, the numerate arts student, the socially aware engineer, for computer literacy and for communication and social skills.

There may be a latent demand for work experience: for example, about half the students surveyed in economics, physics and electrical engineering, whose course did not include work placements, thought this would have been valuable.

Courses reflect four general approaches to work-related skills. One is to prepare the student for work in specific areas of the labour market, to transmit highly relevant knowledge, including the teaching of applicable skills and, in some cases, work placements. For example, an applied physics course at a polytechnic was geared to industrial relevance. Work placements were a compulsory part of the degree programme, and the contextual studies course provided more general work skills and orientation.

A second type of course provides skills that help students to obtain good employment rather than to offer specific training. One college established an institution-wide programme of work orientation. A university course in physics included job seeking and work-related skills. Many courses recognise the generic value of communication skills (verbal and written ability, numeracy, computer literacy), and social skills (teamwork and self-presentation), although not all adapt curricula accordingly.

Third, courses can include knowledge applicable to employment without the teaching taking a vocational orientation. Most economists contend (although our survey suggested that students thought differently) that the vocational benefits of their courses come primarily from acquiring the core tools of economic analysis rather than from 'applied' options. Two well-established university physics departments recognised that problem solving skills could be taught by using 'real life' as well as theoretical material to demonstrate application of the methods.

A fourth pattern emphasises knowledge and acquisition of cognitive skills, with no particular reference to employment. Many staff in the academic subjects believe that courses should not have work related aims, or that obtaining a degree is sufficient preparation for employment and that discipline conferred skills are, in any case, transferable and attractive to employers. For example, in history the skills involved in collecting and weighing evidence and presenting a reasoned argument are thought relevant to any setting.

Vocational shift

Both the colleges of higher education in our study had instituted college-wide curriculum changes to make their undergraduate courses more relevant to employment. At one this entailed wholesale restructuring of the curriculum and staff retraining. At the other it consisted of more modest additions to an otherwise unchanged curriculum. None of the larger institutions had attempted across-the-board curriculum changes, but there were examples of employment-related developments initiated from the centre. A university had recently brought about closer links between the careers service and the academic staff. The new director of a polytechnic was concerned to establish employment objectives as part of the polytechnic's educational policy. Almost everywhere institutional concerns about graduate employment formed an important part of the 'atmospherics'.

These concerns were not, however, equally strong everywhere and the evidence suggests that they partly reflected the degree of vulnerability and traditional differences in institutional 'mission'. Application and vocationalism have been part of the ethos of the polytechnics and the technological universities since their foundation and were well established among our nine institutions, for acceptance or challenge by the basic units.

Several basic units were concerned about employability. New degree programmes in retail marketing or finance and banking were developed to meet specific labour market needs. But course development in pursuit of such ends was often less comprehensive. It might involve new options, the repackaging of existing courses, and moves to secure exemptions from professional bodies. Such changes were found in both directed and individualistic curriculum models.

The individualistic model displayed several kinds of influence. Many staff reported growing student preferences for employment-related options. But demand might also vary with ability. The study suggests, for example, that the best applicants to physics departments wanted strong academic rather than applied courses.

If the academic interests of individual staff play a particularly strong role in the individualistic curriculum, here, too, vocational shifts are discernible. Where, as in physics and engineering, research depends heavily on external funding, staff have tended to follow funding into applied areas. The effects of these shifts are discernible, both in the orientation of existing courses and in the new options which are proposed.

Curriculum development in the directed model reflects similar influences. Changes instituted at departmental or faculty levels took account of institutional priorities, not least because of their relationship to resource allocations. Particularly in the universities, heads of department were anxious to maximise external earnings to help compensate for losses from funding council sources. Thus, developments which could find an external sponsor to fund a lectureship, a chair or a research fellowship were especially desirable. This was a part of a growing entrepreneurial approach in some departments that included the pursuit of research contracts, consultancies and overseas students.

These developments do not usually derive from considered institutional policies but emerge opportunistically as individuals and departments pursue what they see as their best interests: to secure survival; to maintain academic status and identity; to secure resources; to fend off external threats; to sustain individual and collective disciplinary advancement.

In considering the preparation of students for employment Silver and Brennan (1988) have created a hierarchy of relationships between courses and potential employment with an ordering of specificity and explicitness in the design and presentation of courses. They point out that, irrespective of a liberal vocational dichotomy, academic qualifications are being used to regulate entry into employment. From the employer's standpoint a degree in a particular subject is essential, desirable, or irrelevant for selection. They then note three kinds of degree qualifications: a specified degree as a sole regulator; a specified degree as a partial regulator, and an unspecified degree. They also note the relevance of the extent to which courses contain different degrees of completed job preparation. For the most part, these concerns are not strongly present in the thinking of curriculum makers, who largely feel able to respond to intuition and the hidden hand of employment demands.

Changes in particular disciplines

The Brunel study (Boys *et al.* 1988) traced curriculum change in six subject areas, including history, economics, engineering and physics. In summary the findings were as follows.

History remained strongly 'internalist' in its development, but budget cuts caused some rearrangements, even in the stronger departments, including closure. An emphasis on employability was internalised by teachers who were concerned about students' prospects. The logic of the discipline continued to prevail but movement was evident towards more thematic treatments and socially relevant topics, including Britain's economic plight. Some teachers ensured attention to development of oracy, self-presentation and the use of IT (information technology). But individual development continued as the main claim of the subject to employability.

Physics was under pressure. Physicists remained in control of the taught discipline but had to take account of external pressures and constraints. The agenda for research was subject to external pressure from funders but the rules of scientific enquiry were not affected. But economically-led research might begin to affect the undergraduate curriculum. There was a growing demand for inter- and multidisciplinary scientists and for work in areas shaped by both academic science and industry. Physicists were concerned to preserve a distinct identity from engineering whilst taking note of external demands.

In electrical engineering there was broad consensus between academics and employers and differences were of emphasis. The departments were directed to producing graduates for the engineering profession, although not all went into it and not all proved satisfied about their preparation (Brennan 1991). Employers influenced curriculum through research funding rather than through guidance offered through committees or other explicit mechanisms. Departments found it difficult to interpret employers' wishes and there were differences on the proper division between academic and employment skills.

Economics' strong sense of disciplinary identity might make it unresponsive to external influences. Yet its subject matter was relevant to the world of work and, for some, application was the main thrust. They seemed able to make strategic changes in their courses without losing academic authority and recognised that opportunities lay in business or financial institutions whilst sustaining the belief that good 'academic' economists were valued in the labour market. They did not act, or find it necessary to do so, on messages received in any coherent form from employers. But labour market considerations played a part in shaping developments in undergraduate teaching.

It will be seen, therefore, that whilst the four subject areas were certainly responding to employment considerations they were able to do so without shifting from their own value base. But both physics and history were less secure than in the past. Electrical engineering was a growth area. Some traditionally strong subjects, (economics was an exception), were losing ground to newer subjects in the organisation of degrees.

The Enterprise Initiative

Thus far we have described modes of curriculum formation and control in which the main actors are higher education staff and students, even though they are increasingly affected by the assumed needs of the labour market. Such mechanisms as exist for connection with employers assume that IHEs and basic units will internalise external pressures in their own ways. Traditionally, government has not attempted to influence the curriculum, even when making gestures about some of its overall objectives.

The Enterprise in Higher Education Initiative, sponsored by the Department of Employment rather than the Department of Education and Science however, represented a far bolder governmental attempt than hitherto to insinuate market values. It aimed 'to encourage the development of qualities of enterprise amongst those seeking higher education qualifications'. Forty-one institutions have received substantial funding to support five-year Enterprise Plans. No less than 90 per cent of those eligible to do so applied for EHE funding, which was awarded competitively (Department of Employment 1991); their motivation was presumably sharpened by the reduction in funding from the main sources.

The Initiative promotes changes in the learning processes, and in the relationships with employers so that (Jones 1991): 'Every person should be able to develop competencies and attitudes relevant to enterprise' through the acquisitions of personal transferable skills, which are 'generic capabilities which allow people to succeed in a wide range of different tasks and jobs'. The competencies are to be acquired in part through project-based work designed to take place in 'real' economic settings and jointly assessed by employers and institutions.

The relationship with employers is the 'cornerstone' of the initiative: they are to collaborate by providing placements and projects and also cash or kind support for the programmes. The programmes provide for staff development programmes which are 'aimed at raising awareness ... exploring the meaning of "enterprise" in the higher education context; developing staff abilities in...curriculum development and student-centred teaching and learning... Behind this apparently benign agenda is another more political motive...the implicit intent to change the culture of higher education by developing the spirit of enterprise amongst academic staff' (Department of Employment 1991). Enterprise in Higher Education (EHE) is to be managed and integrated within existing management structures; monitoring and evaluation provide feedback for further development of the curriculum, and all institutions must demonstrate how they will keep up the good work once government funding ends.

Evaluations of the initiative have been mounted (Department of Employment 1991) but it is too early to say what the ultimate effects of this astonishingly energetic government activity will be. But some general observations on its import can be made. First, the educational assumptions connected with student- and project-based learning are not revolutionary, although they figure at present in only a substantial minority of higher education courses; such modelling can be found in some of the courses in the Brunel study. Second, the emphasis on 'enterprise' can be dismissed as conservative rhetoric and it will be surprising if it does not simply convert itself into an emphasis on experiential learning. What is new is, however, the attempt by government to implant a value-laden vocabulary into higher education. Third, it gives employers a lead role in determining the curriculum, at least where they can be persuaded to play such a role. Finally, the initiative has enabled government to buy its way into detailed interference in some parts of higher education, through persistent audit and evaluation of the programmes. The British treasury, who probably felt sandbagged by a favoured minister into funding it, was determined that the initiative should not be exploited to restore the cuts suffered by institutions.

Power and control: effects on infrastructures

From an analysis of the influences on substantive content, particularly the curriculum, we next consider the impact on forms of control in institutions.

The individual academic

The prime mover in academic production, the individual academic, is a bizarre organisational and political phenomenon. In British national law he hardly gets a mention, and the policy influences on him, once appointed, scarcely touch the normative core of his work. But they may operate with increasing power through shifting opportunity costs, resource constraints and changes in rewards and sanctions. Traditionally the curriculum is determined and developed bottom-up by the teaching staff and the discipline. The curriculum is one way in which teachers can maintain academic credibility and make public their interests and worth.

The power of individual academics resides in their knowledge and in the conventions of academic freedom. But in the directed curriculum, while the detailed content of teaching is unlikely to be monitored, the design of course units is subject to the overall aims of the degree programme. In the individualistic curriculum constraints follow from patterns of student choice, and the lecturer still has to work within the broad frameworks set by academic decision making levels within – and in some cases outside – the institution. For some academics, getting enough students to secure the financial base has become a prime requisite. For others, preserving the pursuit of pure science, with constant applications for reduced research monies, remains their *raison d'être*. Others must keep the enterprise afloat by earning money from short courses and consultancy.

Changes in conditions of employment may change the balance of power between the individual and the system. Government has removed the legal power to confer tenure and has insisted on appraisal schemes and on salary differentials in order to reward the meritorious and punish the laggards. These measures will inevitably give more power to managers at all levels. But the individual's freedom in teaching and research will remain a dominant criterion of change.

The entry of external influences

There are several potential points of entry for external influences. Davies (1985) notes two groups in the external environment, the controllers and the consumers, who pursue relationships with higher education based in public accountability, in political or consumer interests. Internal and external modes may need to be reconciled. Institutional leaders, concerned to develop or retain a corporate reputation and maintain sponsorship, seek strategies capable of modifying internal systems of values, relationships and attitudes in order to meet external demands and expectations. Depending on the strength of external sanctions or inducements and the relative autonomy of the IHE, different strategies can be expected. However, recent policy moves have induced IHEs to seek their own resources and this has moved them towards a clearer recognition of actual and potential consumers.

The entrepreneurial strategy, one of the reconciliation modes described by Lockwood and Davies (1985), could be found in individual departments which we studied. Institutions encouraged basic units, through financial inducements and sanctions, to increase external earnings through, for example, industrial liaison, research contracts, consultancies, new post-qualifying courses and Science Parks. IHEs were thus increasingly being forced to adjust to the environment, to become more outward looking and to recognise the influence of the consumer.

Effects on internal governance and structure

In determining the effects of external pressures on internal governance and structure we can depend to only a limited extent upon empirical evidence, because whilst changes proposed from the outside have accelerated, new power relationships may take a long time to emerge.

At the time of the Brunel study, whilst there was certainly an atmosphere of change, there were 'still large gaps between the dominant government rhetoric and the ways in which institutions themselves operate' (Boys *et al.* 1988). The classic and autonomous model of academic government was giving way, but only in part, to the concept of the responsive and dependent institution.

To what extent has power shifted from departments to the institution? Concepts of academic autonomy have, in the classic models of higher education, tended to typify the institution as complementary to, rather than in control of, the departments and other basic units; they have been regarded as the prime institutions and the IHE virtually as a holding company. Does this construct still hold or is the institution conceptually and operationally independent of the sub-units with which they relate? Does it have a mission which is more than the aggregate of departmental and individual missions? (Becher and Kogan 1991).

The classic view probably understated the role of the institution, except in the most prestigious collegial universities. Mostly the institution legitimated itself and the activities of its component parts; it maintained the integrity of academic activities by administering rules and due process; it mediated with sponsors, governmental and otherwise. It set the rules by which the basic units work, distributed funding, and acted as a protector of the basic units from the external environment. But its agenda has become greatly expanded with the setting of supra-departmental objectives, and the handling of an environment, both prescriptive and volatile.

The institution's course portfolio is an expression of mission, a public statement about the range and type of education it offers. The institutional ethos may affect the range of courses, but external bodies continue to assume departmental autonomy in course planning and academic development. It is doubtful whether the institution can influence the development of specific courses; the curriculum becomes a matter for institutional decision-making only in terms of the overall balance of courses and in responding to system level requirements or restrictions.

Managerial patterns are changing fast and our study may not have captured some of the more heroic examples. The new bidding procedures are requiring institutions to make a searching inspection of what will 'pay' and what will not. And such externally devised influences as the Enterprise Initiative may enter the curriculum bloodstream through institutional pressure.

The setting of objectives

The setting of objectives for both the DES and individual universities was proposed by the Jarratt Report (1985) and Croham Report (1987) as a way of ensuring that institutional policies will be negotiated and secured.

Whilst the most prestigious and powerful institutions eschewed collective statements of purpose, some IHEs in the study had produced statements of objectives with implications for course development directed to meeting more external community, industrial, commercial or service needs. Most institutions presented some form of statement for public display, as in undergraduate prospectuses. The study of eight public sector institutions by Pratt and Silverman (1986) supports our view that setting institutional objectives was not common but was on the increase; the requirement on universities to produce institutional plans has now made it universal. Statements made in response to earlier planning and evaluation exercises were thought by many to be rhetorical and to fall short of operational statements. We emphasise, however, that the pressure has grown greatly since we or Pratt and Silverman completed the fieldwork for our studies.

At one university, an attempt in the early 1980s to persuade Senate to produce a policy statement 'led to uproar' because it was feared this might pave the way to interference with academic freedom. If an ancient university found it difficult to answer UGC (University Grants Committee) enquiries about priorities, at another moves from the centre to promote industrial links and improve the record on graduate employment resulted in organisational changes, although there too the centre stopped short of making a formal institutional statement of objectives. At a polytechnic a comprehensive statement was prepared to 'make visible' existing goals with some increased emphasis on community objectives. It sought to establish an agreed agenda within the polytechnic as a planning guide, as a framework for evaluation and as a mission statement projecting the image which could be presented to attract funding. Similarly, a college of higher education produced a policy statement which was an essential part of restructuring; objectives were part of a five-year plan committing the institution to policies which were then followed through by a strong directorate.

In setting objectives relating to the essential tasks of higher education institutions may encroach on what has hitherto been the province of the basic units or of individual academics (Becher and Kogan 1992), although institutions may seek to influence them in the name of particular traditions. A church college will hope to sustain a religious ethos and a polytechnic may adopt access policies originally emanating from its controlling local authority. For the most part, however, value setting has belonged to the basic units and individuals.

If recent policies insist that the institution will more determinedly state its objectives, our 1988 study did not find that interactions across the boundaries were largely engendered at institutional level. The IHE remains dependent on the profiles created and sustained by its basic units within Clark's classic 'matrix' (1983); staff belong 'simultaneously to a field of study ('discipline') and to a university or college ('the enterprise'): they identify with an academic peer community as well as an institution. The basic unit still negotiates approvals from professional bodies, generates clientele among prospective students and grants and contracts. Yet, in some of the institutions in our study, particularly those most vulnerable to outside pressures, determined action was taken to change the academic profile of departments and deference to the institution was more decisively placed alongside loyalty to the discipline.

Effects on leadership

In differing degrees these attempts were reinforced or initiated by institutional leadership. The basic units might have internalised and acted on the need to respond to external demands, but also would struggle to reconcile them with academic values. The institution would be more concerned with securing positive responses to the external demands.

But management lines are one part only of the intra-institutional governmental system. Traditional policy making rests on the interaction between powerful groups and individuals located mainly in the basic units (Baldridge *et al.* 1978) and systems change through political negotiation. As familiar issues follow increasingly familiar paths they become 'structurated' into accepted procedures. Thus the writing of a mission statement would have seemed a bizarre exercise twenty years ago. By now it has become formalised into a committee task in which individuals' research plans or departments' course planning may become subject to new disciplines. The political mode of negotiation will thus partly yield to the managerial role of leaders and administrators already strengthened, before the new policies, by an emphasis on planning to reconcile the spontaneous development of basic units with institutional projections of resources, student numbers and research activities.

Thus the institutions, save for the very strongest, have moved from the diarchy of collegium and management to an emphasis on management and the assumption that the institution's objectives can subsume those of the basic and individual units. At the time of our research (1988) there were clear examples of this assumption at work in one of our nine institutions and in others, including universities, outside our sample (Sizer 1987) although most would claim to be, and mainly were, collegial in the way they determined educational policies.

The role of lay leaders – governing bodies

The government's policy supported by the Jarratt and Croham Reports has been to reduce the power of the professionals and increase that of outside lay people, particularly employers. All public sector institutions and almost all universities have governing bodies or councils with lay majorities. Our research uncovered conflicting evidence about them as a source of external influence in the IHE. At key points in institutional histories councils and governors became more active, when conflicts could not be resolved or when a polytechnic needed defence against its controlling local authority's encroachments. They could, and often decisively did, affect the future of the institution most in the appointment of its leader.

Generally, the councillors and governors interviewed doubted the extent to which they could or should attempt to initiate or influence policy, although the chairman emerged as significant in managing meetings and in his relationships with senior officers. Governors expected to follow the recommendations of the officers and committees and to confine themselves to 'giving advice, warning and consent' and not to generate policy or be interventionist; while recognising their residual powers, they thought they should react to and support institutional leadership.

Industrial members were often drawn from a wide range of work and not necessarily from local firms. Several of those interviewed regretted that this made it difficult for them to develop any kind of group perspective. Most members also doubted that the governing body was an avenue through which they could put forward views or ideas about the needs of industry. They referred to the agendas being firmly in the hands of the academics and the committee system; this was felt to be appropriate in view of their lay status in relation to the experience and expertise of the academics and educationalists. However, where they were able to link more directly to departmental staff, industrial governors considered they had a useful, if informal, contribution to make.

Overall, the laymen appeared to be growing in power but were not a primary source of external influence. Although in at least one university outside our sample, council argued the institution case at the time of the 1981 allocations, governors and councillors have only recently begun to lodge arguments within the national political system (Butler 1983).

Leadership

The performance of the institutional leader helped determine how well institutions sustained their position during the period of contraction (Sizer 1987). In eight of our institutions, that is excepting an ancient collegial university, the quality of leadership was seen as affecting the direction of institutional change. Lockwood and Davies (1985) refer to 'limited manageability', but also refer to what they see as the growing challenge for leadership in the need to manage change and reduce uncertainty within a 'turbulent' environment. In the case of at least three (one vice-chancellor and two directors) of the five recent appointments among our nine IHEs, the criteria included not only academic qualities but also leadership, public relations and institutional representation, an entrepreneurial and a stronger managerial approach. The new men shared a perception of the institution as a whole, of the need for stronger central initiatives in order to establish a coordinated institutional profile. For the most part, the leaders in our sample did not adopt a simple hierarchical style: leadership lay as much in the exercise of coordination, team building, committee skills and a sense of overall vision in policy setting.

In three of our IHEs, leaders initiated such changes as organisational restructuring to strengthen the centre; faculty restructuring to facilitate devolution; changes in the committee structure to give the vice-chancellor a more decisive role; the introduction of research and finance committees to allow more prominence to research and to resource allocation. Moves to strengthen the leader's hand in committees and in the administration, to build a 'top team' or directorate, to establish closer links with the chairman of the governing body or council, all indicated attempts to promote active and authoritative leadership.

It was the larger and most prestigious institutions in both sectors which displayed the most diffused patterns of leadership. Leaders of institutions offering the more vocational courses or with expressed community objectives were more likely to look to external relationships. The institutions most under pressure from lost revenue or courses displayed strong leadership. But we repeat that their influence on the curriculum could be only on its outer frames, through decisions on resources, on which departments and courses might survive or start up and at which level, and, more recently, on different forms of quality assurance. The basic units remained the guardians and originators of the bulk of the curriculum and of the research programme.

Faculties and departments

All our institutions except for the ancient university, where the colleges played a particular role, began the period of cuts with departments, or their equivalents, as the principal organisational entity for bringing into collective control the work of individuals. As institutions have been compelled to make reductions, the faculty has become stronger, particularly in the larger institutions. It is seen as a grouping of departments on the basis of academic kinship, 'the embodiment of the larger view' (Moodie and Eustace 1974) and thus eligible for a stronger role as institutions seek to become more centralised. It is sufficiently removed from departments to be able to override specific interests. It is the only level with sufficient expertise to challenge the defences mounted by constituent groups. With contraction and the government's emphasis on employability, the sovereignty of individual disciplines has come under challenge and it is at the faculty level that proposals for the combination, modularisation or combining of teaching or research disciplines can be considered. Locating greater power with the faculty can also give greater autonomy to lecturers and students who wish to pursue multidisciplinary interests.

Lockwood and Davies (1985) have introduced a terminology and normative model custom-made for the new policies. In their view, deans are middle managers: 'Academia expects its middle managers...to be credible academics and administrators. Senior management expects them to be the general officers of their units, able to implement institutional policy...and to defend the veracity and desirability of those policies.' They are 'middle men in a complicated communication network'. These mid-institution posts represent and execute central initiatives. It is improbable that deans think of themselves mainly in these terms: many are appointed for three-year periods, and are unlikely to lose touch with their own disciplinary and academic base.

The basic unit

The curriculum represents the teaching output of a group of academics and, as such, is closely linked with departmental identity, status and power within the institution, and the interests of the discipline. It is at this level that course offerings are worked out and formalised for ratification through faculty boards and senate or academic board. The initiative for new courses continues to reflect the individual and collective interests of lecturers; but some departments, as we have noted, are having to shape their teaching in relation to other interests. There may also be conflicts between departmental and institutional interests. The department's autonomy rests on its control of its research and teaching programmes. The development of the modular programme at a polytechnic, or the subordination of disciplines to employment related courses in a college cut across the interests of subject groups. Modular or faculty programmes, an institution-wide ethos or corporate mission are all likely to erode such autonomy. It is primarily at the level of the basic unit that the interests of the professional institutions and industrial consumers enter, in those subjects where academics are dependent on them for validation or placements.

If basic units, in some subjects and institutions, are undergoing changes, there was little evidence, at least in 1988, that heads of departments exercise much power in setting departmental priorities, although there were decisive individual initiatives in, for example, economics. Most changes result from more or less democratic processes, often prompted by curriculum review. Such review was built into the public sector by CNAA (Council for National Academic Awards) validation but several universities have set up comprehensive reviews of undergraduate teaching. Thus departments may still remain guardians of their subject interests, for example, through their control of student assessments, whilst more vigorously internalising the pressures and needs of the external environment.

Factors affecting the role of the institution in change

Institutional responses to external pressures are affected to a large extent by their status and history. The high status institutions are concerned with maintaining academic positions, and we noted in our project some anxiety in the universities on that score. Less confident IHEs are more likely to assess their sources of support and change their offerings accordingly. The lower the status, the more change is concerned with recruiting external support, and in making sure that undergraduate preparation is 'relevant' to the labour market.

In responding to external pressures, the largest and oldest institutions tended to strengthen faculties rather than to redirect policies from the centre. Some IHEs had become exceedingly vulnerable since the 1981 reductions. Others, particularly if originally concerned with teacher training, had been vulnerable far earlier to reduction and merger and to 'bolt-on' developments. Some institutions had the opportunity to develop 'organically', that is to say, to move according to their own value systems, assessments of markets and resources.

We thus found a spectrum of vulnerability among our nine institutions which could be roughly correlated with their status. The more vulnerable tended to display the stronger leadership.

Summary and conclusion

In the period of our study no academics – at any level within any institution – could doubt that changes in the environment were affecting their ways of working. It was, however, as much the frames of action as the formal structure which determined responsiveness to the labour market. Responses varied according to their status, which helped determine vulnerability, and their histories as well as the style of leadership and its relationship with the other forces operating within and on institutions. Because of this complex combination of factors, generalisations cannot easily be made, but some are offered as follows:

- The setting of objectives by institutional leaders promoted change only when the threat from the outside was severe. This opened the way for determined leadership, or allowed a consensus to build up between leadership and the basic units. Otherwise objectives setting tended to remain as largely rhetorical.

- Institutional responsiveness was not markedly influenced by the activities of lay governors although their part in the appointment of institutional leaders might critically affect the overall style and responsiveness of an institution.
- As institutions responded to external pressures they centralised power, sometimes through an increase in leadership influence, but also through the strengthening of the intermediary, usually faculty, level. The means employed was associated with the size of the institution, and with other factors which might affect its vulnerability and its need to respond to external influences.
- At a time of reductions the importance of leadership became paramount. At the same time, however, the IHE still depended upon the basic unit to generate external support, to determine curricula and research agendas.
- For the most part, academics remained true to their own values in developing and delivering the curriculum, but there were important concerns about skills desirable for employment which varied according to the subject area. Subjects varied in self-confidence according to their status and paradigmal certainties; some (e.g. economics and history) felt able to meet the demands of employability by sustaining their disciplinary stances, whilst others, such as physics, if making no concessions on scientific standards, felt constrained to respond to the perceived demands of the market. Except for such subjects as engineering and business studies, however, most subjects did not receive and act on direct messages about curriculum content from employers.

Thus, academics do not work within a system encapsulated from the influences of the wider socio-economic environment. They read the changes and adapt in order to sustain their positions. Where they can, they are coopting external funders, and strengthening their currency in the institutional and student market place. Many are internalising new norms, as boundaries become more fluid and the persuasions of the institutional mission more powerful. Their own perceptions of student needs and of their own reputational and reward systems are changing.

CHAPTER 3

The Reshaping of the Academic Curriculum in the United Kingdom

Tony Becher and Ronald Barnett

Introduction

The higher education system in the UK has over the past decade been subject to major structural changes. In particular, there has been a steady shift from a 'binary' system of universities and polytechnics towards a 'unitary' system in which many of the previous institutional distinctions between the two sectors will soon be eliminated. Numerous other adjustments have also taken place, some of them in common with changes in other countries: closer control over research allocations, and more selective funding for research; a relative deterioration in academic salaries; reduced levels of per capita expenditure; less favourable staff:student ratios; a substantial increase in student numbers, with further rapid increases projected.

None of these structural changes led by the state will have a direct impact on the curriculum, but a number of curriculum changes are currently being introduced by higher education institutions, including less specialised undergraduate courses, credit transfer arrangements, access programmes, distance learning, interdisciplinary curricula, and modular degree schemes. The take-up of these innovations has been uneven across subjects, institutions and especially as between universities and polytechnics, the latter showing a greater propensity to innovate. Some initiatives have been the subject of extensive development work for over a decade but are only now beginning to have a significant impact. For example, credit transfer schemes operating across institutions are in place, but are not yet extensively used; access courses account for a small, but growing, proportion of entrants.

One major initiative is the government-sponsored Enterprise in Higher Education programme, inaugurated in 1988, in which up to one million pounds has been given to individual institutions (both universities and polytechnics) to fund work over a period of five years designed to promote economic awareness and entrepreneurial aptitudes across all courses, and to bring the business community into a closer partnership with the relevant developments. Overall, however, changes in the processes of teaching and learning, and in the content of courses, have been modest, gradual and unsystematic.

The incremental nature of curricular change is in large part a consequence of decentralisation. The academic curriculum has always been the responsibility of the individual institutions within the system. The two main qualifications to this statement do not invalidate it. The first is that, until very recently, new course proposals in the polytechnic sector had to be approved by the Council for National Academic Awards (CNAA), which also monitored the quality of existing courses. The second is that many professional programmes still remain subject to accreditation by the relevant professional body. Thus, mechanical engineering courses are not approved unless they satisfy the criteria laid down by the Institution of Mechanical Engineers; law degrees have to be acceptable to the Law Society; and so on. But approvals in the case of the CNAA and the professional bodies are permissive rather than directive: certain conditions have to be met, but the method of meeting them is not prescribed. The same is true of other forms of quality check. The recent government White Paper (DES 1991) proposes an external Quality Audit System and a parallel Quality Assessment System: but neither development is likely to remove curricular autonomy, let alone promote curricular innovation.

The components of the mainstream undergraduate curriculum have remained largely unchanged over a long period (Squires 1987, 1990). The typical form of teaching provision is the lecture, supplemented on the humanities side by seminars and individual or small group tutorials (deriving from the Oxbridge tradition) and in the sciences and professional subjects by practical classes and problem-solving sessions. Fieldwork is a further characteristic of subjects such as archaeology, biology, geography and the earth sciences. Assessment methods have changed more than teaching methods: most students now submit coursework and individual projects for adjudication as well as sitting the conventional form of three-hour written examination. As yet, few institutions have had recourse to mass lectures, self-study programmes or computer-marked testing, though the signs are that their day is coming as student numbers increase. There is still (outside the Open University, which is far and away the largest higher education institution in Britain) little exploitation of the facilities of educational technology and even less use of distance learning techniques.

Tradition dies hard in British higher education. Change is not easy to bring about, especially in institutions and departments which are prestigious and successful, and which may see themselves as having little to gain from departures from the *status quo*. Conversely, those who have least to lose in the way of an established reputation, and who stand most to benefit from some special differentiating feature, are the most likely to be open to experimentation. It is therefore in fields such as media studies and management that innovative approaches to the curriculum are the most likely to develop; and it is among post-war universities and polytechnics that innovations such as cooperative teaching programmes with industry, learning contracts, independent learning and problem-based enquiry are most commonly to be found. Relatively high-status subjects (including economics, history and physics, if not engineering), especially when offered in the older and more prestigious universities, tend to prove resilient to changes which are not clearly seen to bring them some substantial advantage.

Postgraduates

In the UK, postgraduate provision is organisationally separate from first degree courses. It is divided mainly into Master's and doctoral programmes, though there is a minority of diploma and certificate courses below the Master's level. PhD programmes have not changed significantly in recent years, except in relation to an increased element of formal research training (which is currently a requirement of the funding bodies providing student grants). Master's courses have however shown a rapid growth in the fields of economics, history and physics as elsewhere (Henkel and Kogan 1992). The growth has been noticeably more limited in engineering, where high starting salaries in industry for recent graduates make it economically unattractive to embark on work for a second degree. In this field, postgraduate study is commonly undertaken to update technical knowledge in mid-career.

The typical timespan for a Master's degree is one year (more rarely two years) full time, and two or three years part time (the latter courses are usually taken in mid-career). Doctorates typically take at least three (usually four) years full time and five or more part time. In the main, staff who teach on Master's courses are the same as those who teach undergraduate degrees (unlike the US system, where graduate school faculty are often distinct from undergraduate teachers). The teaching pattern usually comprises lectures, seminars and tutorials, but with less reliance on the first than in the case of undergraduate courses. There have been some recent experiments with distance learning and independent study approaches, particularly for part-time students. Assessment for Master's degrees usually combines an element of written examinations and a project report or dissertation; most doctorates follow a long tradition of a written thesis and a viva voce examination, though some economics departments have begun to allow the thesis to be replaced by three separate articles of publishable standard.

Master's programmes serve three main functions: providing an academic opportunity for advanced study in specialist areas of the discipline (especially common in history, on such themes as local history or women's history); offering advanced job qualifications in predominantly vocational courses (examples in physics include applied optics, and in economics econometric techniques); making available general research training as a prelude to a doctorate (as in the case of a number of Master's courses in economics).

Master's courses are strongly market oriented, in that they have no captive audience of school leavers, as in the case of undergraduate degrees. This means that they have to adapt to ensure their continuing attractiveness to a relatively limited – though growing – population of those with a first degree who wish to pursue further studies. In curricular terms, they therefore tend to represent the most innovative features of the discipline in question.

Undergraduates

It is implicit in what has already been said that the British higher education system is very heterogeneous (in this it approximates to, though it does not rival, US higher education). In consequence, it does not allow any easy generalisation. So when reference is made in what follows to trends in particular subject areas, it needs to be understood that these relate to a number of specific instances, rather than denoting universal – or even necessarily widespread – developments. Moreover, since there has been no systematic survey in the UK of curricular developments in any of the particular subjects under consideration, the authors are necessarily dependent more on their own informed impressions than on documented factual evidence. Nor does the broad-brush picture painted here do justice to institutional diversity. Despite their awards having equivalent formal status, there exists a hierarchy of esteem across institutions, and especially across the university–polytechnic divide. Accordingly, as we have already intimated, those institutions lower down the hierarchy have had greater recourse to innovative programmes (both in content and in curricular processes). It is those institutions, too, which have been faced with higher staff:student ratios, another source of pressure for innovation.

We shall, in what follows, focus on each chosen discipline in turn, taking them in alphabetical sequence: economics, engineering, history and physics. We shall then conclude with a general review and commentary, adding a postscript on graduate education.

By way of background, it may be helpful to understand some of the student numbers involved. Table 3.1 shows full-time students, split between the university and polytechnic sectors.

Table 3.1 Full-time students in the chosen disciplines

Full-time 1st degree students 1989–90 (1988–89)	Physics	Engineering	Economics	History	Multi-disciplinary
Universities	7253 (6967)	34008 (32743)	8077 (7787)	9893 (9243)	37603 (34884)
Polytechnics and Colleges	724 (769)	23790 (21581)	4299 (3854)	849 (684)	31530 (27221)
Total	7977 (7736)	57798 (54324)	12376 (11641)	10742 (9927)	69133 (62105)

Source: CNAA 1990, Table 5; USR 1990, Table 5.

The final column shows students taking multidisciplinary programmes, since it is probable that many students studying the four subjects, especially taking history in the polytechnics and colleges sector, are following mixed-subject programmes.

The striking feature of the table is that, for every figure, an increase in student numbers between the two years is shown. This growth in student numbers is indicative of the current move towards a mass higher education system in the UK, which in turn provides relevant background in understanding some of the features pointed out below.

To help shape the discussion, and to prevent it from becoming too fragmented, we propose to adopt a framework designed to order the material in a reasonably coherent way. The categories we shall adopt are, along one dimension, subject-specific developments and cross-subject developments; and along the other dimension intrinsic factors and extrinsic factors (Barnett 1992).

	Subject-specific developments	**Cross-subject developments**
Intrinsic factors	1	2
Extrinsic factors	3	4

Source: Barnett.

The first cell of the matrix identifies developments related directly to the disciplinary contexts in question which are triggered off primarily by forces internal to the discipline itself. The second relates to items of a more general, less subject-specific kind which are nonetheless generated in a similar way by factors internal to the academic community. The third cell denotes curricular issues specifically related to the discipline but occasioned by outside pressures; while the fourth embraces general, non-subject-specific developments also occasioned by outside factors.

This framework will now be applied to each of our four disciplines, in terms of a variety of recent developments to which they have been subject. The identification of such elements is to a limited extent arbitrary, but all of them have a basis in the history of the past decade in higher education. Other authors might have made a different choice of items, or opted to give different items a higher priority, but the validity of those put forward is not, we believe, likely to be contested.

The components forming the basis of our analysis are: conceptual change, emphasis shifts, Europeanisation, transferable skills, interdisciplinarity, information technology, access, work links, extended courses, relevance (to the world of work), post-experience provision and modularity.

Economics

	Subject-specific developments	**General developments**
Intrinsic factors	Conceptual change Emphasis shifts Europeanisation	Information technology
Extrinsic factors	Relevance (Post-experience provision)	(Modularity)

(*Note*: Brackets indicate a partial or limited development.)

The matrix in this case suggests a fairly substantial degree of subject-specific, intrinsic change. As a discipline, economics has in recent years evolved in two main directions (Becher 1992; Brennan and Henkel 1988). First, it has become, at the 'pure' end of the subject continuum, increasingly mathematical, to a point at which critics complain that it has lost touch with all economic reality. This is a clear conceptual change which has affected the curriculum, relegating the earlier approach based on political economy to a marginal position within the discipline.

Second, at the 'applied' end of the spectrum, economists have become closely involved in contributing to the newly emerging fields of management and business studies. This change may be characterised as intrinsic rather than extrinsic, since it has taken place as a result of colonising ambitions on the part of academic economists, rather than of pressures put on them from outside. It is however more in the category of a shift of emphasis than of a change in the concept of the subject.

Europeanisation has been included as a further item. Even though economics in the UK has always been open to continental influences, and is in a genuine sense multinational in its make-up, the existence of the European dimension has been emphasised and underlined as a result of the increasing numbers of non-British students now studying in UK economics departments, particularly at the postgraduate level where in some cases (Becher 1992) they outnumber the home students.

Only one entry appears in the second cell of the matrix, since the only evident development promoted as extrinsic to the discipline but having a cross-subject rather than a subject-specific influence on the curriculum is information technology. The ability to handle and process complex data through the use of computer techniques is a widely applicable skill developed by most contemporary economics graduates: for the rest, their capabilities tend to be rather specialised.

A subject-specific, extrinsic item is the emphasis given, in response to outside pressures, to the relevance of economics curricula to the world of work (preparing graduates for careers in finance and commerce); a more debatable, because less widespread, phenomenon is the provision of post-experience courses (often as aspects of higher degrees in management).

Finally, modularity is cited in the cross-subject, extrinsic category: unlike interdisciplinarity, which has its origins within academic enquiry, modular programmes stem from organisational or managerial considerations. Again, it appears in brackets as a tentative item, limited in its incidence. As a subject, economics lends itself to modularisation, and is in some institutions part of a wider modular degree structure: but economists tend to be less than enthusiastic about abdicating any part of their territory in this way.

Engineering

	Subject-specific developments	**Cross-subject developments**
Intrinsic factors	Conceptual change Emphasis shifts (Europeanisation)	Transferable skills Interdisciplinarity Information technology
Extrinsic factors	Access Work links Extended courses (Relevance) Post-experience provision	Modularity

Engineering emerges as a fairly volatile subject. Perhaps this reflects, as much as anything else, its relatively low status in the UK academic scene, at least as compared with the longer-established 'pure' disciplines of economics, history and physics (Becher 1989a; Kirkland 1988). Partly, too, it reflects the fact that engineering is a predominantly vocational subject and, as an academic enterprise, is inevitably shaped by the external demands of its parent profession.

Some quite significant conceptual changes have taken place in the subject as a whole, particularly within electronic engineering and computer design, as increasingly sophisticated techniques are developed for coding, storing and transmitting data. Partly reflecting this rising level of activity in microengineering applications, there has been a shift of emphasis away from the more traditional specialisms in mechanical, civil and power engineering. Such changes are reflected in undergraduate curricula as well as in patterns of enrolment. Europeanisation is bracketed as a tentative entry in this category, in that academic engineers have begun to look at comparability of qualifications across the Community and to anticipate the recruitment of students from across the channel. This tendency has not yet however developed into a significant feature of engineering courses – most non-British students are at present drawn from Middle Eastern countries.

Among their cross-subject, intrinsic elements, engineering curricula can fairly lay claim to developing transferable skills, in that engineering graduates are both numerate and practically competent. It is a point often emphasised by defenders of the subject that several UK university vice-chancellors and polytechnic directors now have engineering backgrounds. This aspect of the transferability of engineering skills has been emphasised in recent years, partly in response to recruitment problems (see below), but also partly in response to pressure to give greater emphasis in the curriculum to broader qualities required by professional engineers. The subject is interdisciplinary, embracing as it does both creative design elements and an understanding of scientific principles: again, this aspect has been given greater attention in recent years. And as in the case of economics, modern engineering degrees produce graduates competent in the skills associated with information technology.

Subject-specific, extrinsic developments include a particular concern with access arrangements. Despite the attempts of successive governments to improve recruitment into engineering courses, most engineering departments remain considerably under-subscribed. They are therefore ready to recruit applicants – and particularly women – without orthodox entry qualifications, and to organise suitable preparatory courses for them. Another steadily growing tendency is for engineering departments to provide work placements for periods of up to a full year for students in industry as an integral part of the course. Some institutions now offer a special four-year academic programme (as against the norm of three years), with government funding, to improve the qualifications of the most able students. This arrangement is atypical of the system as a whole, where the pressure is to minimise the length of courses.

Relevance, another item in this category, is bracketed because it is not an especially novel feature. Over the years, the curriculum has been restructured by the professional bodies to give greater emphasis to practical applications. Moves are currently underway to reduce the academic overloading of degree courses. As a professional and vocational field, engineering has always tended to emphasise its usefulness in terms of graduate employment, and the accreditation of curricula by professional bodies has helped to ensure that they are kept in line with current requirements (though the complaint is made by some academics that the resulting tendency is to be excessively conservative). Finally, post-experience provision (or 'continuing professional development') is becoming a strong feature of engineering departments, often in the form of short courses commissioned by individual companies, and sometimes in partnership with them (CIHE 1990).

Modularity appears in the fourth category, reflecting the ways in which engineering programmes have been complemented by offerings in subjects deemed to enhance professional competence. Modern languages and management are examples of other subjects incorporated in engineering courses as a result of external cross-subject influences.

History

	Subject-specific developments	**Cross-subject developments**
Intrinsic factors	Conceptual change Emphasis shifts Europeanisation	Transferable skills Interdisciplinarity (Information technology)
Extrinsic factors	Access Relevance	Modularity Transferable skills

As a stable, well-subscribed subject in the humanities (Becher 1989b; Becher 1992; Kogan 1988), one might expect history to carry an image of conservatism and resistance to change. Yet in actuality the range of recent developments is at least as wide as that of economics, and more so than that of physics.

The most notable conceptual changes in recent years have been associated with the French *Annales* school – and in particular, an opening up of the range of admissible historical evidence to include sociological, archaeological and demographic data. A further (indirectly related) change has been in the techniques of oral history. These developments have been accompanied by a change of curricular emphasis towards modern history and a move away from traditional narrative history (which has tended to focus on the deeds of national monarchs and leaders and to neglect the everyday life of the period). The shift to Europeanisation is at least to some extent independent of Britain's membership of the European Community, and reflects a reaction among academic historians against the strongly chauvinist approaches of the past (though it should be noted that there has been an accompanying tendency to embrace studies of other previously neglected parts of the globe).

Among cross-subject developments intrinsic to the discipline, history lays claim to the promotion of transferable skills based on the close study and careful interpretation of data as well as on a high degree of linguistic competence. The subject field is characterised by its open, permeable boundaries, which lends it to new interdisciplinary approaches within undergraduate history programmes themselves as well as enabling it to accommodate well to broader interdisciplinary degree structures. Competence in information technology is not a universal feature of history graduates, though a small but growing number now go beyond simple wordprocessing to handle computerised data, particularly in economic history and population studies.

We have listed access and relevance under specific, extrinsic developments. As far as the former is concerned, history departments (unlike their engineering counterparts) have no shortage of applicants. However, their long-established attitude of open acceptance of qualified candidates as well as the non-linear nature of the subject makes history departments receptive to the increasing numbers of non-traditional and mature entrants. In the case of history, the claim to relevance is based on different considerations from those of economics and engineering, in that it concerns a general understanding of contemporary society rather than having a specific bearing on the world of industry and commerce.

The first entry under general, extrinsic developments refers to modularity. History can be more easily incorporated than most degree subjects into a modular structure, in that it is readily divisible into both chronological periods and specialist topics. Unlike many 'linear' subjects, it can be taken up at almost any point and fitted into almost any context. It is, in short, a highly versatile discipline.

Transferable skills appears as a second entry here (as well as under intrinsic factors), in that recent years have seen deliberate attempts in some departments to develop general communication skills, enterprising aptitudes and self-motivating capacities among students. Units or modules have been introduced calling for project work and links with outside agencies such as local museums and record offices. These developments can be seen as a response to the general challenge faced by the humanities to establish the 'transferability' of their degree courses to the world of work.

Physics

	Subject-specific developments	**Cross-subject developments**
Intrinsic factors		Transferable skills Information technology
Extrinsic factors	Emphasis shifts (Relevance) (Access)	

If history is characterised by openness and adaptability, physics is in contrast a relatively closed and specialised field of enquiry (Becher 1990; Becher 1992; Youll 1988). Its high academic status (stemming partly from its 'purity') defends it against most forms of external intervention, and that defensiveness is reinforced by the close political unity which academic physicists generally succeed in achieving. The subject is, however, seriously under threat in Britain from two main sources: the high and increasing costs of some of the key areas of research and the deterioration in the quality of physics teaching in schools. There is little sign that the discipline is adjusting successfully to either challenge.

The overall pattern is a conservative one, with few significant curricular developments to record in any category. There have been no major conceptual changes in recent years, though many steady developments have taken place in the understanding of the underlying nature of physical matter at the micro end of the subject and in the fields of astrophysics and cosmology at the macro. There have been some shifts of curricular emphasis, but these are more appropriately classified as extrinsic than as intrinsic.

Cross-subject developments in the curriculum resulting from intrinsic factors include the deliberate promotion during the 1980s of transferable skills, particularly in terms of advanced capabilities in numeracy, and the acquisition of a wide variety of techniques associated with information technology. There has also recently been some acknowledgement that physics courses have not been sufficiently thought through in educational terms, and are overloaded with technical concepts and routines calling for rote learning rather than analytic thought. Wider educational aims are now being debated, if not yet implemented.

Perhaps the most significant subject-specific, extrinsic development follows the change in research emphasis occasioned by recent shifts in funding policy. 'Pure' areas (some of which, such as high-energy physics and radio astronomy, are particularly expensive to maintain) are less favoured by governmental or industrial funding sources than are topics with evident commercial applications such as optics, superconductivity and plasma physics. This has led to a relative research bias towards the latter fields, which is to some extent reflected in changes in undergraduate curricula. Relevance and access are bracketed as somewhat limited trends. While the physics curriculum does have some relevance to an industrial society, and indeed to a deeper understanding of the physical environment, these aspects tend not to be given much emphasis: the teaching is usually closely bound within the conceptual framework of the discipline itself. Most physics departments are as short of students as are departments of engineering, but unlike the latter they are reluctant to make any concessions in entry qualifications: applicants who do not meet conventional criteria are turned away as unworthy of studying the subject to degree level.

The regrettable process of slow, steady attrition continues, with new departmental closures announced each year. There could indeed come a time when physics, like classics, becomes a minority subject which once enjoyed supremacy in its field.

Conclusion

These four brief vignettes indicate how differently each discipline has fared in the contemporary context of British higher education. Even when the same general label can be attached to innovative developments in different fields, that label will often have a distinctive meaning. For example, as we have suggested, Europeanisation means a bringing out of shared conceptual traditions in economics, a concern with common professional qualifications in engineering and a move away from narrowly ethnocentric emphases in history; relevance has to be identified in history as relating to social awareness, as against the more utilitarian interpretation in the case of economics and engineering. Once attention turns to the micro scale, subtle distinctions emerge which are effectively concealed at the macro level. Some areas are open to numerous curricular changes; others show relatively little adaptation to circumstance. Detailed analysis overturns some easy assumptions. Thus, as we have seen, history is far from being a static bastion of traditional values, impervious to outside influence; physics better fits that description, though one might have attributed physicists with being a highly adaptable, modern-minded community, open to novel ideas.

Academic prestige does perhaps play some significant part in a readiness for innovation, as Boys *et al.* (1988) have suggested. To take the obvious case in point, physics, which still undoubtedly enjoys high disciplinary prestige, has so far been able (even if at a considerable price) to resist change, while engineering, which is in Britain low in the pecking order, has innovated to preserve – and indeed to some extent to enhance – its institutional standing. Other considerations clearly apply, however, in the case of history and economics, both of which have shown themselves reasonably adaptable, but which are the pre-eminent disciplines in, respectively, the humanities and social sciences. Here, one might argue, it is the recent changes in the nature of the disciplines in question which has made them particularly amenable to new developments – the exploitation of the possibilities opened up by business and management studies in the case of economics, and the widening of conceptual boundaries in the case of history.

From this analysis, four features stand out as determinants of curriculum change, and perhaps in the following order of significance:

type of institution, (polytechnics more than universities, new universities more than older ones); sciences or humanities-oriented (humanities more than scientific disciplines); purity of discipline (impure more than pure disciplines); and market position (weakly recruiting courses more than popular programmes). These suggested determinants can only serve as hypotheses for further investigation. It may be noted that they are all related, in one sense or another, to issues of socio-academic status.

Whatever the causes – and in reality they are likely to be multiple and complex – it seems clear that curricular innovation in British higher education is characterised more by piecemeal, specific, subject- by-subject change than by any grand overall design. This unevenness of curriculum change is inevitable in a decentralised structure of the kind described in our introductory comments, and given the disciplinary differences, both in their internal coherence and in their relationship to the world of work.

It would seem from the evidence presented here that the rhetoric of the system-wide planners and missionary reformist groups – backing their campaigns for lifelong learning, the promotion of an enterprise culture and other well-intentioned causes – has had a limited impact on the everyday curricular concerns of staff and students. As Burton Clark (1983) has observed, higher education is a bottom-heavy and loosely coupled enterprise, and as such not easily receptive to attempts at top-down reformation. Nor, we would argue, is its relationship with its external environment susceptible to simple generalisations. But, as we have also suggested, there are many indications that the academic community is, perhaps in spite of itself, responding more readily than before to extrinsic influences and messages, and so becoming more permeable in relation to the wider society.

CHAPTER 4

Impacts of Social and Political Changes on Higher Education Curricula

Structural Comments on the German Situation

Ewald Berning

This article does not attempt to describe recent changes in the four higher education curricula treated in this volume (history, engineering, physics, and economics) in any detail. On the contrary, it tries to indicate the structural conditions for reforms and adaptation of study courses at the micro-level of higher education. This approach is preferred, because the German higher education system is rather formalised and bound into tight structures of political competencies and responsibility, and of administrative and financial dependency. The opportunities of designing and adapting higher education curricula in such a system are more limited than in other, market oriented, systems which are characterised by more competition, autonomy, and dependency from demands of students and society.

Presuppositions

To understand how individual institutions and higher education as a whole have coped with social, economic, and political changes one should bear the following basic conditions ruling the higher education system in Germany in mind.

The dual character of institutions of higher education

Most of the institutions of higher education, except a few private ones, are state institutions though at the same time corporations under public law (Dallinger, Bode and Gieseke 1978). They enjoy a certain autonomy in conducting their own affairs, for example in research, teaching, studies, staff recruitment and administration. On the other hand, they are in many ways dependent on the state authorities. Regarding studies, the institutions draw up study and examination regulations only for part of their curricula except those concluding with a state examination: e.g. medicine, law, pharmacy, teacher training, food and drug chemistry. These regulations have to be approved by the respective *Länder* ministries for education. Regulations governing state examinations are set up by the state authorities themselves. As a result of these overlapping competencies there are problems of coordination, delays, conflicts about contents of curricula and legal interpretation of regulations.

Germany, a federation of partly autonomous states

The political and administrative competencies for education and cultural affairs rest completely with individual *Länder.* The federal authorities (*Bund*) are active only in limited sectors such as professional education or financial assistance for students. The *Länder* are responsible for higher education legislation, administration, planning and development, and financing, except for some joint tasks which are to be carried out together with the *Bund* and laid down in the constitution of the Federal Republic of Germany (*Grundgesetz der Bundesrepublik Deutschland* art. 91a, b). To guarantee a nationwide harmonisation of secondary and higher education at least to a certain degree, there are so called institutions at the third level between *Bund* and *Länder,* such as the Standing Conference of Ministers of Education and Cultural Affairs, the *Bund-Länder*-Conference for Educational Planning and Research Promotion, and the *Wissenschaftsrat* (Science Council).

Traditional philosophy of German university studies

One of the essentials of the Humboldtian university is 'education by science': the best way to prepare students for the most ambitious professional and political tasks is participation in science and research (König 1970). This research orientation was certainly one of the reasons for the success of German universities and research in the past. By and by this ideal had to be given up. Universities have become institutions where research still carries fundamental weight, but where academic teaching has shifted from participation in pure science and research towards professional education by means of scientifically based instruments (Gellert 1988).

The lack of inter-institutional competition

The concept of scientific equality of all universities or all *Fachhochschulen* in Germany, their almost complete legal and financial dependency on the state, and not very high student numbers prevent competition in any serious form, particularly in the field of teaching and curricula. Institutions are not accustomed and not forced to attract students by means of quality of their curricula and courses and by their permanent adaptation to actual demand. Quality of curricula and teaching are considered to flow directly from highly qualified research.

Higher education institutions do not compete for gifted students; they do not even have the means to select their students, except those study courses under *numerus clausus* where admission depends on the marks gained in final secondary school examinations. The school system, not the higher education institutions, establishes the student's ability to study.

Underestimation of teaching compared with research

Teaching and didactics and, as a consequence, quality assessment have little weight in German universities. Recently, there has been broad public discussion to improve university teaching (*Arbeitgemeinschaft für Hochschuldidaktik* 1991). The concerns behind this discussion are not to be found in a new appreciation of teaching but in some negative developments blamed on bad teaching, such as long duration of studies, increasing drop-out rates, decreasing numbers of successful students. In fact the professional career of higher education teachers has almost nothing to do with their didactic abilities but is exclusively based on the quality of their research.

Lack of evaluation of teaching

There are no formal instruments of evaluation and quality assessment of teaching, neither for individual professors nor for institutions as a whole. Certainly, there is informal feedback on the part of students, academic colleagues, the labour market, professional associations and so on, but efficient measures to reward good and to penalise and improve bad teaching are still unknown.

Expansion of student numbers: mass institutions

Extremely high student numbers (1992: 1,820,000 students accommodated within an infrastructure for only 810,000 student units) are severely burdening all institutions of higher education (*Bundesminister fürBildung und Wissenschaft* 1992). However, many institutions are abusing these difficulties by using them as an excuse for failing to improve teaching and to revise curricula.

The structure of higher education studies

In 1976 the Framework Act for Higher Education reorganised the higher education system (*Hochschulrahmengesetz* art. 1 and 2). It recognises the following types of institutions:

- universities, technical universities, comprehensive universities, teacher training colleges (in the following this group is called 'universities')
- *Fachhochschulen*
- *Kunsthochschulen* (institutions of fine arts and music; not discussed in this article).

Although the boundaries may be fluid, the individual types of institutions have to fulfil particular tasks in studies and teaching (*Deutscher Akademischer Austauschdienst* 1991). Most of the study courses are given at only one type of institution (either universities or *Fachhochschulen*). Some others, such as engineering and economics, can be studied at both types but then there are clear differences between the two: a high theoretical level and research orientation at universities and lower theoretical demand and strong orientation towards practical and professional application at *Fachhochschulen.*

Admission

There are three types of secondary school certificates entitling students to take up higher education studies:

- the *Allgemeine Hochschulreife* (general higher education entrance qualification), normally obtained after the final examinations at secondary schools following 13 years of schooling, provides access to all study courses at all institutions

- the *Fachgebundene Hochschulreife* (subject-restricted higher education entrance qualification), mostly acquired at a secondary school with vocational specialisation, gives access to the study of certain subjects
- the *Fachhochschulreife* (entrance qualification for studies at *Fachhochschulen*), obtained by taking a final examination after 12 years of schooling, including two years at a *Fachoberschule* (higher professional school). It provides access to *Fachhochschulen* and corresponding courses at comprehensive universities.

The individual *Länder* have issued detailed regulations particularly to enable transition from lower levels of education to higher ones.

Studies at Fachhochschulen

Depending on the *Land*, studies at *Fachhochschulen* last three or four years (six to eight semesters). In most of the *Länder* they are organised as sandwich studies, containing six theoretical plus one or two practical semesters. During the practical semesters students are supervised by their *Fachhochschule*.

In the *Grundstudium* (the first one or two years) students are taught basic contents and methods of the chosen field of subjects. It ends with an examination called *Vordiplom* (pre-diploma). The *Hauptstudium* (second part of the curriculum) prepares students directly for future professional practice as engineers, economists, social workers and so on. An important part of the final examination (*Diplomprüfung*) is the *Diplomarbeit* (thesis), by which the examinee has to demonstrate capability of treating a problem in his or her field of study, working independently and using practical and scientific methods.

Graduates from *Fachhochschulen* are awarded the academic degree of *Diplom-Ingenieur*, *-Betriebswirt*, *-Designer*, *-Sozialpädagoge* (engineer, applied economist, designer, social worker). The additional abbreviation (FH) indicates the graduation from a *Fachhochschule* (*Fachhochschulführer* 1989).

Study courses at universities

Two groups of university study courses can be distinguished: those leading up to a state examination and those leading up to an academic examination.

Courses concluded by a state examination (*Staatsprüfung, Staatsexamen*) are teacher training courses, human and veterinary medicine, dentistry, pharmacy, law, food and drug chemistry. Curricula and examination regulations for these courses are issued by the state authorities (*Bund* or *Länder*). The state examination is a prerequisite for entering the respective professions. Actually about 30–40 per cent of all university students take state examination courses, predominantly teacher students.

Courses concluded by an academic examination (*Hochschulprüfung*) form the majority of university courses (and all courses at *Fachhochschulen*). Study courses in natural, technical, social, and economic sciences end with the *Diplom* examination (diploma). Students choose one field of subjects, specialising in stage II, the *Hauptstudium*. Most of the courses in humanities (*Geisteswissenschaften*) are terminated by the *Magister* examination (MA = *Magister Artium*). Studies are broader than diploma courses and students have to choose a main subject plus one or two auxiliary subjects (*Haupt- und Nebenfach* e.g. history and philosophy, political sciences and economics).

Regulations for studies and examinations are set up by the universities which are relatively free in organising the respective curricula according to their scientific capacities and special fields of research. The regulations have to be approved by the responsible ministry of the individual *Land*, which not only checks formal and legal aspects but also tries to achieve a certain comparability with similar courses offered by other universities in the *Land*. This is to guarantee the mobility of students and the opportunity to study efficiently at various institutions.

Many study courses are offered with both types of examination: as diploma/master courses and as teacher training (state examination) courses. Students are free to choose the kind of examination. As a rule teacher students have to take at least two fields of subjects.

Regarding history, physics, engineering and economics there are the following study opportunities (cf. Table 4.1):

History:

- master course at universities (MA)

- teacher training course in combination with other subjects at universities.

Physics:

- diploma course at universities (*Diplom-Physiker*)
- teacher training course in combination with other subjects at universities
- diploma course at *Fachhochschulen* (*Diplom-Ingenieur FH*).

Engineering:

- diploma course at universities/technical universities (*Diplom-Ingenieur*)
- diploma course at *Fachhochschulen* (*Diplom-Ingenieur FH*).

Economics:

- diploma course 'industrial economics/business and management studies' at universities (*Diplom-Betriebswirt*)
- diploma course economics at universities (*Diplom-Volkswirt*)
- teacher training course in combination with other subjects at universities
- diploma course at *Fachhochschulen* (*Diplom-Betriebswirt FH*).

Table 4.1 Placement of the four study courses in a list of the 15 most chosen courses at universities and *Fachhochschulen* in 1989

	Universities		*Fachhochschulen*	
	rank	*percentage of studies*	*rank*	*percentage of studies*
History	14	2.4%		-
Physics	11	3.2%		-
Engineering	2	11.0%	1	41.6%
Economics	1	13.7%	2	15.5%

Source: Bundesminister für Bildung und Wissenschaft 1992.

Organisation of university studies

Times have passed when students were absolutely free in selecting single subjects and courses within the frame of the chosen discipline. Most of the curricula in higher education are defined by study and examination regulations, very strictly in medicine, natural and technical sciences, still rather open in humanities. Diploma courses are divided in basic and advances studies (stage I and II: *Grundstudium*, *Hauptstudium*). Stage I ends with an intermediate examination (*Vordiplom*), stage II with the final diploma examination, which often lasts several months. Part of this final examination is, similar to *Fachhochschulen*, an ambitious scientific thesis, which takes the students at least half a year and often more. Common didactic teaching methods are lectures, seminars, practical courses, project work, group and team-work.

It is important to underline that the first graduation level at *Fachhochschulen* and universities is the *Diplom*, *Magister Artium*, *Staatsexamen*. There is no intermediate qualification leading to academic professions. Thus, German students have to study at least three or four years (at *Fachhochschulen*) or more (at universities) to get an academic degree and the respective professional qualification. A Bachelor's degree like in the Anglo-American higher education system is unknown. Leaving higher education without a final examination is dropping out without any qualification. Postgraduate studies, finally, are offered at various levels, as postgraduate studies in a stricter sense (e.g. supplementary courses, specialisation courses), as a complete second study, as doctoral studies to achieve the doctoral degree, and as continuing education courses for those who have gained professional experience.

Social, economic and political changes – challenges for curricula reforms

Among the factors deeply influencing university curricula and teaching the following certainly have to be mentioned: growth in student numbers, aims of higher education studies, changes in labour market demands and the process of European unification.

Public discussion in the 1960s and 1970s on educational politics – growth in student numbers

In the 1960s, as in other Western industrial countries, there was an increasing awareness in German society and industry that besides capital and labour, education is a decisive third factor enabling and sustaining economic welfare and therefore social stability. Some practical consequences of this new insight were the beginning of educational planning, the establishment of the *Wissenschaftrat* (German Science Council) as a consulting and steering board for the development of higher education and research, and not least a growing interest of industry in educational politics. The latter interest in processes of higher education went beyond a superficial demand that research results be applicable and that the system produces well trained young people.

In 1964, Georg Picht, from the University of Heidelberg, received considerable attention postulating enlargement of the education sector at various levels to cope with national and international demand for well trained people in many sectors (Picht 1964). The necessity to enlarge particularly the higher education sector was supported by philosophical and political arguments: Rolf Dahrendorf talked of a civil right to education (Dahrendorf 1965). More and more education was regarded as one of the best ways to achieve a broader and successful participation in the economic and social development of the country.

The enormous quantitative development of student numbers could only be managed by expanding existing higher education institutions and by founding new ones (cf. Table 4.2). Unification of former Eastern and Western parts of Germany in October 1990 is a further challenge for higher education institutions and politics to cope with. In 1991, the total number of students in Germany was about 1,780,000, about 135,000 of them in Eastern Germany. Change has to be managed not only in terms of quantity but also in terms of quality, particularly where institutions on the territory of the former German Democratic Republic are concerned.

Table 4.2 Indicators to illustrate the expansion of higher education at secondary and tertiary level

	1965	*1990*
School leavers holding a higher education entrance qualification (percentage)	6.9%	38.0%
Portion of study beginners within an age group	10.0%	35.6%
Students (total numbers; *Fachhochschulen* in brackets)	384,000 (76,000)	1,585,000 (372,600)

Source: Westdeutsche Rektorenkonferenz, 1989; figures are valid for Germany before unification.

Aims of higher education studies

Study reforms are always accompanied by discussions about aims of studies and curricula. During the economic boom in the 1950s and 1960s German employers expected higher education graduates to be well trained and immediately able to carry out their jobs from the first day on. In German this was called *Berufsfertigkeit* (skills for a specific profession). Universities always rejected this expectation, but even *Fachhochschulen* are not able to realise this aim and to offer 'completely ready graduates'. By and by a certain consensus was achieved, that higher education graduates should be basically able to cope with a broad range of tasks and challenges in future professions (*Berufsfähigkeit*). This means a number of things:

1. Students have to learn basic knowledge/contents and scientific methods and instruments, which characterise the discipline itself and potential fields of application. Because of the simultaneous explosion and obsolescence of knowledge learning in higher education is always exemplary. Students must learn how to learn and why by means of examples and selection.

2. Students have to learn how to recognise and to analyse problems, to find new approaches, measures and instruments, to discuss possible solutions and to defend the final decision.

3. Students must learn how to use the so-called third cultural techniques: computers, mathematics and statistics in many fields, network and ecological thinking, presentation of results and so on. In some curricula this is already tradition, for others it is rather new.

4. Students should be trained in multifunctional abilities, not bound to certain scientific fields or approaches; necessary where complex and difficult tasks must be solved by means of scientific and practical measures. In addition to the ability of problem analysing and solving, social competencies, critical judgement, readiness for corporate identity as well as for distance from the social and technological mainstream also belong to these qualifications.

Changes in labour market demands

The structure of Western labour markets and the professional qualifications expected from those seeking employment have changed profoundly. The decrease of production industries and simultaneous increase of highly qualified professions in the sector of services and high technologies, and internationalisation of the economy pose enormous challenges for higher education.

The process of European unification

In the past, European ideas and the development of the European Community did not touch academic curricula and teaching in Germany too much. Until a short time ago there were almost no courses referring to special subjects with a European perspective, e.g. in law, economics, politics or history, although some technical studies courses included the harmonisation of technical norms and standards. Since the European Community has become more active in the field of higher education, institutions have begun to understand that internationalisation also has to become practical in curricula and teaching.

The answer of higher education: study and curricula reform and adaptation

State and higher education institutions seek to answer these challenges in three ways. First, by quantitative measures such as raising the participation rate in education at various levels, enlarging public financing for education in general and particularly for higher education, or founding new institutions and reorganising quantitatively the existing ones. Second, by qualitative and structural measures such as differentiation of higher education by creating new types of institutions, mainly the *Fachhochschulen* or by reform conceptions for new institutions. Finally, higher education institutions try to meet changing demands by study and curricula reform and adaptation.

General study reform at federal and Länder level

The history of general study reforms in Germany is complicated and in great part an adventure of non-implementation of decisions and of failure (Webler 1983, pp.169–192; Ellwein 1985, pp.236–251).

Autonomy of higher education institutions in research and teaching includes a responsibility or even obligation to carry out a permanent adaptation of studies. Universities in particular have proved to be unable to realise necessary reforms for many reasons. Therefore, since 1978 the state authorities, accusing universities of inactivity, have started some reform initiatives themselves, which could be legitimised by the federal Framework Act for Higher Education. They installed study reform committees at the levels of *Bund* and *Länder* to develop guidelines for higher education studies as a whole and formulate recommendations for individual curricula to be transferred into study plans and examination regulations by the institutions.

Only a few committees succeeded. A central Standing Committee for Study Reforms was not even able to come to a consensus regarding the basic guidelines. After some years the top-down study reform was buried in silence, accompanied by calm applause on the part of many higher education institutions (Meier 1982).

The reasons for the failure of these initiatives are manifold. First of all, universities and professors are still mainly interested in research; many of them are not ready or prepared to emphasise practice and profession oriented teaching. Furthermore, members of the reform committees came from rather differing interest groups, such as universities, *Fachhochschulen*, industry, trade unions, politicians of different wings and so on, thus the conflict potential was very high and the scope for consensus small. In addition, the results of the committees' work did not find the necessary appreciation and acceptance on the part of state and higher education authorities to be successfully transferred into practice.

Fundamentally, there was no nationwide movement towards a new conception of what science, research and higher education studies should mean for modern society. 'Piecemeal working' (Popper 1970, p.296), reforms in small steps, instead of a critical theory of scientific institutions and practice seemed to remain as the only alternative. This is, roughly speaking, the destiny of general study reform efforts.

Decentralised study and curricula reform

The failure of a general and nationwide top-down study reform is in part to blame on a lack of motivation for bottom-up activities on the part of institutions. Nevertheless, curricula have changed and are steadily changing, although difficulties are being encountered and some resistance and immobility persists. The *Länder* ministries try to push institutions to fulfil their tasks. Institutions themselves, professional boards, university teacher and industrial associations share these efforts, although sometimes with mixed interests and therefore counterproductively.

Indeed, there are formalised instruments to carry out study and curricula reforms at institutional and interinstitutional level. To begin with, every university or *Fachhochschule* has an academic senate commission responsible for curricula affairs and teaching (*Kommission für Lehre und Studium*). Membership consists of professors, other faculty delegates and students. Similar commissions are sometimes installed at faculty or departmental level. In addition, special teacher training commissions are responsible for the implementation of examination regulations and have to take care that the faculties offer the respective curricula.

Furthermore, individual faculties of universities and *Fachhochschulen* are members of so called *Fakultätentage* (Association of faculties/departments) operating at federal and *Land* level. These associations discuss the state of the art and development and contents of study courses and curricula. They then issue recommendations to institutions as regards study and examination regulations. Standing rectors' conferences (federal and *Land*) also deal with reform problems. Finally, the Standing Conference of Ministers of Education and Cultural Affairs in Bonn outlines study and examination regulations with a view to guaranteeing a minimum of comparability of study conditions in Germany.

Besides these formal bodies there are others sharing reform activities, such as industry, trade unions, professional associations and working parties for higher education didactics.

Main obstacles hampering study reforms

Besides institutional and individual inability and hesitation there are factual obstacles impeding far-reaching reforms. One of them is high student numbers. Some faculties are overburdened up to 200 per cent if you compare actual student population with official teaching capacity. Some of the consequences are lectures for hundreds of students at a time, seminars with up to 100 participants, lack of rooms and working places and bottlenecks in libraries and other study facilities.

Increase of scientific knowledge and study contents, which make it very difficult to define the topics for what is called 'exemplary learning', is another factor impeding reform. This is in addition to the permanent conflict between research orientation of most professors (at least at universities) on the one hand, and practice orientation of students and respective expectations of future employers on the other.

Another structural problem is that most institutions lack internal instruments of gratification and sanction which might result in a better commitment to teaching.

Finally, there are several factors working against efforts to reduce actual study time. One of them is the incompatibility between theoretical conceptions of full-time studies (in study and examination regulations) and the reality that about 60 per cent of all students work in addition to their studies and are more or less part-time students. Furthermore, specialisation in general and an increase in the number of specialised teachers interested in giving courses terminating with compulsory examinations in particular, are blowing up the total number of examinations. Finally, there is a lack of external pressure on institutions to create realistic curricula and to motivate and help their students to finish their studies in reasonable time.

Who does the reform job in the individual institution?

With the exception of those covered by state examination, all curricula are planned and organised by the institutions themselves. Single faculties or departments are responsible for formulating study and examination regulations to be approved by the respective ministry. Although, as already said, the ministry demands comparability with similar courses at other institutions in the *Land*, there is considerable room for manoeuvre to design courses, their contents, specialisations and organisation. As a rule, study regulations of universities indicate study subjects rather superficially without formulating single contents.

The latter may be interpreted positively as freedom of academic teaching according to the scientific capacities and standards of an institution. There is a danger, however, of mere formal comparability of courses whilst actual contents depend on availability of teachers and subjects; of additional curricula following broad specialisations in big universities.

Since *Fachhochschulen* are rather young institutions, only incorporated into the higher education sector in 1973, state authorities have tried to lead them on a tight rein since the beginning (Wissenschaftsrat 1991a, pp.9–19). Although formally autonomous like universities, *Fachhochschulen* have not been given the same freedom by the ministries. Thus, in terms of strictness of regulations, their study regulations and plans are more similar to the plans of secondary schools than to university plans (Gellert 1991a).

Single measures in decentralised study and curricula reforms

Structure and organisation of studies

To cope with the increase of knowledge and study contents and to achieve the feasibility of completing a study course within a reasonable time, the legislator fixes standard periods of study (*Regelstudienzeit*) which must be sufficient for an average student to take the necessary courses, to prepare examinations, and to have a fair chance to pass. Complying with standard periods is obligatory for institutions, rather than for individual students. Institutions have to guarantee that completing study courses within the fixed time limit is feasible. Standard periods range from four to six years, depending on the study course (most of them run for four years, engineering and sciences for five years, medicine for six years).

Feasibility of completing studies within the fixed time demands restriction of content, which is one of the most difficult aims in study reform to achieve. Although German universities are proud of their extensively trained graduates, there will be no alternative in the future than to restrict study content, to reorganise graduate studies and to turn some parts of the undergraduate curriculum into postgraduate studies and/or continuing education. Particularly in the case of rapidly changing study courses such as physics and engineering this will be the only option to effectively reduce the length of studies, which in practice is 50–60 per cent longer than the standard study periods allow. Supplementary studies for specialisation and practical purposes have a long tradition in Germany. They take between two and four semesters. As a rule, this type of postgraduate course is organised as full-time study (Berning 1992).

Since a few years ago universities have been able to apply for a new type of postgraduate study, the *Graduiertenkollegs*, which is financed by additional federal funds. These are doctoral studies, which give postgraduate students the opportunity to prepare their doctorate (*Promotion*) within a well-organised and systematically ordered scientific postgraduate curriculum. Thus they should be able to channel their special interests into a broader range of research subjects. The *Graduiertenkollegs* are primarily destined to cure the problem of isolation – both personal and scientific – which many doctoral students have felt in Germany because of a lack of structure, courses and opportunities for scientific exchange for students preparing a thesis. This problem of isolation is widespread in the humanities, less in natural sciences and engineering (Berning 1992).

Further education at scientific level is becoming a new challenge which higher education institutions have to meet. Individual professors and other teaching personnel have traditionally been working in this field, not least because much money can be made by cooperating with industry in further education. However, only recently have universities and *Fachhochschulen* begun to create organisational structures to cope with an increasing demand for further education courses. At present this demand particularly concerns economics and technical disciplines (Lullies and Berning 1991).

Approximation of theory and practice

Curricula in physics, economics and engineering traditionally contain many practical- and profession-related elements. These can be found in, for instance: compulsory professional experience of at least six months before the beginning of studies, and further practical stages or practical semesters and strong relations of professors with industry and economy, in many cases via private firms and laboratories run by professors themselves. Furthermore, close relations exist between faculties and professional associations and the latter take part in the permanent discussion on innovation and adaptation in curricula. Finally, specific project work shared by students, assistants and professors and close relations between research and practice by means of applied research in many *Diplomarbeiten* (theses) constitute an important part of the approximation of theory and practice (Dusch and Müllner 1989).

In history and other courses in the humanities however, students are not trained for concrete professional fields. The profile of most of the *Magister* curricula is still very closely linked to research, not least to certain scientific schools, depending on scientific orientation of individual professors and institutions. Changes and adaptations are mainly due to internal changes of the discipline and its self-conception. Certainly, some universities try to prepare their Master's students as well as possible for concrete professional tasks, but these are additional and complementary efforts in the sense of special skills (data processing; marketing and organisation; psychology, pedagogics and didactics for adult education, etc.) which do not really touch the substance of the curriculum itself.

Linking studies and labour market

Universities and *Fachhochschulen*, particularly state institutions, are woven into a network of complicated relations and traditions, and usually are not able to react quickly to changes and problems on the labour market. However, in the longer term many changes in higher education curricula are the result of developments on the labour market.

First of all, public labour administration and higher education institutions offer a dense network of counselling and information to young people who intend to study. This gives them an initial idea of what to study, where and how.

Second, students usually observe developments and shifts on the labour market very carefully. This affects the basic decision of whether to study or not, as well as the choice of discipline, curricula and single courses. In some cases students remain in the same field of subjects but choose another type of graduation. For example, some years ago many students with low expectations of getting jobs as teachers gave up their teacher training, but remained within the chosen study area taking a diploma or master's curriculum. This happened very often in natural sciences, economics and technical courses, less often in *Magister* courses (Schmidt and Schindler 1988).

Third, in the past, the state, aware of the narrow labour market for teachers, has reduced teaching capacities for teacher training curricula in favour of other disciplines such as economics, law and engineering. At present higher education must increase teacher curricula because of the increasing demand for teachers for demographic reasons.

Fourth, universities and *Fachhochschulen* offer new curricula expecting new or supplementary professional opportunities. Their realization is a long and often difficult process because it takes time for planning, agreement with state authorities, organisation and implementation. In some cases, higher education institutions can apply for so-called model-curricula (*Modellversuche*), which are in part funded by the

Bund-Länder-Conference for Educational Planning and Research Promotion. After some years of experience a decision has to be made whether to transfer these model-curricula into ordinary curricula or to cancel them.

Finally, changes and developments on the labour market create new demands for specialisation and further education. Universities and *Fachhochschulen* offer new study areas within existing curricula, partly for free choice, partly for compulsory choice among several subjects. This happens mainly in stage II, the *Hauptstudium*.

Studying for Europe

In recent years some universities and *Fachhochschulen* in Germany have tried to find part of their profile in research and teaching by stressing international relations and introducing cross-country aspects in many curricula. Some of these institutions are located close to the borders and have created frontier-crossing scientific regions, for example Saarbrücken with France, Konstanz with Switzerland, Stuttgart/Reutlingen with Straßbourg, and Passau with Austria. Years before the ERASMUS programme started some institutions participated in efforts to create integrated study programmes in Europe. In a few instances they succeeded in setting up a common curriculum involving two or three institutions in different countries. The *Fachhochschule* Reutlingen for instance is cooperating with a French institution in an integrated curriculum of economics, where students spend part of their studies at the partner institution and receive a double degree at the end, a German and a French one. Finally the ECTS pilot programme (European Community Course Credit Transfer System) of the European Community links universities from all EC member states by means of integrated study programmes, guaranteeing mutual recognition of studies and examinations and granting multiple degrees to the participating students.

Taking part in European student mobility and similar programmes such as ERASMUS, ECTS, COMETT, LINGUA can be one of the first steps an institution takes to introduce international aspects into their curricula. On the other hand, a real and substantial opening of curricula for European perspectives is only at the very beginning. Study courses such as economics, law, modern history and some technical disciplines are among the first to introduce European elements into the basic contents of studies.

Conclusion

Adaptation of higher education curricula is dependent on the structural and political conditions of the higher education system itself and, moreover, on the awareness of problems of individuals and interest groups and from their preparedness to modify things which must be changed. What is the horizon of alternatives for study and higher education reforms in Germany? It ranges from shirt-sleeve recommendations to run higher education like a big industrial company, cutting off ineffective branches and kicking out lazy professors and students (Etzold 1992), through childish hopes that with decreasing student numbers one day things will get better, up to the sophisticated self-consciousness of universities that only public administration and politics are hampering them to run things at their best.

No one of these caricatured alternatives is serious. The author is not very confident that the problems described in this article will change very soon. This would mean the realisation of certain basic prerequisites, which is not very likely to happen and for which a political consensus seems to be far away. Some questions which have to be addressed are, for example: How can student flows from secondary education be canalised so that they reach that field of advanced professional or higher education they really need and want? How can the imbalance of 24 per cent of all students in Germany studying at *Fachhochschulen* and more than 70 per cent studying at universities be inverted? How could this be done whilst institutions have no possibility of choosing their students and offering realistic alternatives to those not able to study? Huge student numbers are frustrating any effort towards competition and differentiation among institutions – how can institutions be moved towards a market-oriented behaviour in teaching as long as evaluation and accountability in teaching, research and administration are widely unknown or strongly undesired? How can serious efforts towards study reforms really be supported and rewarded within a system of ideological equality and untouchability? How can politicians be motivated to honestly begin the Sisyphean task of reshaping higher education legislation, necessary for a modern and functioning system of higher education? Many questions and few perspectives: this is the present situation in Germany.

CHAPTER 5

Radical Restructuration

The Consequences of West German Interventionism for the East German Higher Education System

Einhard Rau

Introduction

After years of quiescence inside higher education, the winter term of 1988–89 brought disturbances into the higher education system of the Federal Republic of Germany (FRG). The roots of these upheavals can – at least in part – be traced back to a decision taken by the conference of state prime ministers (*Konferenz der Ministerpräsidenten der Länder*) in 1977, which had defined a policy of 'opening of higher education'. The problem with this decision was that it did not include 'a program of extending resources, but rather one of persuading universities to accept more students on their existing resources. Universities were urged to accept an additional "load" of about 30 per cent for a limited time span of about a decade' (Teichler 1987). Leaving the overall structure of higher education, the organisation of studies and the content of courses more or less untouched, it is no wonder that this policy led to criticism, unrest and protest.

In 1988, the German Science Council (*Wissenschaftsrat*) published its recommendations *Higher Education Perspectives in the Nineties* which identified four major problems in West German higher education:

1. the high age of university graduates
2. the long duration of studies
3. the high drop-out rates
4. the inadequate functioning of examinations and grading as means of selectivity.

The Science Council referred to the 'opening policy' and to the inadequate number and amount of scholarships for students which forced many of them to earn their living besides their studies, as causes for these problems. At the same time, the Council identified an incapability of institutions of higher education to adapt organisation and contents of their study programmes to changed circumstances, a different student body and the alteration of demands of the labour market as the most important causes for the inefficiency of teaching and learning.

The students who articulated their dissatisfaction during the winter term of 1988–89 also referred to those causes and added complaints about a widespread disinterest of their professors in teaching, guiding and counselling them.

As had happened many times before, the visible expression of discontent led to activities in the political arena. When *Der Spiegel*, the influential weekly magazine, published first results of a survey on conditions of teaching and learning at universities in the FRG in December 1990, plans for better financing of higher education and for improving teaching at universities became more specific and urgent. About six months after the student protests the Berlin Wall came down and the border crossings between the FRG and the German Democratic Republic (GDR) opened, and in less than a year Germany became formally reunited.

This paper sketches the situation of higher education in both German states before the Wall came down, the intentions and plans as they were discussed and developed between November 1989 and 3 October 1990 (reunification day), and the reality of the Winter of 1991.

Naturally, an immense number of problems are connected with the integration of two very different systems, and these are problems which cannot be solved in a time span of two or three years. This paper, therefore, concentrates on developments in Berlin, where the integration of the two systems culminated and can be made most explicit.

The situation of German higher education in 1990

To get an idea of the huge task of restructuring the East German system of higher education and its reintegration into a unified higher education system, it is necessary to sketch a picture of the two parts. But it is difficult to define the boundaries of the higher education system. Which of the institutions are institutions of higher education and which are of university type and non-university type respectively? Such questions must be answered by analysing contents of study programmes and by comparing job perspectives of graduates of respective institutions, something which has not been done until today. Because of that we have to be satisfied with preliminary observations. The basic problems of restructuration and reintegration exist besides those classificatory issues and are in principle independent of those.

The FRG with its 248,678 square kilometres and a population of about 61 million people, was more than twice as large as the GDR (108,333 square kilometres) and had a population nearly four times as large (GDR: 16 million).

The higher education systems of the two states to a certain extent reflect the overall quantitative relations. The following tables give an impression of the quantitative relations with respect to the number of institutions (Table 5.1), the number of freshmen (Table 5.2), the number of students (Table 5.3) and the number of graduates (Table 5.4) through the years 1980 to 1988. Different institutional types are taken into account.

Table 5.1 Number of higher education institutions in the two Germanies

	Univers.		*Compr. U.*		*Teach. Coll.*		*Art Schools*		*Fachhs.*		*All*	
	FRG	GDR	FRG	GDR	FRG	GDR	FRG	GDR	FRG	GDR	FRG	GDR
1980	55	9	9	–	13	9	26	11	115	24	229	53
1985	59	9	8	–	11	9	26	12	122	24	241	54
1988	67	9	1	–	8	9	29	12	122	24	243	54

Source: BMBW: Grund- und Strukturdaten 1989/90. Bonn, 1989 and HIS: Hochschulstudium in der DDR, n.p., n.y.
Note: the total number for the FRG includes theological seminaries, which are university type institutions (11 in 1980; 15 in 1985; 16 in 1988).

Table 5.2 Number of freshmen at institutions in the two Germanies

	Universities		*Art Schools*		*Fachhochschulen*		*All*	
	FRG	GDR	FRG	GDR	FRG	GDR	FRG	GDR
1980	126300	16773	2600	919	54200	10017	183100	31094
1985	129300	16841	2400	862	61200	10143	192900	31306
1988	154500	17298	2400	1023	70600	9977	227500	31528

Source: see Table 5.1.
Note: The total numbers for the GDR include freshmen at teacher colleges (3,385 in 1980; 3,460 in 1985; 3,230 in 1988)

Table 5.3 Number of students at institutions of higher education in the two Germanies

	Universities		*Fachhochschulen*		*All*	
	FRG	GDR	FRG	GDR	FRG	GDR
1980	842207	72438	202003	38164	1044210	126023
1985	1036774	73298	301268	37850	1338042	127052
1988	1127627	76276	343111	36124	1470738	130456

Source: see Table 5.1.
Note: The total numbers for the GDR include 11,761 students at teacher colleges and 3660 at art schools in 1980, 12057 and 3847 in 1985 and 13973 and 4083 respectively in 1988.

Table 5.4 Number of graduates from institutions of higher education in the two Germanies

	Universities		*Fachhochschulen*		*All*	
	FRG	GDR	FRG	GDR	FRG	GDR
1980	77823	12012	33473	7912	111296	23442
1985	81740	13230	46543	7338	128283	24305
1988	83777	13620	51200	7554	134977	24616

Source: see Table 5.1.
Note: The total numbers for the GDR include graduates from teacher colleges and art schools (2,844 and 674 in 1980; 2,966 and 771 in 1985; 2,696 and 746 in 1988.)

A comparison of these data shows that in 1988 the FRG had about 4.5 times more institutions of higher education than the GDR, more than five times more graduates, about seven times more freshmen and more than ten times more students.

However, quantities are only one aspect of higher education. They have to be complemented with structural features of the system in question. Higher education, science and research in the GDR were structured and organised quite differently. Compared with the FRG, higher education in the GDR was totally centralised and rigidly organised.

Educational planning followed the 'manpower approach', that is to say, the number of graduates from the *Gymnasium* (*Abiturienten*) was planned centrally and implemented rigidly. Likewise, the number of admissions to the different types of institutions of higher education as well as to the different disciplines and programmes was an important part of higher education planning. The institutions of higher education, in the first place, were places of education and training and not primarily engaged in research. Unlike the universities and university-type institutions in the FRG, the universities in the GDR did not aim at a unity of teaching and research. Since the third higher education reform of 1968, research in the GDR was mainly concentrated in the Academies of Sciences. It is also worth mentioning that the overwhelming majority of academic staff had tenured positions.

Besides these structural features, higher education in the GDR – like all education – was an integrated part of Socialist society. The reservation of about 20 per cent of the credit hours in all disciplines and programmes for the study of Marxism–Leninism must be seen in this context. To restructure and to adapt such a system to a democratic and market environment is an enormous task.

Unfortunately, such a task cannot simply be done according to planning theories – starting with long-range goal planning, continuing with middle-range programme planning and ending with short range project planning – by using the approved instruments of planning. On the contrary, the restructuration of the higher education system in the 'new states' (*neue Bundesländer*) has been happening in an unsystematic and controversial way, not much different from the restructuration of East German society in general.

Some measures have already been taken. The Treaty on German Unity (*Einheitsvertrag*) deals with education and science/research in article 37, which covers mainly the recognition of grades and exams and in article 38 which deals with the research institutions in the former GDR (Academies of Sciences) and their future. Institutions of higher education are not mentioned in these articles. This is in accordance with the Constitution (*Grundgesetz*) of the FRG which stipulates that matters of education (including higher education) are the responsibility of the individual states (*Länder*). Nevertheless, a principle as stated in article 38 is of importance for higher education. It says that the necessary restoration of science and research should be guaranteed through an evaluation of the research institutions of the former GDR. The Science Council was chosen to carry out these evaluations by December 1991.

Another provision, article 13, is relevant for the restructuration of the higher education system too. It deals with bringing former GDR public affairs institutions under the jurisdiction of the governments of the 'new states' (*neue Länder*) in which they are located. Furthermore it establishes that the appropriate federal agency will decide upon the future of these institutions, that is, whether they will be kept alive or whether they will be closed down. Institutions of education and research are explicitly mentioned as public affairs institutions in the Treaty.

Looking at the Treaty and trying to catch its spirit leaves no doubt that the standards of the former FRG define the development of the former GDR. This is true with respect to adaptation of the Constitution, laws of the Federal Republic, financial matters and not least standards of evaluation in science and research.

Goals of restructuration

The huge demands which were placed on the higher education system of the Federal Republic came at a time when this system was criticised rather heavily from outside as well as from inside. University teaching was a major focus of that critique. Students blamed their teachers for uninteresting, poorly prepared courses, industry blamed institutions for the long duration of studies and inadequate preparation of students for the job market, politicians blamed institutions for inefficient use of resources, and the institutions blamed the state for continuously rising demands whilst at the same time continuously failing to provide necessary resources.

Some reformers inside the higher education community were tempted to use this situation as a chance not only to restructure the East

German system but also to implement necessary reforms in West Germany in order to build a unified, modern system of higher education. Whatever their plans and intentions were, a number of problems had to be solved in any case.

First, the transformation of a planned – into a 'market' system of higher education brought about open admission and an increase in the number of students as well as more competition for the already scarce resources in restricted programmes (*numerus clausus*).

Second, in order to restore science and research in East Germany, it was necessary to retain 'useful' and successful research activities (including the people who were engaged in them) and, at the same time, to get rid of highly 'ideologised' areas of research such as the social sciences, law, education and some of the humanities. Another aim was to reintegrate research into universities which in many cases made it necessary to invest in laboratories, libraries and equipment. Furthermore, it was considered necessary to build relations between research and industry as well as between university and non-university research.

Finally, it rather quickly became obvious that the general situation of higher education in the former GDR with respect to condition of buildings, necessary machines, books and elementary resources, as well as support of students and student housing, needed a close look and significant investment. At that point it seemed that it would be possible to deal rationally and pragmatically with those problems. The Federal Republic had elaborated the instruments and institutions of counselling at its disposal. Consensus was soon found that these bodies, especially the German Science Council, should responsibly guide the restoration of East German science and research which would have to be successfully completed by 31 December 1991.

The universities were given three years for the adaptation to West German regulations and laws especially with respect to admission. Being within the jurisdiction of several states (*Länder*), higher education is not a homogeneous system. This means that the 'new' East German *Länder* are able to opt for different ways to deal with the above problems. They have each chosen one of the 'old' *Länder* as partner and 'sponsor' for the restructuration of their respective higher education system. This has led to slightly different solutions in each respective *Länder*. At the moment, the relevant problems can best be seen and studied in Berlin were the two systems closely meet and confront each other. Because of that the situation in Berlin is taken as an example of the restructuration of East German higher education and the consequences of West German Interventionism for the East.

The case of Berlin

In the late 1980s East Berlin encompassed 555 square kilometres and about 1.2 million inhabitants (approximately 2.114 people per square kilometre). Compared with this, West Berlin encompassed 480 square kilometres and 2.1 million inhabitants (4.288 people per square kilometre). The quantitative situation of the higher education system in the two parts of the city at the end of the 1980s can be described as follows: East Berlin had a university (*Humboldt Universität*), three schools of art/music, three *Fachhochschulen* (among them the quantitatively important School of Economics), and a school of theology. West Berlin on the other hand had two universities (*Technische Universität* and *Freie Universität*), an arts school, a school of theology, seven *Fachhochschulen* and a private school of economics.

It is worth mentioning that one of the two universities in West Berlin, the Technical University, emphasises engineering and natural sciences and possesses a distinct profile. In comparison, the other two universities, the *Freie Universität* and the *Humboldt Universität*, are rather similar in their disciplinary profiles. Both of them house important schools of medicine and departments of social sciences. Some data will give an idea of the quantitative differences between the two systems (see Tables 5.5–5.9).

Table 5.5 Number of students at institutions of higher education in 1989

	West Berlin	*East Berlin**
Universities	90730	15810
Arts schools	4662	1266
Fachhochschulen	13100	4710
School of Theology	529	130
All	109021	21916

* included are students of distant-study programmes

Table 5.6: Number of freshmen at institutions of higher education in 1989

	West Berlin	*East Berlin**
Universities	9127	3046
Arts schools	319	311
Fachhochschulen	3205	1376
School of Theology	67	20
All	12718	4753

* included are students of distant-study programmes

Table 5.7: Number of graduates at institutions of higher education 1988/89

	West Berlin	*East Berlin**
Universities	5181	2678
Arts schools	456**	241
Fachhochschulen	2199	763
School of Theology	23	16
All	7017	3698

* included are graduates of distant-study programmes
** included are 104 teacher exams

Table 5.8: Number of personnel at institutions of higher education West Berlin (1990)

	Univ.	*Arts schools*	*School of Theol.*	*Fachhs.*
Professors	1701	323	19	554
Research staff (tenured)	1205	57	4	–
Research staff (non-tenured)	3090	75	12	–
Other	14235	344	27	465
All	20231	799	62	1019
Faculty	6096	455	35	554
Student/faculty ratio	14.9	10.2	15.1	23.6

Table 5.9 Number of personnel at institutions of higher education East Berlin 1989

	Univ.	*Arts schools*	*School of Theol.*	*Fachhs.*
Professors	947	132	11	256
Research staff (tenured)	3146	196	2	928
Research staff (non-tenured)	527	10	7	147
Other	7189	242	15	1388
All	11809	580	35	2719
Faculty	4620	338	20	1331
Student/faculty ration	2.9	3.0	6.7	2.6

In 1989, the institutions of higher education in East Berlin had a budget of about DM 1.2 billion. Compared with this, in 1990 the institutions in West Berlin had a budget of about DM 2.7 billion. It should be noted that an amount of about DM 345 million (in East Berlin) and roughly the same amount (in West Berlin) of the total budget for the universities is spent in the medical schools and covers some of the costs of medical care for the population of the city. The three university hospitals are the major institutions of medical care in Berlin. Because of that a significant number of personnel, which is classified as 'other' in the tables, are nurses (male and female).

The former GDR as a centralised state, concentrated the major part of its research in the capital in the Academy of Sciences. Forty-eight institutes with a total of 15,000 people were situated in Berlin. Altogether there are 27,000 people working in research or research-oriented education and training in East Berlin (15,000 in the Academy of Sciences and 12,000 at the Humboldt University), whilst West Berlin, besides also being a centre of research and education, employed an additional 22,000 people in research, university teaching and research-oriented training.

After reunification the question was whether it would be possible to pay nearly 50,000 people and provide the necessary resources for effective research. And how should it be decided which institutions, or parts of them, would be transferred or closed down? The last question had a direct relevance for the higher education system of the city. Both parts of the city had a well-developed infrastructure, especially with respect to public transportation, and it had been relatively easy to merge the two systems into one.

Following the Treaty on German Unity (*Einheitsvertrag*), procedures had been developed to realise the restructuration of the East German higher education system. The German Science Council, the most influential agency in German science and higher education policy and planning, took the initiative to implement West German standards in the East German system and provided the necessary data and information. The reconstruction of democratic and efficient institutions of higher education, as well as social care for the people working at these institutions, were identified as the most urgent problems. The Science Council put a number of disciplinary oriented evaluation commissions together and sent them on visits to various institutions to evaluate people, products and their future perspectives in a unified system. Beyond that, the Council proposed the institutionalisation of expert commissions for each state (*Landestrukturkommission*) which would cope with necessities of establishing and/or re-establishing of institutions, with the development of new disciplines and programmes, the development of new curricula in existing disciplines and programmes, as well as the installation of commissions for the appointment of faculty.

The expert commissions consisted of 10 to 12 members, all reputable researchers and representatives of public life, none of whom were living or working in the respective state. The commissions for the appointment of faculty working directly at the institutions consisted of six professors, three of whom were not to be members of the institution, one teaching or research assistant and one student.

The situation in Berlin was, and still is, a special one. Since the end of World War II, higher education has been highly politicised and ideologised and often used (by all political parties and interest groups) for aims and goals which only indirectly, if at all, had to do with higher education. This climate heavily influenced the restructuration of the higher education system in the city.

Several stages of discussion and planning the restructuration can be identified, with differing interests attached to them respectively. In the following we will briefly sketch the administrative and legal procedures, the forces which push the whole process ahead and those which slow it down, and the plans and restrictions which are part of the radical restructuration.

The process started with reciprocal visits, with exchanges of ideas, plans for cooperation and mutual projects. 'They' wanted to know how 'we' did things, asked us for advice and support, described their admiration for the way we had organised and developed the system often not realising that many of 'us' were very sceptical of the state of the educational system and its reforms. It was a very pleasant – in no way threatening – situation in the first weeks of 1990. This changed when reality started to influence daily life once again.

On 18 March 1990, free elections were held in the GDR for the first time and brought a surprising victory for the CDU, the East German sister party of the governing party of the Federal Republic. A coalition government (CDU, SPD, Liberals and two minor conservative parties) was formed which committed itself to the reunification of the two Germanies according to Article 23 of the Constitution (*Grundgesetz*) of the FRG. This effectively meant that the GDR decided to join the Federal Republic and to comply with its laws. On 1 July 1990, the two Germanies became an economic union with one currency and equal social rights for all people living in the two parts. The Treaty on German Unity (*Einheitsvertrag*) went into effect on 3 October 1990.

But initial euphoria was soon replaced by different emotions and public feelings. Relations became more official, and institutions were being scrutinised. It became clear that planning for higher education in Berlin would from now on mean thinking of more institutions, more students, more resources and more money. There was a widely felt need for information, compiling of data and having talks about what had been done in the past and what had to be done in the future.

During the first half of 1990, the process of restructuring the higher education system in Berlin was seen by many of those who had been involved in the respective discussions as a chance to restructure the system in general, that is to carry through some reforms that were long overdue. An atmosphere of cooperation, community spirit and mutual support could be felt at this time. This changed when it became obvious that there would not be much room for improvement and reform, that there would not be enough funds for all and that only Western standards and laws would determine the future fate of higher education in Berlin.

Higher education institutions in East Berlin, most prominently the *Humboldt Universität*, after a phase of stiffness and speechlessness, reanimated themselves and started to regain the initiative in developing plans and perspectives for their own future. The new rector, Professor Heinrich Fink, together with a group of active and reform-oriented students as well as some faculty, claimed with self-confidence the reconstruction and renewal of the university. They claimed a new ethic and a new culture of communication, renewal in the spirit of Wilhelm von Humboldt. Referring to failures which had been made in the Western part of the city, Professor Fink stated that the *Humboldt Universität* did not intend to become a 'mass institution' (like the *Freie Universität* in West Berlin).

Having in the meantime learned something about the situation at the *Humboldt Universität,* the other universities, especially the *Freie Universität,* reacted angrily, pointing to the 'ideal' teaching conditions at Humboldt and comparing them with the rather bad ones in the West. They accused the leaders of Humboldt university of trying to erect an élite institution at the cost of the *Freie Universität.*

Basically, the *Humboldt Universität* claimed to be able to autonomously reconstruct itself without the interference from outside, especially from the West. Its members accepted the advice and support of the Science Council and colleagues from the West, but at the same time they held the view that real reform and a future-oriented, constructive renewal would only be possible from within. They acknowledged the problem of those who had been too deeply involved in the ideologisation of the university but claimed to be able to get rid of them without outside interference.

The responsible department of the state government saw these issues differently and pursued another policy. Referring to article 13 of the Treaty on German Unity, it decided to close down a number of departments of the *Humboldt Universität* because of their ideological nature. The departments of law, economics, history, philosophy and education were to close on 31 March 1991, in order to reopen on 1 October 1991 with new faculty, new programmes and new structures. Teaching during the summer term of 1991 was to be done mostly by guest professors from the West and by 'old' faculty which had been offered contracts until 30 September 1991.

Humboldt University did not accept this procedure and demanded the right to solve its problems without state intervention in the tradition of autonomy and self-evaluation. It said that more than 10,000 students and about 1500 members of the departments involved would be affected and proposed individual investigations into the 'political past' of each and every one working at the institution. It went to court which declared the governmental procedures illegal, especially those with respect to the closing down of departments.

The university installed a commission which, through hearings and individual interviews, was to identify those members of the faculty which, for ideological and political reasons, had permanently violated the rules of the community of scholars. Those identified would be asked to voluntary retreat or their discharge would be recommended. Besides that the university installed a central and a number of departmental commissions which was to cope with the development of plans and procedures for the reconstruction of the institution. These commissions consisted of 15 members of which four were professors from outside and the other 11 (four professors, three teaching assistants, three students and one staff member) were members of the university. These commissions had a difficult task in presenting convincing results in a reasonable time span. In addition, there were problems which had to be resolved directly. Students wanted to continue their studies, freshers wished to begin with their studies, faculty wanted to know if they could keep their jobs and what they were expected to teach.

In principle, all students had the opportunity to apply to the *Freie Universität* or the *Technische Universität*. However, those possibilities were restricted as students from the West were not eager to share the study places, and faculty in the West were not willing to work under steadily worsening conditions. Politicians and administrators had to do something in order to calm down unrest and protest. As it turned out, the state government and the responsible secretary of science and research (*Senator für Wissenschaft und Forschung*) were not willing to supply *Humboldt Universität* with the necessary funding to successfully carry through the process of restructuration.

The government aimed for restructuration through the appointment of deans who were responsible for the new departments, especially a shake-up of personnel, and the installation of a commission which was to design the overall structure of the higher education system, including recommendations for the future profiles of the respective institutions.

These deans and their committees for the appointment of new professors did their work successfully. They had many applications, including those of prominent members of the respective disciplines. Within less than three months they were able to name those who should get the respective chairs. Nevertheless, legal problems accompanied by an enormous lack of financial resources complicated and delayed the appointment of those who had been named and with that the start of the active restructuration of the disciplines.

The case of economics studies

A closer look at a certain field of studies – economics in this case – gives a clearer impression of the problems of restructuration. For many years the study of economics (*Volkswirtschaftslehre*) and business administration (*Betriebswirtschaftslehre*) at Western universities has been an area of controversy. In the early 1950s criticism was raised against the heterogeneity of study programmes and the multiplicity of options for study and examination. This criticism has been on the agenda ever since. Plans and proposals to relate studies and future work closer, to connect teaching and goals of study closer and to place a distinct accent on practical work were not carried through.

However, this dissatisfaction with economics studies did not affect the number of applications for places in economics programmes at institutions of higher education. Since the early 1980s, the study of economics has attracted the highest number of students. A former domination of male students has been balanced since the mid-1980s and now economics is the most popular discipline among both male and female students.

When student numbers are differentiated according to the major sub-disciplines of economics and business administration, it becomes clear that business administration dominates the field (see Table 5.10). Since the mid-1970s more than two-thirds of all economics students have studied business administration, a quota which continuously rose to more than three-quarters of all economics students in the late 1980s. Although there are other reasons which might explain this, it is a clear sign of the domination of job-related and practically oriented motives and intentions of students.

A sketch of the picture of economics studies in the former GDR has to be based on less detailed information. A number of approaches for the reform of higher education which have been conceptualised during the late 1960s, the so-called third higher education reform, became relevant for the study of economics in the GDR. From 1972, a standardised curriculum existed which included obligatory goals and emphasis on studies as well as organisation. This curriculum was revised in 1976 and 1982. In 1983 it was again given a new direction in that ideologically accentuated fields such as Marxism–Leninism and the history of the working class, foreign languages (primarily Russian) and physical education were reduced and time for disciplinary studies and self-study increased.

Table 5.10 Number of students in economics/business administration at universities in the FRG

	Business administration		*Economics*	
	students	*freshmen*	*students*	*freshmen*
1983	35680	2253	15915	1131
1984	41302	2754	15955	1119
1985	46671	2865	17181	1165
1986	52261	3397	17290	1215
1987	57359	3715	17854	1263
1988	64799	4620	18458	1445

Source: Statistisches Bundesamt, Fachserie 11 Bildung und Kultur, Reihe 4.1 Studenten an Hochschulen, Stuttgart.

A comparison between study programmes in the FRG and the former GDR shows that students in the East had to study 520 (business administration) and 400 (economics) contact hours more than their colleagues in the West. They did this in fewer years. Studies in the GDR placed a stronger emphasis on mathematics and foreign languages (primarily Russian) and claimed less hours in law.

Twenty-one institutions of higher education in the GDR offered 31 economics programmes, of which 20 were related to business administration and 11 to economics. Not all programmes were offered at all institutions. In fact, most institutions offered only a small number of programmes. The most important institution was the School of Economics (*Hochschule für Ökonomie*) in Berlin, an independent institution which trained most of the future middle- and upper-level management in business and industry.

The restructuration of the School of Economics (like that of the comparable School of Commerce in Leipzig) has encountered special problems. In times of the still existing GDR, these schools were of 'university type'. From the FRG point of view, however, they had to be classified as *Fachhochschulen* (polytechnics). The members of these schools interpreted this as a downgrading and were, naturally, heavily opposed to this classification. Nevertheless, it was decided that the

School of Economics was to become part of a new *Fachhochschule* for engineering and economics which has since been founded.

Two-thirds (about 2400) of the school's former students decided to continue their studies at the school and in fact switched from a university type to a non-university type programme. Personnel had to be recruited, which was, because of the ideologisation of the field, a difficult task.

Conclusion

The restructuration of a system of higher education is always a complicated task, especially when not equal partners but 'winners' and 'losers' are the subjects of the process in question.

Doubts must be raised whether the East German higher education system was in every respect worse than the West German one. Even the Science Council pointed out in its recommendations (*Wissenschaftsrat* 1990) that the reunification of the two research systems should be seen as a chance to improve the structural and organisational prerequisites of research in Germany and that this process should be more than the unreflected transfer of the West German research system to East Germany. Moreover, the West German higher education system should have taken the chance to assess critically and reorganise parts of its own educational and research system. The case of Berlin is – at least until today – a good example of the incapability to restructure a complex system of higher education.

More generally, it can be said that institutions have tried to keep their assets, primarily defending what they have, perhaps hoping to gain some ground. Until today there is no 'master-plan' for the efficient and future oriented use of the enormous potential which is at the city's disposal. It is a fact that there are not enough funds to finance everything. Nevertheless, plans should be developed. Plans on what kind of research, what kind of education and training, how much of that, for how many students and with how many people. Plans on what to share and how to share, on profiles and perspectives.

Who is to blame for all this? The Western imperialists, the Eastern orthodox hard liners, or the inflexible people? Is somebody to blame at all? Nobody has been able to stop (or at least slow down) the process of reunification after it had started to develop dynamically. Everybody wanted this process, although not knowing where it would lead to, what it would cost physically, psychologically and financially.

Things could have developed more smoothly, could have been better planned and organised. It is difficult to predict the future development of the higher education system in the East. In many ways it will be like the West German one. However, this will not only be a result of Western interventionism but in many respects a consequence of helplessness, inflexibility and lack of creativity in the West as well as in the East.

CHAPTER 6

Intended and Real Changes in Italy's Higher Education System

The Case of Engineering and Economics

Roberto Moscati

The changing process of Italian higher education

The Italian system of higher education remained stable for a long period of time, adhering to the traditional form it had acquired before World War II, despite the fact that Italy, like its Western counterparts, was experiencing rapid political, social and economic evolution. This form consisted of universities alone offering one level of degree, with an 'open-door' admission system for all pupils who had successfully completed any kind of upper-secondary school (five years in length).

The lack of modernisation in the entire educational system – including the upper-secondary levels, where the only change, at the end of the 1960s, was to unify the various secondary diplomas to offer equal access to university – can easily be explained.

In the other European countries, social pressure insisted upon education as a means to gain equality and to reduce social differences. This was combined with economic demands for more modern methods of workforce training. The result was the creation of comprehensive schools and 'short cycles', differentiating diplomas and courses at post-secondary level. In Italy during the same period of time – the 1960s and 1970s – strong social and political pressures in favour of education as a mainstay for equality were supported by the particular factors at play in Italy – remarkable economic growth and strong social/ideological divergences. However, these factors were not offset by traditional economic rules, namely by an obvious demand for a more highly qualified and specialised workforce.

The reason for this was not so much bound up in the relative weakness of the political forces representing the principal economic interests, but rather in the effectively low demand for highly qualified personnel. In those years, Italy's economic system was characterised by a weakness in the modernisation process, especially regarding services to firms and society as a whole. In addition, industry basically consisted of small and medium-sized enterprises, and the general training policy of entrepreneurship was more inclined towards hands-on job experience and internal promotion of technical staff (the career ladder), than to forming functional links with the state education system. Finally, within the education system, the onus was on maintaining an independent system, i.e. a public service, a structure free from any practical and instrumental purpose, with the sole aim of imparting knowledge.

For a long period of time the structure of higher education has been influenced by this ideological background, which rose to a peak during the student and union movements between 1968 and 1972.

The consequences of this lack of change became magnified by the growing demands for higher education. First of all, the open-door university admission policy did not take into account differences in secondary school preparation. The *licei*, and technical and professional schools, were originally correlated to different professional careers, and accordingly admission to university was limited to pupils from the *liceo*. Together with the weakness of the structures (unprepared to cope with rapidly increasing enrolment), these differences between the various types of upper-secondary schools strongly penalised those students coming from schools which were not originally conceived to prepare students for university. As a result, the drop-out rate in the first university year in all faculties has been incredibly high, sometimes over 30 per cent of total students enrolled. These figures refer mainly to students from the lower social classes who traditionally attended technical and vocational schools.

In general terms it is possible to distinguish two main periods, the 1970s and the 1980s.

In the 1970s, economic stagnation created a mismatch between supply and demand of graduates on the labour market. The market was not able to absorb the demand (or rather, it only partially satisfied demand, giving rise to the phenomenon of 'overeducation'), yet the university graduation rate was very low. The collective drive towards education was not diminished, even though the surplus of graduates grew steadily due to the social prestige of academic qualifications.

During the 1980s economic growth caused an increase in the supply of highly skilled positions, but at the same time highlighted the lack of quality in the training system's results when compared with the changing needs of various professional sectors. On the one hand, this was related to the lack of any sort of orientation or counselling on university entrance which often led to choices which were not relevant to the existing opportunities in professional fields. This created a severe shortage of qualified graduates in the scientific domains and a surplus in other fields such as medicine and the humanities. On the other hand, much was caused by a lack of flexibility and the fixed structure of the university curricula and training courses.

To complete the picture, it is worth pointing out that initially industry was somewhat late in modifying its demands on higher education (for reasons mentioned above), but in the second half of the 1980s, the strong industrial renewal process and the modernisation of several economic sectors brought to the attention of the entrepreneurial world the need for new professional material which could no longer be provided by traditional training inside factories.

In addition, the advent of the liberalisation of European markets emphasised the singularities of the Italian system. In particular, several major inadequacies emerged. One of them was the lack of managers and supervisors able to deal with the restructuring process and with European innovation and competition, and another the lack of intermediate technicians open to new procedures and able to control new methods of production and sales organisation. In this situation, the entrepreneurial world realised that the traditional internal training process in large firms was inadequate, both because of the rapid development of technical know-how and its growing impact on production costs. This aspect was reinforced by the growing tendency of labour forces, following training periods in large companies, to search for interesting career options in many small and medium-sized companies.

Since 1987, the political milieu has been made aware, in one way or another, of international and domestic pressures in favour of modernisation of the higher education system. Measures taken or underway are now affecting legislation as is to be expected, since they refer to an almost completely state system.

Basically these measures follow two main tendencies. The first is a move towards a real autonomy of each single university, freeing them of bureaucratic central control and bringing them closer to the local community. The second is a move towards changing curricula in order to satisfy the changing needs of society and economy.

University autonomy should be introduced formally by a law which is currently under discussion in Parliament; whilst the transformation of the teaching organisation has been achieved through a special law which has already been passed and should become operative during the next academic year (1992–93).

From the point of view of this paper, the most interesting aspect of this law is related to the introduction of the 'short cycle' (first level degree, or *laurea di primo livello*). The new structure of studies thus emerging includes the existing degree or *laurea* (becoming a second level degree) and the research doctorate (as a third level).

The aim of the new structure is twofold. On the one hand, it should provide an answer to the need for intermediate technicians with a post-secondary education, who are required in several economic sectors in line with a general European trend. On the other hand, it should bring back – either directly or indirectly – a substantial percentage of students who currently drop out of university during the first two years of studies. In this respect, it is worth pointing out that just over 30 per cent of students actually graduate from Italian universities within an average of two years behind the schedule officially established in the curriculum. It is therefore understandable that the crucial aim is to make the higher education system more productive and less onerous for the state budget.

One of the fundamental aspects of the Italian version of the 'short cycle' is its correlation in sequence with the existing 'long cycle'. The decision to opt for the creation of a sequence rather than of a parallel structure was determined by the strong fear of introducing two culturally and scientifically different levels. In addition, the academic world was concerned that professors would object to teaching in what may be considered as 'second-rate' institutions and was also concerned with providing prospective drop-outs with the choice of an alternative course with a real chance of transferring to the longer one.

In the following tables (6.1–6.3), an overview is given on overall student numbers in the respective disciplines, and on the problems of 'slow study progress'.

Table 6.1: University students on schedule and behind schedule

	Academic year 1987–88			*Academic Year 1989–90*	
	Students on schedule		*Students behind schedule*	*Students on schedule*	
	Total	*1st Year*		*Total*	*1st Year*
Natural sciences	96173	31497	42858	102703	35475
Medicine	69993	10618	40316	53266	8034
Engineering	129583	38642	46626	151432	48489
Agricultural sciences	20374	5788	11843	19776	5115
Economics	133710	48515	46922	147578	53610
Political & social sciences	62016	25618	17382	77782	32213
Law	127294	42903	57783	135798	45352
Humanities	157682	50796	71114	164338	58721
Diplomas (short cycles)	16116	6008	6059	14757	5280
Total	812871	260365	340903	867430	292289

Source: ISTAT (Italian Institute for Statistics).

Table 6.2: Number of graduates by scientific areas

	1984	*1985*	*1986*	*1987*	*1988*	*1989*
Natural sciences	10758	9945	10112	10391	10993	11690
Medicine	14387	13489	13518	12603	12198	12204
Engineering	10328	9615	10295	9845	10469	11867
Agricultural sciences	2840	3034	3016	2842	2765	2882
Economics & political/ social science	9070	9784	11591	12618	13527	15854
Law	8232	8599	9353	9959	10988	12554
Humanities	13803	14149	15085	15827	16098	16985
Diplomas (short cycles)	3790	3533	2840	3784	3996	3678
Total	73208	72148	75810	77869	80794	87714

Table 6.2 continued

	1984	*1985*	*1986*	*1987*	*1988*	*1989*
Percentage values						
Natural sciences	14.7	13.8	13.3	13.3	13.5	13.3
Medicine	19.6	18.7	17.8	16.2	15.1	13.9
Engineering	14.1	13.3	13.6	12.6	12.9	13.5
Agricultural sciences	3.0	4.2	4.0	3.7	3.4	3.3
Economics & political/ social science	12.4	13.6	15.3	16.2	16.7	18.0
Humanities	18.9	19.6	19.9	20.3	19.9	19.4
Law	11.2	11.9	12.3	12.8	13.6	14.3
Diplomas (short cycles)	5.2	4.9	3.6	4.9	4.9	4.3
Total	100.0	100.0	100.0	100.0	100.0	100.0

Source: MURST (Ministry for University and Scientific Research) 1990.

Table 6.3: Academic staff and students in per cent

				Students		Graduates	
	Full* Prof.	Assoc.* Prof	Re-search-ers	Total	1st year	on sched.	1988
Natural science	18.50	20.31	30.96	17.30	10.76	10.00	10.87
Pharmacy	2.87	3.46	4.88	2.82	1.97	2.34	3.41
Medicine	20.58	24.73	51.11	25.09	2.90	6.40	15.74
Engineering	13.95	12.72	21.60	11.27	11.35	11.28	7.95
Architecture	3.11	4.03	8.12	4.06	5.48	6.61	5.75
Agric. Science	4.58	3.87	7.75	3.73	1.36	1.54	2.28
Veterin. med.	1.87	1.61	3.18	1.47	0.45	0.83	1.32
Economics	6.04	5.10	11.28	5.21	16.79	15.79	11.93
Statistics	0.73	0.53	0.77	0.53	0.28	0.24	0.47
Political Science	3.29	3.37	6.70	3.48	9.02	6.95	3.26
Law	7.29	2.67	12.07	5.05	17.61	17.66	15.00
Humanities	10.40	9.97	24.98	11.95	10.77	10.83	11.78
Teacher's College	5.62	6.25	13.80	6.75	9.38	8.04	8.63
Foreign Lang.	1.18	1.39	2.80	1.27	1.89	1.49	1.60
Total	100.00	100.00	100.00	100.00	100.00	100.00	100.00

Source: MURST 1990.

Table: 6.3: Percentage composition of professors, researchers, students and graduates according to faculty

				Students		Graduates	
	Full* Prof.	Assoc.* Prof.	Researchers*	Total	1st Year	on schedule	1988
Natural science	18.5	20.31	30.96	17.30	10.76	10.00	10.87
Pharmacy	2.87	3.46	4.88	2.82	1.97	2.34	3.41
Medicine	20.58	24.73	51.11	25.09	2.90	6.40	15.74
Engineering	13.95	12.72	21.6	11.27	11.35	11.28	7.95
Architecture	3.11	4.03	8.12	4.06	5.48	6.61	5.75
Agricultural science	4.58	3.87	7.75	3.73	1.36	1.54	2.28
Veterinary medicine	1.87	1.61	3.18	1.47	0.45	0.83	1.32
Economics	6.04	5.10	11.28	5.21	16.79	15.79	11.93
Statistics	0.73	0.53	0.77	0.53	0.28	0.24	0.47
Political science	3.29	3.37	6.70	3.48	9.02	6.95	3.26
Law	7.29	2.67	12.07	5.05	17.61	17.66	15.00
Humanities	10.40	9.97	24.98	11.95	10.77	10.83	11.78
Teachers' college	5.62	6.25	13.8	6.75	9.38	8.04	8.63
Foreign Language	1.18	1.39	2.80	1.27	1.89	1.49	1.60
Total	100.00	100.00	100.00	100.00	100.00	100.00	100.00

Innovative areas: engineering and economics

In the light of the above situation, it is interesting to explore in greater detail two specific cases, the faculties of engineering and economics. Above all others, these two faculties have recently felt the need to modify their structure and to take advantage of the innovations introduced by the new law.

Engineering

During the last decade, the Faculty of Engineering has grown constantly in terms of enrolment, reaching a maximum of 32,000 new students in 1989–90 for a total of 150,000 students enrolled. Almost one-third of these students were behind schedule, indeed the average length of time to obtain a degree is seven years, although the official schedule is five. Selectivity is rather high, as the percentage of graduates amounts to only 35 per cent of new enrolments.

Another characteristic of the faculty is the small number of women enrolled – just over 6 per cent. This is coherent with the traditional male dominance in the professional field related to this degree (such as engineers), but also with the type of upper-secondary school which provides the faculty with its students. The majority of students come from technical institutes (46.6%) traditionally attended by males, then from the *Liceo Scientifico* (38.9%); the *Liceo Classico* accounts for only 8.4 per cent. On the other hand, in 1984, out of 100 graduates, 48 were from the *Liceo Classico,* 32 from the *Liceo Scientifico* and only 20 from technical institutes. This data supports the well-known trend in all Italian universities by which those students who did not attend the *Liceo* have fewer chances of completing their studies and graduating.

The majority of engineering graduates are happy with the training they received, although they point to a need for the updating of professional training. This leads us to the problem of the lack of exchange between university and the production field, a factor that is becoming more accentuated due to the almost complete lack of continuous training and of updating/refresher facilities at all levels within the Italian system.

In Italy currently, 28 universities offer a degree (*laurea*) in engineering. The structure of the faculty includes an initial two-year course comprising nine compulsory courses and exams common to all universities, the further courses may differ according to a particular specialisation. In order to proceed to a thesis and obtain a degree, a total of 30 courses must be taken and passed. After the first two years, there are 15 different course combinations which may be taken to obtain a degree, and these are split into three sectors: 'Environmental and regional engineering', 'Telecommunications', and 'Economical and organisational engineering' (relating to economics and to the organisational aspects of business administration, with reference to the new professional position of manager-engineers). This latter specialisation was introduced a few years ago by the Polytechnic of Milan and is now being developed through an extremely promising joint venture together with the private Bocconi University (we will return to this point later on).

Not all specialisations, courses and degrees are offered by the 28 engineering faculties. Quite the opposite; there are substantial differences between universities in the type of curricula offered, structures available, informal ranking and scientific repute. This last factor often coincides with the surrounding labour market in terms of engineering.

These differences must be considered in the light of the general structure of the Italian university system, which consists of (a) large universities located in the main urban centres (like Rome, Milan, Turin and Bologna) which are very crowded and poorly organised but which are of 'central' importance for economic and social reasons; (b) crowded but 'peripheral' universities mostly located in the south (such as Cagliari, Sassari, Lecce, Salerno, Messina, Catania); (c) medium-sized, less crowded universities, with a good scientific reputation, which are less appealing being located in medium-sized urban areas. This last category has the best teacher:student ratio, and by far the best conditions from a pedagogical point of view (examples are Pavia, Parma, Ferrara, Trento, Perugia, Trieste).

As far as engineering is concerned, situations differ from 17,000 students enrolled at Milan Polytechnic (with 1160 graduates in 1988), 10,000 at Rome I (674 graduates), to 8100 students at Naples (610 graduates), down to approximately 3000 students at Genoa, Cagliari and Pisa and to even fewer students in Bologna, Catania, Palermo and Pavia. The teacher:student ratio also varies considerably, going from 125 at the new University of Cassino to 14 in Pavia, 16 in Genoa; the national average is of 25.3 'on schedule' students per professor (Table 6.4).

In keeping with the new atmosphere of modernisation and updating of the entire higher education system which has been developing over the past few years, the recently created Ministry of University and

Table 6.4 Faculty of Engineering: basic data per university

	A *Researchers & Professors*	*B* *Students on Schedule*	*C* *Graduates 1988*	*B/A*	*C/A*
Turin (Polytechnic)	376	6832	572	18.17	1.52
Genoa	250	3347	297	13.39	1.19
Milan (Polytechnic)	482	17,091	1160	35.46	2.41
Brescia	68	1057	44	15.54	0.65
Pavia	113	1261	123	11.16	1.09
Trento	61	886	4	14.52	0.07
Padua	267	6429	473	24.08	1.77
Udine	68	596	24	8.76	0.35
Trieste	133	938	66	7.05	0.50
Parma	34	1229	0	36.15	0.00
Modena	14	0	0	0.00	0.00
Bologna	309	6110	551	19.77	1.78
Ferrara	11	0	0	0.00	0.00
Ancona	135	2034	134	15.07	0.99
Firenze	142	2777	179	19.56	1.26
Pisa	243	3640	238	14.98	0.98
Perugia	21	1232	0	58.67	0.00
Roma I	394	10,008	674	25.40	1.71
Roma II	122	1457	10	11.94	0.08
Cassino	7	628	0	0.00	0.00
Naples	411	8128	610	19.78	1.48
Salerno	72	1407	15	19.54	0.21
L'Aquila	111	1543	60	13.90	0.54
Bari	200	4180	245	20.90	1.23
Basilicata	49	667	0	13.61	0.00

Table 6.4 continued

Calabria	90	1569	134	17.43	1.49
Reggio Calabria	27	565	0	20.93	0.00
Palermo	263	2623	221	9.97	0.84
Catania	115	2751	164	23.92	1.43
Cagliari	175	3326	109	19.01	0.62
Totals	4763	94,311	6107	19.80	1.28

Source: MURST 1990.

Scientific Research put together a special committee to study the possible changes to be introduced in the Faculty of Engineering. The committee put forward several proposals during the summer of 1990, basically related to the creation of the first level degree and the diversification of degree courses offered, but also to the new professional positions for which training is to be offered in the restructured faculty.

The general proposal is based on the consideration that an engineer who successfully completes the five-year training course today has reached a good level and can compete with his or her European counterparts. In a European perspective this kind of engineer (who will be equipped with a II level degree) should be a highly qualified technician, able to run different activities related to research, planning and to the development of technological innovation. To achieve these results requires a wide theoretical background. This professional position requires the specific ability to carry out research to organise and promote innovation. In this perspective, the teaching activities at the Faculty of Engineering must improve experimental instruction and laboratory activities (severely compromised by the excessive number of students). At the same time, greater student support is required – with diffuse tutorship and small group seminars instead of large classes – in order to improve productivity and to bring the effective length of studies in line with the theoretical schedule.

On his part, the new first level degree graduate will have to be a highly qualified technician in order to cope with technical–industrial problems, and at the same time, must be equipped with sufficient extended training to allow him to accept and utilise innovations. To this purpose basic training in mathematics and physics is necessary (with particular reference to practical application) together with engineering training with a good level of specialisation. In fact, the curriculum is not designed to train an expert in one limited section of technology, neglecting basic training, nor to train an engineer with just a broad/generic competence. Such training will allow flexible adaptation of the professional engineer and prevent him from becoming obsolete in a short span of time. Accordingly, the ability of the new engineer to adapt to a productive process will be connected largely to a new pedagogical procedure, supported strongly by laboratory activities and related strictly to professional activities.

This cultural and professional profile means that first level engineers are trained almost exclusively within the faculty; thus the need for new teachers and academic structures, although external support for teaching activities will also be required.

These external resources will be used mainly as part of training courses outside the university. These parallel courses will provide a type of practical knowledge on specific operative activities. They will be in the form of two-year courses relating to specific professional positions and be organised by combined associations (public and private) locally and comprising universities, chambers of commerce, relevant factories and companies and so on.

The structure of courses foreseen by the committee for the Faculty of Engineering following the introduction of the first level degree takes into account the necessity to maintain correlation between the two courses, which in principle both lead to a second level degree (the new, real *laurea* in engineering). Two alternative solutions are offered.

The first one comprises a curriculum leading to the second level degree (*laurea*), and a parallel curriculum leading to the first level degree ('university diploma'); for those who wish to continue their studies beyond the first level, a 'post-diploma' curriculum is offered. The first traditional course covers a span of five years and involves 29 exams (or 'teaching units'); the second course includes an initial three-year section with 15 teaching units which leads to the 'diploma', after which it is possible to enrol in a further three-year section with 17 teaching units to obtain a second level degree (*laurea*). The latter course will be purposefully kept within the faculty of engineering in order to maintain a sufficiently high level of training (and to this aim teaching staff will be required to rotate between the two courses). Despite these attempts, this alternative may not appeal to students and for this reason a second solution has been considered.

This solution includes (a) a first year of preparation common to both courses, after which there will be (b) a four-year course leading to the traditional *laurea* or, alternatively, (c) a two-year course leading to the 'diploma', to be followed, if desired by (d) the three-year course leading to the second level degree (Figures 6.1 and 6.2).

Laurea (II level)	Diploma (I level)		
A	B	C	D
5 years	3 years	3 years	2 years
29 courses	15courses	17 courses	

A = Long Cycle; B = Short Cycle; C = 'Post Diploma' Cycle and
D = Post-secondary vocational cycle (not at university)

Laurea (II level) Diploma (I level)

Figure 6.1 Engineering: new organisation of courses (hypothesis I)

B	C	D	E
4 years	2 years	3 years	2 years
24 courses	11 courses	17 courses	
A			
1 year			
5 courses			

A = Orientation Year; B = Long Cycle; C = Short Cycle;
D = Post Diploma Cycle and E = Post-secondary vocational cycle

Figure 6.2 Engineering: new organisation of courses (hypothesis II)

The second solution is justified by the difficulty of introducing the first level degree without depreciating it too much in comparison with the existing degree. It also aims to create new preparation procedures to reduce the consequences of the open-door admission policy and the consequent phenomenon of dropping-out and transferring from one faculty to another during the first year (at least 10% of total students enrolled in the university system transfer during their first year).

Increasing the acceptability of the first level degree implies substantial changes in pedagogical structure. The problem lies in connecting the two courses in a sequence. This is particularly complicated due to the Italian educational tradition which (contrary to the British one) is based on progressive transition from general to specific concepts. In this respect, the general structure of the present engineering curriculum represents a valid example. Its structure pursues the following steps:

1. acquisition of a *fundamental* background in mathematics, physics and chemistry
2. the acquisition of the *basic* elements of general engineering
3. the acquisition of knowledge of *basic* professional instruments relating to one of the *fundamental* sectors of engineering
4. the first broadening of knowledge in a chosen specific section of engineering
5. acquisition of advanced specific elements of knowledge in mathematics, physics and chemistry relating to a specific professional area
6. complete command of special professional knowledge, including the pursuit of a specific scientific activity.

This sequence is representative of a particular learning philosophy which cannot be whittled down to a simplified version, although substantial assistance should come from the introduction of the brand new 'credit system' which will bring the Italian system in line with the ERASMUS project.

On this same pedagogical side, the Committee predicted a substantial increase in teaching staff in order to introduce diffuse assisted instruction through seminars, laboratory activities and so on, in addition to or to substitute for the traditional lessons to large classes. The latter teaching method is now considered very unsuitable, especially during the first year of studies when the overwhelming number of students adversely affects the teacher:student ratio and prevents any kind of meaningful contact with adverse consequences for the continuation of studies.

The new teaching procedure to be created includes a different process of assessment, a different class composition, a new teaching schedule, an increase in teaching staff and a strong growth in faculty graduates. The current process of assessment is based on oral exams in each discipline at the end of the course. Instead, a new assessment procedure has been conceived, based on checking and supporting the student throughout the academic year and leading to a global assessment (including a final exam in completion of the assessment). In this way, the possibility of introducing a remedial exam (in the event of a negative assessment during the year) will reduce the drop-out rate and will require students to attend pedagogical activities on a more regular basis (currently students are accustomed to a very irregular university life).

The different class composition means a maximum attendance of between 50–100 students and practical exercise groups of 25 at the most and laboratory activities with one assistant per 12–13 students.

The new teaching schedule prescribes a minimum of 100 hours per semester for each teacher, within new pedagogical mechanism-based teaching modules which involve from 130 to 220 teaching hours per module. This implies a slight increase of teaching duty in class activities in comparison to the current average in the Italian university (currently about 70 hours for a single course).

As regards the substantial increase in teaching and technical staff (apart from the space for new laboratories and classrooms), the committee also envisages a change in ratio among the three levels of teaching staff which is currently – at a national level – based on a 1:1:1 ratio (full professors, associate professors and researchers). The committee foresees instead a 1:1.3:1.7 ratio. In this respect, there will be an increase of full professors (in the faculties of engineering) from the current 1919 to 3600, of associate professors from 2141 to 4700 and of researchers from 1700 to 6100. Technical and administrative staff will also increase from 5000 to 14,000.

Finally, there will be a strong growth in faculty graduates from the current number of 6000 to reach 9000 graduates with a second level

Table 6.5 Engineering: perspectives for the year 2000 after the reforms

	Current situation	*Year 2000*
1st year enrolment	22957 (1)	28000
Students on schedule	73746 (1)	100000
Students in all	105000 (1)	110000
Graduates	5770 (2)	9000
level I degree graduates		12000 (6)
Full professors	1919 (3)	3600
Associate professors	2141 (4)	4700
Researchers	1700 (4)	6100
Technicians	2000 (5)	7500
Administrative personnel	3000 (5)	6500
Square metres	850000 (5)	2100000

Notes: (1) academic year 1987/8; (2) 1987: (3) in service at 3.3.89; (4) in service at 3.3.89; (5) estimated data;(6) including 3000 graduates.

degree, plus 12,000 with a new first level degree ('university diploma') by the year 2000, according to projections based on the current trend and the expected increase of the social demand for training in engineering (coming particularly from females) and taking into account the declining demographic trend (see Table 6.5).

Economics

The Faculty of Economics offers courses in 31 universities. It is structured in eight courses, and in the academic year 1988–89 accounted for 16.1 per cent of total enrolment in the Italian university system (with a total of 196,320 students, 53,707 of whom were behind the regular schedule of their courses).

Economics represents a steadily growing section in the Italian academic world with an average rate of growth of +5.9 per cent in the last five years (1986–1990), against an average increase in the entire university system of +2.6 per cent during the same period (Table 6.6).

Table 6.6: Trend of first year enrolment according to scientific areas

	1985–6	*1989–90*	*Index 1985–86 =100*	*Percentage of total*
Natural sciences	29278	35475	121.2	12.3
Medicine	13206	8034	60.8	2.8
Engineering (Architecture)	34300	48489	141.4	16.8
Agricultural sciences	6509	5115	78.6	1.8
Economics	42308	53610	126.7	18.6
Political & social sciences	18665	32213	172.6	11.2
Law	41874	45352	108.3	15.7
Humanities	50956	58721	115.2	20.4
Diplomas (short cycles)	1347	1180	87.6	0.4
Total	238443	288189	120.9	100.0

Source: MURST on ISTAT data 1990.

The percentage of females enrolled in economics is significant, reaching 36 per cent (the general overall average reached 49.0% in 1989, see Table 6.8).

The Faculty of Economics in Italy has been traditionally characterised by a strong tendency towards a theoretical approach to

Table 6.7: Economics: basic data per university

	A *Researchers & Professors*	*B* *Students on Schedule*	*C* *Graduates 1988*	*B/A*	*C/A*
Turin (Polytechnic)	87	6410	450	73.68	5.17
Genoa	71	3343	235	47.08	3.31
Milan (Bocconi)	97	6659	1184	68.65	12.21
Milan (Cath. U.)	100	6466	429	64.66	4.29

Table 6.7 continued

Bergamo	35	2146	157	61.31	4.49
Brescia	61	2636	98	43.21	1.61
Pavia	58	3966	179	68.38	3.09
Trento	67	1612	96	24.04	1.43
Verona	89	4302	318	48.34	3.57
Venezia	93	4180	321	44.95	3.45
Trieste	53	1516	157	28.60	2.96
Parma	58	2884	240	49.72	4.14
Modena	61	1769	191	29.00	3.13
Bologna	89	6703	659	75.31	7.40
Urbino	26	999	58	38.42	2.23
Ancona	53	2508	229	47.32	4.32
Firenze	107	4078	270	38.11	2.52
Pisa	75	3508	206	46.77	2.75
Perugia	53	2230	100	42.08	1.89
Roma I	178	15897	926	89.31	5.20
Roma II	19	1425	0	75.00	0.00
Roma (LUISS)	17	1247	265	73.35	15.59
Cassino	37	2736	53	73.95	1.43
Napoli	136	9531	489	70.08	3.60
Salerno	31	3965	157	127.90	5.06
Pescara	68	3690	184	54.26	2.71
Bari	89	7008	484	78.74	5.44
Palermo	100	3676	267	36.76	2.67
Messina	93	7941	491	85.39	5.28
Catania	60	3689	141	61.48	2.35
Cagliari	42	3267	130	77.79	3.10
Total	2203	131987	9164	59.91	4.16

Source: MURST 1990.

Table 6.8: Graduates according to sex and scientific areas – 1989

	MF	*F*	*%F/MF*
Natural Sciences	11690	6670	57.1
Medicine	12204	4723	38.7
Engineering	11867	2432	20.5
Agricultural sciences	2882	791	27.5
Economics	11612	4136	35.6
Political and social sciences	4242	2043	48.2
Law	12554	5942	47.3
Humanities	16985	13925	82.0
Diplomas (short cycles)	3678	2116	57.5

Source: Augusti, 1991.

the economic reality and the study of economic behaviour rather than by direct training of professionals related to the area. The absence of business schools can be seen as a typical example of this approach. In fact, management training has been introduced only in the last 20 years as a postgraduate course in just a few private universities like the Bocconi in Milan and LUISS (The Free International University of Social Sciences) in Rome.

There have been several proposals for the changing of curricula in economics in the past few years: in 1986 a special ministerial commission suggested a division into four areas: management, economics, law, mathematics and statistics. Each area was to have just four courses in common and a basic series of compulsory courses dealing specifically with each area; a substantial number of other courses could be freely chosen by each individual faculty.

Each degree course would be able to create a teaching programme specifying compulsory exams and optional exams chosen from several subject sets. The degree courses consisted of two steps: (a) a first step consisting of 18 annual units to be completed within a three-year period leading to the first level degree (diploma); and, (b) a second step, available after the first level degree, consisting of six annual units and the discussion of a written thesis (to be completed within two years).

This project has never been implemented and has now become obsolete following the introduction of the new bill on educational structures (law 341/90). Nevertheless it is worth dwelling upon two of its main points. First, the division of the curriculum into two levels, introducing the first degree level and, second, the proposal to grant the faculty the freedom and responsibility to offer alternative units and different combinations of compulsory and optional courses, instead of leaving such an option to the individual student (as imposed by the student movement from 1968). This latter point is linked – within the context of the overall system – to a rather contradictory situation: on the one hand the centralised, state university system is required to provide homogeneous training and curricula to ensure nationwide legal recognition of the degree. On the other hand each individual university needs to blend into its local surroundings through a flexible and differentiated series of training courses and curricula.

At the moment, the Faculty of Economics is faced with some crucial alternatives concerning the process of modernisation:

1. The mix of scientific areas (interdisciplinary) – a traditional feature of the faculty in Italy – which combines law, accountancy, mathematics and statistics, pure and applied economics, has still proved to be useful today, but could create problems were specialisations to be introduced.

2. The traditional interest in pure economics studies has now been combined with managerial economics (and the latter may well replace the former in the not too distant future). Managerial economics is becoming more and more necessary due to the current demand in various universities for specific courses in business administration, banking and insurance.

3. The proposal (made in 1986) to split the curriculum into two phases (three years + two) anticipated the current move towards the first level degree in accordance with a typically Italian philosophy. It suggested that the basic training be reduced from four to three years and eliminated any sort of direct professional use and sophisticated technical content. These features should, instead, be included in short post-degree courses (approximately six months long) to be held outside the university like any other direct job training courses. This philosophy originated from the idea that four years were not enough to guarantee completion of both

broad background training and the in-depth knowledge of a specific field required to produce the final written thesis.

This proposal has now been opposed by those universities – such as the private Bocconi University – which have already implemented (or are about to do so) new professionally oriented Master's programmes. The increase of the basic length of the curriculum to five years (3+2) could undermine the success of the Master's programme, especially in terms of time needed to complete studies and obtain a degree (but it is worth pointing out that the percentage of students at the Bocconi who graduate within the scheduled four years is below 10%).

4. The implementation of the recent law on curricula and teaching programmes (law 341/90) suggests a new structure of courses with a first two-year course of basic studies common to all universities followed by a wide selection of degree courses from which each university is free to choose those which most appeal.

5. On this key, each individual university will create curricula and establish the limits to the students' options in order to ensure nationwide compatibility and equality of degrees.

6. The same philosophy will lead to the creation of combined training courses composed of 'credit courses' which, for the first time in the entire system, will encourage transversal specialisation.

Towards a combination of sector modernisation

A good example of this new trend is a joint project agreed between the Polytechnic of Milan and Bocconi University. According to this agreement, students of engineering and architecture at the Polytechnic and engineering students at the Bocconi have been allowed, as from the academic year 1991–92, to add to their curricula 'integrated courses' (jointly held by professors of both universities) and 'exchange courses' (specifically offered in just one of the two universities) in order to promote a spirit of integration between technological and organisational subjects. This joint programme specifically refers to management training for both private companies and public administration and pays special attention to current topics such as ecological problems, urban and land planning, factory management, computer science and management of public services.

The basic aim of the programme is twofold: to combine the training of engineers and architects with the awareness of the managerial process in the productive system, and to equip economists with the ability to better manage the entire industrial production process.

It is worth remembering that this joint project can also be considered as a reciprocal action following the introduction of management courses in the special 'economic and organisational engineering course' created a few years ago at the Polytechnic of Milan (as mentioned above). In a way, it anticipates a new trend which will develop widely in the near future, underlining both the key role of engineers in the Italian economic system (especially as regards business administration), and the feasibility of forming effective partnerships between state and private universities or institutions in a totally unique way for the Italian system of higher education.

The force of tradition in other disciplinary fields

Very few changes are being implemented in other disciplinary sectors of Italian university. The main reason for this widespread inertia may be attributed to a lack of outside pressure on the academic milieu. Under these circumstances each disciplinary sector adheres to its traditional dynamics and rules. Apart from medicine, where the *numerus clausus* has been introduced following requests from the medical doctors' association, and without considering the new, recently introduced fields such as computer science, the only other field to undergo a transformation process has been teacher training.

After twenty years of debates, the faculty created especially for this purpose in 1935 (*Facoltà di Magistero*) is now about to be split into two new branches of 'Humanities' (*Scienze Umane*) and 'Education' (*Scienze dell'educazione*). The purpose is to update the curricula for teachers at different levels, taking into consideration – among other things – that teacher training in Italy has traditionally been very poor and inefficient in terms of pedagogical and teaching methods. To be more precise, it would be fair to say that all graduates from any field have always been entitled to apply for a teaching position on the basis that knowledge of a scientific topic automatically provides the right (and the competence) to teach it.

Besides the Faculty of Teacher Training (*Magistero*), teachers mainly come from the Faculty of Letters and Philosophy (*Facoltà di Lettere e Filosofia*). This basically included the teaching of history divided either according to chronological order (Greek, Roman, medieval, modern, contemporary) or according to specific sectors (from palaeography to diplomatics or history of economics). History is considered a special area of studies inside the faculty, and it combines a number of specific curricula, in some cases linked to geography of archaeology through 'classical' or 'modern' courses. Only nine universities provide a degree in history within the Faculty of Letters and Philosophy, since a specialisation in history can be obtained from the Faculty of Political Science. Examples of the resistance to change in these fields can be seen from the refusal to introduce 'short cycles' (first level degree) in the Faculty of Letters and Philosophy due to the lack of professional positions available on the market. Another example is the opposition to course structure divided into semesters (instead of traditionally running the whole academic year), and the scepticism towards written exams.

Physics is also static, although for very different reasons. Formally included in the Faculty of Mathematics, Physics and Natural Sciences, it enjoys a peculiar situation of prestige and an extremely high reputation thanks to its organisation of studies and the pursuit of quality in close relation to the international scientific network. This is true for practically all 26 universities offering a degree in physics, and explains why this field is not affected by the pressure of reforms. Having now introduced most changes under debate years ago in order to keep up with international partners (the experimental nature of the department is a good example), physics represents a positive exception to the rule of inertia as its approach is progressive rather than conservative.

Conclusions

The Italian higher education system has, for a long period of time, adhered to old elitarian and pre-industrial models. The introduction of the open-door university admission policy has widened the gap between the system and changing social circumstances (and other European models), though it was conceived to achieve the opposite.

In the past few years, strong pressure has arisen in favour of modernisation of the system both in anticipation of the liberalisation and unification of the European labour market (the 1993 syndrome), and also because of the growing awareness (among entrepreneurs) of the increasing impact on overall production costs of professional training costs at an intermediate and high level.

These two processes, both relating to the rules of international competition, have contributed to the triggering of a general review of the university system, the best example of which is currently the introduction of the first level degree. This is a relevant reform as it modifies the egalitarian view of the tasks of higher education, traditionally geared to keeping universities free from any possible affiliation and submission from external society, either at a local level (through an excess of independence of the individual university from centralised control), or at a national level (through an excessively stringent correlation with extra-scientific interests of any kind).

Nevertheless, such traditional fears linger on and are exemplified by the choice of the two-level system of sequential courses within the university in order to permit transfers from one course to the other and to maintain the scientific and cultural quality of the first (or short) cycle.

All in all, the Italian innovation seems to resemble the French model (including a third post-secondary professional level which is similar to the STS example) rather than the German *Fachhochschulen*.

In this modernisation process, the new training requirements (in line with European models) can be exemplified above all by the training courses of the Faculties of Engineering and Economics. In these two areas, the need for short cycles and intermediate professional preparation has been evident for several years.

A specific and particular side of these training requirements is represented by the attempt to combine engineering and managing skills on the (typically Italian) premise that company management is best handled by an engineering mentality backed up by business administration training. This connection (e.g. the recent partnership between the Polytechnic of Milan and the Bocconi University) between apparently and traditionally distant disciplinary sectors is perhaps the most interesting Italian contribution to the modernisation of Europe's higher education system.

CHAPTER 7

Evaluation and Organisational Change in Selected Disciplines of Portuguese Higher Education

Eduardo Marçal Grilo

and Manuel Carmelo Rosa

Introduction

Portugal's higher education system has undergone considerable changes over the last few years and universities and central government have faced major challenges in adapting to changing conditions (Marçal Grilo 1993). In this paper we will pay attention to recent developments and single out four areas that deserve immediate attention. First we will discuss the risks involved in the 'high speed' expansion of the private system of higher education in Portugal. Closely connected to this are the modifications of the legal and political framework of the system and we will briefly examine new trends and issues. Then we will make an assessment of new curricular developments resulting from recent European agreements. Finally, and most importantly in view of the subject matter of this book, we will examine fundamental modifications occurring in engineering, economics and business training courses.

The private sector in the higher education system

One of the most relevant trends in the development of the higher education system is the accelerated expansion of the private sector which, for instance between 1987 and 1991, has admitted a growing number of students, as is shown in Table 7.1.

Table 7.1 Access to higher education, number of places

Institutions: universities + polytechnics	*1987–88*	*1988–89*	*1989–90*	*1990–91*
Public	16216 69%	18186 71%	22300 66%	24000 52.5%
Private	7359 31%	7377 29%	11584 33%	21964 47.5%
Total	23575	25563	33884	45964

Source: Ministry of Education (DGES), Lisbon.

In fact, the percentage of the students admitted in private institutions has moved from 31 per cent in 1987/88 to 47.5 per cent in 1990/91 which shows how fast this system is expanding regarding the global expansion of the higher education system (public plus private). In the public sector the number of places has grown around 48 per cent while the number in the private sector has grown around 198 per cent.

Regarding the number of students in higher education Table 7.2 shows that the percentage of students enrolled in private institutions has also grown from 21 per cent in 1987/88 to 26 per cent in 1990/91 which represents a trend that, in the future and due to the number of students enrolled in the last three years, will be strongly reinforced.

Table 7.2 Number of students in higher education

Institutions	*1987–88*	*1988–89*	*1989–90*	*1990–91*
Public	88114	105531	116003	127011
Private	22917	30531	38234	45005
Total	111031	136531	154237	172061

Source: Ministry of Education (DGES), Lisbon.

The growth of the private system is one of the main issues in higher education in Portugal as this expansion is the result of an enormous proliferation of institutions whose quality of teaching and capacity for research are being questioned. In the last five to six years the number of new, private higher education institutions has increased significantly. Five non-public universities now exist, including the Catholic University which has a special statute under an agreement established between Portugal and the Vatican, and around thirty-five private polytechnics.

However – and this is our main concern – these institutions were created and launched recruiting the academic staff among the professors and lecturers belonging to the public higher education institutions. This means that the private system has not been able to develop their own staff and subsequently the large majority of professors and lecturers are working in these institutions on a part-time basis delivering lectures exclusively and not developing any research programmes as they perform these activities within their duties in the public sector.

In this context it is important to analyse the results of this expansion and suggest a way in which it would be possible to control the quality of teaching activities in the private sector.

The expansion of the private higher education sector is, in real terms, the response to an existing demand from the student population. A large number of those finishing upper secondary school are not able to go into public institutions where a tight *numerus clausus* is in operation. This means that quantitative expansion of the private sector (a) satisfies demand; (b) pleases the government because it makes expansion possible. In four years, the percentage of the age group in higher education has risen from 11 per cent to 20 per cent. In addition, (c) it gives high profits to the institutions where school fees are the norm in contrast with the public sector where fees are negligible; and (d) it allows academic staff members to increase their salaries very significantly, i.e. all the participants in the process have good reasons not to criticise or to question the validity and the quality of diplomas. This aspect is extremely important because by law, in Portugal, the state through the government recognises all institutions – public or private – and is responsible for authorising courses and teaching activities.

In this regard all we can say is that the government should be very cautious in this matter and establish an evaluation process as soon as possible. The results of this evaluation should be publicised in the country in order to avoid misleading situations that can affect the students and the country in general. It is necessary to clarify and inform the public opinion on the performances of these institutions, particularly as regards qualitative indicators. The so-called *brasileirizaçao* (Brazilianisation) of the system is something to be avoided in the future and an effort should be made to impose measures aiming to increase the quality of the private system. Only the setting of rigorous quality standards can ensure the supply of human resources with abilities and qualifications to participate in the development process of the country.

Structural modifications of the legal and political framework of the higher education system

With the approval, by the Portuguese Parliament, of laws granting a large autonomy to the universities institutions (Set. 88) as well as to the polytechnics (Set. 90) belonging to the public sector the legal and political framework of the higher education system has been modified very significantly.

These institutions have gained a large set of legal capacities in different fields such as pedagogics, administration, financing, patrimony. They are now also free to define their own internal institutional statutes. As an outcome of the autonomy granted to the institutions it is important to emphasise the capacity that universities and polytechnics have from now on (a) to establish the administrative and scientific governing bodies as well as to appoint their heads; (b) to define the criteria for selecting students; (c) to create new training courses (graduate or postgraduate); (d) to establish the development planning of the institutions; (e) to select and recruit academic and non-academic staff; and (f) to obtain alternative financial sources through the provision of services such as research and consultation, and from the student users through increases in fees. A new situation with enormous potential has thus been created but reaction of academic authorities has been slow due to financial constraints imposed by the central administration and the low level of experience of administrative staff in dealing with these issues.

The financial constraints are particularly relevant as the central administration controls up to 80 per cent of the total budget of each institution. In the foreseeable future there is a need for the establishment of contract programmes between the central administration as the main financial source of the system and each institution of higher education. These contracts would be essential for the normal running and development of the institutions within the priorities and objectives defined by the central government for the sector whilst at the same time safeguarding their autonomy.

The Ministry of Education has, since the appraisal of the autonomy laws, prepared two important documents containing the guidelines for the modifications to be adopted regarding the financing of the higher education sector as well as the introduction of a system of evaluation.

In Portugal a widespread debate is taking place, first, about the mechanisms and the organisational structure of a new financial system that would set the criteria for the allocation of funds from the national budget but at the same time ensure a certain degree of autonomy of the institutions *vis à vis* the central administration and, second, about the nature and role of the evaluation process.

As regards the latter there is controversy because many members of higher education institutions (public and private) consider evaluation activities as a potential threat to the future of their institutions. The main issues of the debate have been: (a) the list of indicators to be used during the evaluation process; (b) the relationship between the results of the evaluation and the criteria to be adopted on the allocation of the available funds; (c) the freeing of governmental responsibilities because the financial structures proposed in the documents mentioned above entail independent autonomous bodies engaged in the definition of criteria and priorities and in making decisions about the allocation of funds. As mentioned above another important issue under discussion is the increase of fees in the public system. Current fees are negligible (less than seven ECU per year) and do in fact subsidise students in higher education who, with some minor exceptions, come from the most socially and economically advantaged families in the country.

New curricular developments

The integration of Portugal in the EC is bringing to the higher education system a closer cooperation with other systems and direct participation in European Community programmes and projects aiming to stimulate interrelationships among the different higher education systems and institutions.

Interrelationships are to be established through increasing the mobility of students and academic staff. To achieve these goals one of the important issues is the establishment of flexible curricula allowing students to float around Europe without losing study time or missing out on basic elements of the curriculum at home. In order to experiment with this the European Community, within the framework of the ERASMUS programme, has adopted a pilot-scheme aiming the introduction of a generalised credit system in the higher education courses (ECTS – European Credit Transfer System). The programme, as is well-known, is being applied in five subjects – history, mechanical engineering, chemistry, medicine and business and administration – and includes a very small inner-circle of institutions.

This trend towards flexibility of courses and curricula in Europe may give rise to some modifications of the current studies in Portugal, such as general use of the credit system; limitation of the duration of studies; change of the examination system; reinforcement of the tutorial system; development of better integrated courses; diversification of subject matters; modification of study methods; expansion of postgraduate education.

The adoption of these modifications is mainly in the hands of the institutions as a result of the autonomy laws mentioned above. However, it is foreseen that the more dynamic institutions, and particularly those participating more actively in European programmes, will initiate a reforming process of courses and studies in accordance with European trends. From our point of view the adoption of a generalised credit system is the natural consequence of the development of the ECTS projects, while the expansion of postgraduate education is related (a) to the need for specialised manpower with a very solid scientific background, and (b) to the career of academic staff in those universities and polytechnics, where a postgraduate degree is considered a precondition for promotion to the highest positions.

Diversification of subject matters, as forecasted in some reports, is expected to occur in the near future, especially a movement towards the development of multidisciplinary courses is discernible. Examples of this kind are combining economics or a science with a language, or business studies with engineering, in order to produce broader educated individuals suitable for managerial or administrative positions.

There is also a trend towards the development of better integrated courses. Some reports prepared for the Government have suggested that the present structure of degree courses could be changed to make them more the study of a coordinated body of knowledge, in which each constituent subject is integrated into the whole, with the linkages needing to be comprehended by the student as part of his or her studies. Then the student's task would become not only the absorption of the subject, but also the development of the capacity to demonstrate its internal linkages and their significance, and to use this sum of knowledge to arrive at further conclusions through the application of techniques and reasoning and analysis.

The fundamental modifications occurring in engineering and economic and business courses

Over the last twelve years, within the context of an extended reform that encompassed several fields of higher education, engineering and economic and business courses have been submitted to a very thorough reforming process. We will look at engineering and economic and business courses in separate sections.

Engineering

In engineering the reform process has been based on two major presumptions: (a) that since 1979/80 a coherent system of academic courses exists in these disciplines, within which the polytechnics are carrying out technician training courses and the universities are preparing students with a broad scientific background; and (b) that creation and expansion of postgraduate courses can be achieved. In this context the fundamental trends of the reforms introduced in the above mentioned courses at the university level may be summarised as follows:[1] strengthening of the basic subjects such as mathematics and physics; curricula diversification particularly in the fourth and fifth years of courses; increasing autonomy of the student; intensive use of new methodologies; development of better integrated courses; integration of areas of knowledge; development of intensive relationship with industry.

In what concerns the engineering curriculum the basic subjects (basically mathematics and physics) constitute the selection mechanism of the course, i.e. the students who have the capacity and ability to pass the examinations of these subjects can be sure to achieve graduation. This means that in the curriculum these subjects are the big hurdle for the student to take and the knowledge tested is deeper and more detailed than should necessarily be the case if these subjects were exam-

1 The present considerations are the result of an analysis of the curricula offered in the *Instituto Superior Technico* (1991) (Technical University of Lisboa) and follow some interviews with students as well as with members of the academic staff.

ined solely to support scientifically the subsequent subjects covered in the curriculum.

Curricula diversification is relevant in many engineering fields where the student, predominantly in the fourth and fifth academic years, can choose the subjects from a 'menu' which is offered in the course. For example, in civil engineering, the students in the fourth and fifth years have the opportunity to select 12 subjects from a total of 44 included in the 'menu'.

We have to underline that beyond this curricular diversification that occurred within almost all branches the *Instituto Superior Technico* (IST) has also diversified the courses on offer, adding new branches to the classic specialities (civil, mechanical, electric, chemical, mining) such as naval engineering, engineer and industrial management, information and computers.

One of the characteristics of the engineering courses is now the use of new methodologies for teaching. In fact, the student has greater autonomy than before; the content of the subject is less rigid; the student gathers many times with other colleagues in working groups; in a large number of subjects the final examination consists of an analysis and discussion of small dissertations prepared by groups of students; and, finally, the number of subjects with experimental characteristics has increased significantly.

The integration of several fields of knowledge is also a trend in the engineering courses, and it emerged from the interviews with students and professors that many 'bridges' have been established among the different subjects. In particular the so-called 'final dissertation' is an excellent opportunity for the students to test their capacity to bring together different kinds of knowledge in the various subjects.

At the moment we wonder to what extent the engineering courses, like economic and business courses, can in the future merge different subjects into larger scientific areas, or at least teach them together. The creation of these larger scientific areas or even branches (such as mechanics/electronics) would have to go hand in hand with the emergence of a greater number of postgraduate courses where the student may obtain narrow specialisations well-adapted to the needs of the research sector or of the economic world.

Finally, it is important to underline the development in recent years of a close relationship between the engineering courses and the outside world, particularly industry. Universities have developed a large number of activities with industry and many students have more and more opportunities to visit industries, to work in factories for larger or shorter periods, and to benefit from scholarships granted by individual companies.

Representatives from industry are also participating in consultative governing bodies of institutions of higher education and many enterprises are giving support to the re-equipment of laboratories and workshops. In this respect it is important to emphasise the existing needs for equipment in the basic subjects (e.g. physics and chemistry) and the existence of excellent machinery and laboratory equipment in some sectors (e.g. computers and electronics) due mainly to external financial contribution from the industrial sector.

Economics and business studies

In the economics and business courses we note a trend, similar to the one we observed in engineering courses, to make the curriculum more flexible. In this analysis we have considered the situation of two university institutions: the *Instituto Superior de Economia e Gestao* (1991) (ISEG), within the Technical University of Lisbon; and the *Faculdade de Economia* (FE), belonging to the New University of Lisbon.

Although the organisation of the curriculum in the FE is much more flexible than in the ISEG, even in this last institution we notice some efforts in that sense. In ISEG a new curriculum was adopted in 1986. The most relevant aspects of change, compared with the previous curricula, are:

- a reduction in both courses (economics and business) of the common core of subjects – the new common core was reduced from two academic years to one academic year (the first year of each course)
- the introduction of specialised groups of subjects corresponding to the so-called 'conditioned options' as well as some other optional subjects in the fourth and fifth academic years of the curriculum of each course in parallel with the group of compulsory subjects.

In the economics course the scientific areas of the 'conditioned options' available in the last academic year were the following: International economy; Planning and economic policy; Social and economic development; Urban and regional economy. In the business course the options were: Finance; Commerce. In both courses there are two options in the fourth academic year (each one of one semester in length) and seven in the fifth academic year, of the same length.

In the FE the situation in what concerns the curricular organisation is rather different with a larger emphasis on the autonomy of the student. The students have a large range of choice in the menu of the subjects which are available in each course. The subjects are gathered in three different groups according to their relevance and characteristics. Each subject is given a certain number of credits that varies from 4.5 to 3.5 units.

The conditions for completing courses with success are the following:

- to achieve a number of credit units between 124 (minimum) and 140 (maximum)
- to spend at least eight academic semesters on the course
- to pass all subjects of Group I
- to collect a certain number of credit units (between a minimum and a maximum) of the subjects from Group III
- to pass subjects that integrate two of several fields of knowledge belonging to Group II
- to be approved in English language and informatics.

As regards the academic evaluation of the students, the situation also varies from one institution to another. In FE it is compulsory to accomplish a final examination for each subject the student studies. The final mark for each subject is the result of a weighting of the marks obtained in each examination with the marks of a continuous process evaluation. In ISEG the academic evaluation for each subject is based on one or a combination of some of the following alternatives:

- an individual test in a written or oral form
- the analysis of a project or a specific work
- continuous evaluation.

In both institutions looked at here new methodologies in teaching are being used. These new methodologies are aimed at promoting greater autonomy of students, a larger integration of fields of knowledge and the provision of more experience in working in groups.

The relationship between economic and business courses and entrepreneurial activities (public or private) is promoted in each institution through some specific units specialised in cooperation with the industrial world. In these units academic staff and final-year students develop projects together. Some enterprises, in both institutions but particularly in FE, are financing some of these academic activities, mainly at postgraduate level, providing work placements for students, funding the purchase of equipment (mainly computers), and offering scholarships for students.

CHAPTER 8

An Attempt to Diversify University Curricula

The Case of Spain

Emilio Lamo de Espinosa and Inés Alberdi

Introduction

The Spanish curriculum of today is different from that in the past, but changes have taken place within certain limits set by tradition and the democratic process of negotiations. Decisions on educational practices take place at several levels, and concern subjects such as methods of teaching, syllabuses and teaching materials. The changes in the Spanish university curriculum have taken place in a democratic manner, putting as much emphasis on participation in education as on scientific rational conceptions of it. One of the factors underlying the need for reform was a demand by faculty members to be able to share in decision making in society and working life, including university organisational structures and decision making procedures.

Legal Reforms

The 1970 Education General Law, *Ley General de Educación* (LGE) changed a dual system into a unified university structure. The subsequent 1978 constitution maintained the responsibility of central government over degrees. In the 1980s the University Reform Law, *Ley de la Reforma Universitaria* (LRU) was another important step in the transformation of the Spanish university system (Lamo de Espinosa 1993) from a centralised scheme to a more autonomous system. Universities now have the power of initiative in many areas although the Education Department continues to hold some authority over the selection of faculty members and determines the national framework for access to tenure and retribution.

At the same time the 1983 LRU permits the establishment of private universities, which preserve freedom in selecting students and teachers and to develop curricula, although they have to be formally approved by the Council of Universities.

The process of change has resulted in a unification of higher education in the sense that virtually all higher education institutions are now called universities. The 1970 law integrated the technical schools into the university system and within the framework of the 1983 reform the remaining institutions also joined. More recently, some specialised studies like music and drama are also in the process of integrating into the system.

New universities

In April 1991 a new decree authorised and regulated a number of new universities, some of them private and some of them public, in the framework of the LRU. This decree fixed the requirements and general conditions for these universities in order to secure their ability for education and research. The general requirement to establish a new university, public or private, is to offer a minimum of eight degrees of official titles in architecture, engineering or liberal sciences at the first cycle of *Diplomatura* (College) or the second cycle of *Licenciatura* (Graduate), at least three of them at the second cycle, and offering some technical degrees. The decree does not determine what must be the structure of the departments but requires a minimum of research activity and a minimum teacher:student ratio of 1:25. There is also a regulation for the professional requirement of the teachers: at the first cycle (college) 30 per cent of the teachers must have their PhD; at the second cycle (graduates) 70 per cent of the teachers must have their PhD; and for the third cycle (doctorate and master) all the teachers must have it. At any rate at least 50 per cent of the faculty must be doctors.

At the same time the decree determines the incompatibility of teachers working in public and private universities at the same time. This last decision has been contested by the public university teachers who saw the new private institutions as a way to improve their remuneration. There is also a series of regulations on the physical conditions of the new universities premises: they must include community spaces, classrooms, laboratories, seminar rooms, libraries and sport facilities.

The new public universities will eventually be created and organised by the regional and local administrations. The private universities will undergo stricter control than the public in order to assure their ability to offer higher education. All legal requirements will be examined before they are allowed to start to operate, the promise to maintain their activity for a minimum number of years must be signed, and the general planning of activities and the economic assessment of their running possibilities will be examined before the centre is duly authorised.

This decree also regulates the conditions for foreign universities to establish High Studies Centres in Spain. These centres must be submitted to public inspection and they have to prove that they are correctly established in their country of origin. The situation of teachers, students and the general condition of the premises will be treated in the same way as the private universities. However, if the centres want to offer a general degree they must work in partnership with a public university in order to assure its legality.

Research

Going against the traditional character of the Spanish university, the 1983 reform has brought about a greater orientation towards research activities. The departmental structure was introduced to pursue this objective. While the centres organise the whole degree teaching programmes, the department is the unit which organises and produces research.

Research activity is managed with absolute freedom by the universities regulating the internal department structure. Generally universities allow departments great autonomy and their research capacities and orientation depend mostly on their capacity to obtain external financing.

Research activities have increased in Spanish universities over the last few years due to the general support and interest for science among private and public institutions. The 1986 law for Promotion and Coordination of Scientific and Technical Research, *Ley de la Ciencia* (LC), has structured the field and has been backed up by strong financial support. Annually there is a public contest offering a large amount of public money for scientific programmes to be developed inside the university system. These programmes, coordinated by the Education Department, indicate the endorsed fields for research each year.

New national degrees

Within the frame of the LRU, the 1983 University Reform Law, all the proposals for new curricula degrees correspond to the Council of Universities, a public body formed by the principals of most of the Spanish universities and with a secretary appointed by the Education Minister.

One of the first purposes of the Council of Universities has been to update and diversify programmes and curricula. A typical characteristic of the Spanish university system was the small number of degrees offered. When the Council launched its reform plan in 1986 there were only 56 different degrees, most of them regulated by old and traditional programmes (Consejo de Universidades 1986). To change this situation the Council outlined an ambitious project of reform of degrees and curricula. The basic objective of this plan was to diversify the programmes *vertically*, by incorporating new and necessary degrees, and differentiate the studies *horizontally*, establishing a cyclic order in such a way that students could enrol in a programme of two or three years to get a degree, and move on later to the second cycle to get a higher degree, and even to a third to prepare a Master's or doctorate. The aim of that was to make it possible to integrate periods of training and education with periods of work as well as making flexible personal curricula by creating access to various second cycles from each first cycle. An additional objective was to broaden the study programmes offered by the system.

Impact of changes on the curriculum

In 1987 the Council of Universities created several working groups of professors in order to study the current curricula and to propose changes and improvements, as well as to work out a basis for new degrees. The deliberations of these commissions have been subject to debate within the faculty communities (Consejo de Universidades 1987).

The first step of the reform was the definition of a central curricula nucleus, about 30 per cent of the total schooling hours, and to push universities and centres to fill the rest by a process of combining public debate and small working groups. Finally, in 1990 and 1991, the Council of Universities approved, at the request of several working groups, the general regulations of the new university degrees that Spanish universities want to offer. The general idea of the reform is the diversification and the specialisation of Spanish degrees (Consejo de Universidades 1990, 1991).

The first draft of the reform was made public in June 1990, and approved by the Gonzalez cabinet in October of the same year. The new lines for the curriculum of 55 degrees were approved in 1990 and another 41 degrees in 1991. The first 55 degrees were ratified in 1990, with a general outline of their studies programme, and they shape the basic body of university offer.[1] One year later the guidelines for 41 more degrees were approved.[2] The new degrees are meant to align Spanish university degrees with those of our European neighbours who generally have a wider diversification of higher education curricula.

With this reform Spain tries to shape its universities in accordance with European models in order to ease Spanish integration into the European internal market, and to adapt educational facilities on offer to new social needs. Many of these degrees are new in Spanish universities and the changes in traditional degrees have to do with the contents of the curricula, the new system of credits, the maximum and minimum global numbers of credits for each one, and the succession of cycles within the levels of degrees. Indeed this is only the first stage of the process of reform because the universities now have the responsibility to finish the design of the curriculum of the degrees they want to offer.

The curriculum: issues and aspects

Flexibility v rigidity

The programmes of studies have traditionally been strict in Spanish universities. The administrative control of the curriculum stood at the basis of homogeneity and uniformity of all degrees, and they all had similar structures with roughly the same contents in every university. The possibility for innovation and diversity is now open with the LRU because each university is allowed to redefine its curriculum, but it will take some time before the process of curriculum reform is completed.

1 The new degrees approved were, among others: physics (graduate), business administration (graduate), marketing and research techniques (graduate), history (graduate), economics (graduate), agronomy engineering, woods engineering, computering engineering, business administration (BA) etc.

2 These degrees were mainly in the fields of experimental sciences, health, technical engineering, social sciences and humanities.

Even after the reform will have been carried through for the student most of the curriculum will be mandatory since its regulation depends on decisions adopted by the Council of Universities, the university and the centre, and only a maximum of 15 per cent of the curriculum will be of free choice to the student.

Education and the labour market

One of the aims of the reform has been the adjustment of higher education to the needs of the labour market. The public debate over the economic and social aspects of university studies was intense in the early 1980s and a sense of a lack of connection between society and university spread among the growing numbers of graduate unemployed. Some research on this issue has been carried out recently in order to establish the level of work and unemployment among graduates (Consejo de Universidades 1987; VVAA 1989).

A traditional weakness of university studies has been their isolation from the actual workplace. Academics despised applicability as an unnecessary pragmatism, and innovations and new technologies as immature science. Only recently the financial aspect of applied research has produced new interest for recent scientific innovations. The question to what extent universities should be responsive to the needs of the labour market and industry remains open.

Degrees and professional practice

A national degree is the legal requirement to exercise most professions, and that limits the possible curricula innovation as it might meet with opposition of professional corporations.

The influence of professional corporations is quite strong in the Spanish administration and the decisions of the Education Ministry and universities have been influenced by them. They are the institutions that have the responsibility to allow professionals to be introduced into professional activities. The connection between the degree and the legal possibility for professional work produces some difficulties as soon as new degrees are introduced. Corporations are reluctant to accept innovations and sometimes refuse recognition of new degrees.

The cycle system

University studies are structured in three cycles – as established by the University Reform Law (LRU) – which stand for three levels of knowledge or complexity. There is a continuity between cycles, but it is also possible to stop in each of them. The possible communication between cycles and different specialisations is still scarcely developed.

First cycle: Bachelor of Arts, Diplomatura and Technical Engineering

This is considered the basic cycle. The first cycle is composed of those diplomas organised in two or three academic years; they finish with gaining a *Diplomatura*, Technical Engineer or Technical Architect diploma. Most of these diplomas are offered in university schools, centres that offer only three-year programmes. These short studies programmes are especially important in the areas of health and education. Teachers in those centres are often also members of departments where second cycles are offered, and where programmes and curricula are designed. Part of the first cycle programmes are organised as complete and independent units, others as part of a long, full degree programme to which the first three years are a first cycle introduction.

Second cycle: Graduate, Licenciatura, Architect and Engineer

The dominant idea in this cycle is specialisation. The second cycle is made up of those degrees organised in four, five or six academic years (the first three years of them are part of the first cycle) and, after that, students obtain the degree of *Licenciatura*, Graduate, Engineer or Architect. Traditionally it was possible to choose between multiple options of programmes in the last two years of the cycle, but the degree you obtained was not differentiated. The reform already in process tries to improve and to recognise this specialisation.

The Third Cycle: Official and unofficial degrees

In the third cycle there are different options between official and unofficial degrees. This is the most advanced level with the doctorate, always official, and the Master's, unofficial. The postgraduate cycle is, within the framework of the LRU, a priority for the universities from the point of view of research and advanced education. There are also specialisation studies that open the possibility for public and private universities to offer unofficial degrees in all kinds of fields. The open regulation of these studies allows for the introduction in universities of all sorts of subjects, including those traditionally alien to the Spanish university.

The PhD has been reformed on the line of the American model: two years of specialised training within a previously defined programme, two or three years of research and a final dissertation, all of which is performed under the supervision of a tutor member of a department that is the responsible for the authorisation of the final presentation.

There are no official Master's degrees, but the law allows universities and other institutions to offer postgraduate studies in the form of Master's degrees; some of which are organised jointly with foreign universities. This is the field where the development and diversification of curricula has been the most pronounced.

Finally, many universities offer postgraduate studies which are not recognised as part of the doctorate, and which are organised around a subject amidst an oasis of freedom, since they do not prepare for official degrees.

The structure of the academic year

The debate over the academic year is currently being held in Spanish universities. Traditionally the academic year lasted nine months and all subjects were taught within that time span. The universities are now discussing an alternative academic year of two periods, or semesters, and a different division of time for teachers and students. The semester system is very appropriate for an open curriculum in which the student is allowed to choose subjects, but it is only an administrative complication for a closed programme where students are forced to follow most of the programme and are allowed only a small amount of choice.

The duration of degrees

The study programme of every degree determines the number of years within which the degree has to be concluded. There is some flexibility in allowing students to take longer to get the degree, but the maximum programme the student can have each year is officially laid down. In this way the time a good student takes to finish his or her degree is known exactly. The minimum number of years is three for a Bachelor of Arts *Diplomatura*, five for a Graduation *Licenciatura*, and at least two more years for a Master's or doctorate.

The Spanish tradition has been to extend the number of years of studies as much as possible. The five-year programme is the norm for the majority of full degrees and there are six years for medicine and the most prestigious engineering programmes.

The number of years can be changed by the reform that is now being discussed, because the LRU allows universities to introduce their time-scales for the duration of degrees. For instance, Catalonian universities have already approved a four-year scheme for university degrees. Nevertheless, this aspect is of less importance now that the system of credits has been introduced and that the students can organise themselves more freely.

Other higher studies

To improve their financial autonomy the LRU has allowed universities to contract teaching activities with all types of public and private entities, and good results have been obtained not only in polytechnical universities but also in the academic ones. An example of this could be the free humanities curriculum that the Autónoma University in Madrid offers to a very socially select public. Another different case is the Popular University organised by the Complutense University for the Madrid Town Council that offered public lectures in suburban areas. In the more technical departments there is the opportunity to arrange training courses and programmes for private firms, improving resources and external relations in doing so.

The Summer Universities over the last years can be put forward as another form of higher studies. During the long period of summer recess some universities organise short courses or seminars with a large media coverage. The teachers are not only university professors but private firm professionals, well-known politicians, senior public administrators and civil servants, and cultural personalities. These summer courses do not require academic standards and do not result in university diplomas, but they are an excellent place for scientific popularisation and public debate.

Changes in selected disciplines

Physics

The Royal Decree 1425/1990 regulates the official degree in physics, valid in all national territories. The degree in physics is organised in two cycles, each of them with a minimum of two academic years and a maximum of five. It must contain a minimum of 300 credits, each credit meaning 10 class hours.

The maximum number of weekly class hours is 30 with a maximum of 15 theoretical classes.

The compulsory national subjects – 30 per cent of the curriculum – are included in the Decree with an explanation of their contents.

Engineering

The French system was the historical model for engineering studies in Spain, with its high schools linked to the technical administrative departments where engineers always had the possibility to become civil servants at the end of their studies. Schools were very demanding in the standards they set and the number of students was limited through a strict and selective system. In 1957 engineering studies came under the control of the Education Department, and their relationship with the university system increased.

The university system has developed and, since 1970, has incorporated the higher technical schools, *Escuelas Tecnicas Superiores* (ETS) where engineers have traditionally been prepared. Nevertheless, there are some peculiarities about these centres that make them more exclusive and selective than universities. The requirements to enter are higher, the first year of studies is selective (you cannot continue unless you pass every subject), six academic years are needed to get the degree and statistically only one out of four students succeeds in passing. In addition, the number of engineers has not increased as in other diplomas, the ETS receive only 6 per cent of the university students, and the percentage of women is very low: as opposed to the 50 per cent in the entire university, women form only 15 per cent of the students in ETSs.

Several engineering degrees were approved on 26 October 1990, indicating the general requirements for their curricula reform. Since the reform the curriculum has not changed much but it has adjusted to the cycle system, and also a number of new technical engineering diplomas have been created.

The Royal Decree 1451/1990 on agronomy is a model for an engineering diploma. The structure of the full degree diploma includes two cycles, each of them having at least 120 credits and a minimum of 300 credits combined. The universities have to decide on the total amount of credits and on the number of years needed to get a degree in engineering, with a maximum of five years for a full degree diploma (two cycles).

The Council has approved the national compulsory basic subjects for each speciality, about 30 per cent of the credits, and the universities had to decide what other obligatory and optional subjects they want to add. The plan outlines an amount between 20 and 30 hours of class per week, a minimum of 15 of them theoretical. The decree also foresees the connection between technical engineering diplomas and the second cycle of this degree.

Economics

The Royal Decree 1425/1990 regulates the full degree in economics and the general direction for its curricula. Economics is organised in two cycles, with a total of four or five academic years to be decided by each university, and a total amount of 300 credits. The number of hours per week in class must be 30, with a maximum of 15 weekly theoretical class hours. The compulsory subjects, 30 per cent of the total, are stipulated in the decree, and each university has to design the rest of the curricula.

History

The scheme for the history full degree is very similar to the above mentioned. History is regulated by the Royal Decree 1448/1990, in which the general mandatory subjects for the diploma appear as a 30 per cent of the total.

The degree is organised in two cycles with a minimum of 300 credits and a maximum of five academic years, to be decided by each university. Universities have three years to present the studies programme to the Council for its approval. The weekly number of classes, a minimum of 20 and a maximum of 30, must be theoretical and practical. A maximum of 15 theoretical class hours per week is mandatory.

Conclusion

The 1983 University Reform Law has set a reform process in motion which is still ongoing. Once the legal parameters were set it was up to the universities to fill them in and to design curricula that corresponded to the needs of Spanish society. Any innovation meets with some resistance and there are indeed some unresolved questions, e.g.

to what extent the curriculum should be adapted to the needs of the labour market and to what extent academic values and traditions take preference over practical ones, and may be short-term expectations of society at large. Another constraint consists in the time universities need to adjust themselves to their more autonomous role in the Spanish system. In addition, the new public and private universities have to be merged with the established system, possibly catching the carefully balanced *status quo* off guard. In that respect the exact relationship between private and public institutions has not been settled yet. The growth of postgraduate education in its various forms, official or unofficial, is certainly a new feature of the system and goes hand in hand with an increased research orientation in general. Although 1990 Royal Decrees set the framework for new degrees in physics, engineering, history and economics, it is still difficult to draw detailed conclusions as to the changes achieved at micro-level.

CHAPTER 9

Patterns of Studies in Greek Universities

A Micro-Level Approach of Four Disciplines

Stephanos Pesmazoglou

Introduction

The focus of this chapter is to delineate certain modes of adaptation and innovation within Greek universities with point of reference for disparate fields of study. An attempt is being made to detect the teaching and research preconditions that seem to coexist when some sort of collective creative teaching is at work.

As a preliminary warning it is worthwhile noting that within the European context it is not a simple task to determine some common methods, criteria and models for intra-European comparisons. To be more to the point: with no criteria for evaluating teaching staff, researchers or students, no institutionalised research nor really structured postgraduate courses, with teaching staff by necessity tending to consider their jobs as subsidiary and 'undergraduates' who are as a rule (90%) never seen in class it is doubtful if one can really speak of a 'university' in Greece at all. Within the European context, most of the major issues in the ongoing debate on university and/or higher education are non-issues in Greece.

Endemic phenomena of contemporary Greek society – such as the long-standing politics of state patronage and clientelism, the whirlwind of populism in the 1980s – cannot but be reflected in the educational system as a whole and the universities more specifically. Furthermore, teaching staff corporatism and student militancy did not concentrate on educational issues but rather on facilitating their respective problematic conditions within the institutions. The cumulative impact of all the above societal, political and endogenous institutional factors has been, for the university, to operate as a means toward various meta-universitarian ends instead of concentrating on the essence of its major functions as an institution of higher education: i.e. teaching, learning and research.

It is in this sense, that much of the discussion on 'adaptation' and 'renovation' which is offered as an antidote to the political, educational and cultural stalemate of Greek society often sounds rhetorical and pompous. Nevertheless, certain niches of creative work seem to indicate that attempts to overcome inertia exist *en sourdine* at all university levels. Perhaps such phenomena are evidenced with a greater frequency as we move 'downwards' from the university or school level to the departmental and from there on to the sectoral – often around an individual professor or a nucleus of the teaching staff. It is within this micro-level perspective that we shall attempt to outline certain features within the four specific disciplines proposed. As there are no systematic studies at a faculty level (nor at the 'macro' university level), we necessarily have to rely on sources such as conference proceedings, special journal issues, and personal interviews or written communications.

Chemical engineering: the *par excellence* 'productive' field of study

If one had to choose from among the 28 departments the one most linked to and affected by economic trends and, in particular, industrial developments, it would most certainly be the department of chemical engineering. In addition to its interaction with industrial and general economic factors, it is affected by innovation in technology. Furthermore, its relationship to energy and water conservation and other environmental problems makes it even more sensitive to external stimuli: in the Greek context of an 'unproductive' (in the literal economic meaning of the term) higher education, it is quite an exceptional case.

The existing indications concerning employment of graduates from the chemical engineering departments are that around 40–50 per cent work in the industrial sector.[1] This constitutes by far the highest percentage of any polytechnic department in Greece, and simultaneously one of the lowest internationally (in the US in the mid-1980s it was around 87%). What is even more indicative is that among those employed in the industrial sector, only 28 per cent are

1 Estimates are based on statistical information provided by the Greek Chamber of Engineers and the Union of Chemical Engineers.

linked with chemical-industrial research studies and process engineering. The rest are mainly involved in supervision, management, sales and maintenance.[2]

The emerging picture of the links of the chemical engineering departments with production is one of an essentially indirect relationship, and provides additional evidence of the lack of organic links between the Greek economy and higher education. Nevertheless, the departments of chemical engineering (mainly in Athens Polytechnic, now the Technical University of Athens), have since the 1960s been quick to adapt to industrial trends (Kalogirou, Paöayiannaki and Sacharides 1980; Marinos-Kouris 1980). It followed the fifteen-year industrial boom period up to the oil crisis of 1973. The construction industry might have been at the forefront, but the textile and food processing industries commanded an important share of industrial production and employment.

Under the combined influence of technological and economic development, new social and environmental needs in Greece, and Western European trends in the reorganisation of studies in the faculties of chemical engineering, there has been an ongoing debate on the orientation of the curriculum since the early 1980s.

This debate can be summarised as follows (Panhellenic Association 1991): Engineering or technology: Which path to follow and which model to adopt? Very schematically and with the obvious danger of misrepresenting the epistemological dilemmas of a science completely out of my personal horizon and understanding, it seems that there has been an internalisation of diverging or even conflicting trends in the organisation of chemical engineering studies.

On the one hand, a point of reference is the Anglo-Saxon model of solid engineering studies founded on the general methodology of the various physical and chemical systems. On the other hand, there is the emphasis on the technological content of the curriculum. In-depth studies are proposed for very particular industrial sectors and for very specific commodities. Such proposals seem to be influenced by Ger-

2 Most of the information in this paper was obtained through oral and written communications with key people in the Greek university system. Of course, the full responsibility for the final synthesis and the views expressed burden the writer.

man patterns of chemical applications on a sectoral basis, reaching at their limits specific production formulas.

In the newer department of chemical engineering of the University of Patras, the general philosophy of the engineering model seems to have prevailed. In the respective Athens Technical University department (the first in Greek higher education), a mixed system has been adopted, although the engineering model is gaining ground. The mixed nature of the curriculum is reflected in the formation of separate sectors within the department each with a different emphasis, and in the proliferation of optional courses.

A first conclusion to be drawn from the above is that regardless of the particular model or mixture of models adopted, developments in the organisation of studies, in their content and orientation, have been to an important extent affected by the international developments in the specific discipline, irrespective of endogenous developmental exigencies and social needs. Catalysts in this transfer of educational programmes and methodologies have been members of the teaching staff, usually influenced by the school of their own postgraduate studies, research activities or professorial experience. For the post-war period, the countries of reception have been nearly exclusively the United States and Great Britain and, to a lesser, extent Germany.[3]

The second source of stimuli for the reorganisation of the curriculum has undoubtedly been the novel subject matters arising in the last two decades (Diakoulakis 1991):

1. energy conservation through rational use, differentiation of the sources and effective use of its renewable forms
2. management of water resources, rationalisation of its uses and processing of the seawater
3. work hygiene and industrial safety analysis.

All of the above areas, which constitute acute natural, social and environmental problems for Greece, are now represented in the curriculum, especially among the optional courses. With the deep crisis in the

3 It is worth noting that a high percentage of graduates from the department, and more generally of the Technical University of Athens, continue postgraduate studies abroad and many of those who excel academically remain in universities and research institutes of the host countries (uninterrupted post-war phenomenon of brain drain).

chemical industry, these new fields of study have to an extent become prerequisites for the future employment of chemical engineers.

Under the triple impact of new subject areas, new technologies and diverging models of chemical engineering education, the reorganisation of course structure has in recent years affected the relative importance of specific methods of teaching and learning.

First, there has been a tendency to reduce the number of courses (originally between 50 and 60 during five years) and concentrate on a smaller number – but still far from the English model of 15–20 courses within three to four years. The tendency has been to eliminate general courses, like physics.

Second, a drastic reduction in the amount of teaching *ex cathedra* (from 42 to 30 hours) and in the number of courses examined (from nine to less than seven per semester) was followed by growing emphasis on homework, papers and seminars (Skoulikidis 1991).

Third, undergraduate specialisation was instituted as from the fourth year in five areas: design, materials, organic industries, inorganic industries and food-biotechnology. The final diploma obtained is uniform, with no specification of the specialisation (Skoulikidis 1991).

Fourth, in the ninth semester a five-week practicum was initiated on the premises of enterprises, organisations or research institutes linked with the specialisation of the undergraduate. Specialisation can be further strengthened by the choice of a long paper for the diploma and, of course, even more so for those who excel by a doctoral thesis (Skoulikidis 1991).

Finally, the institution of the 'Counselling Professor' has been introduced to supervise or tutor groups of three to four students.

With a staff/student ratio of 1:23 the departments of chemical engineering in Greek universities fare relatively well (Table 9.1). They run structured postgraduate courses, albeit informal, and award doctoral degrees (some of which are at a high level, especially when linked with research programmes), and participate in joint European projects. The departments of chemical engineering in the Athens Technical University and in Patras are examples of cases where innovation and adaptation of course curricula are interlinked with postgraduate and research programmes, international mobility of teaching staff and graduates and participation in European projects, although this is true only in very recent years as the school did not escape some of the blockages of contemporary Greek society. It seems that corresponding forces are at

Table 9.1 Engineering staff:student ratios academic year 1989–1990

Universities/Schools	*Teaching staff:undergraduates (Ratio)*	
	Chemical engineering	*Electrical engineering*
Technical University of Athens	1:19	1:34
University of Thessaloniki Polytechnic School	1:27	1:44
University of Patras Polytechnic School	1:29	1:35
University of Thrace Polytechnic School	–	1:21
Average for engineering	1:18	1:33
In absolute numbers: Teaching staff	120	153
Undergraduates	(2172)	(5112)

Source: MNER (Ministry of National Education), Department of Studies and Statistics, 1991.

work in the much smaller faculties of electrical engineering and shipbuilding engineering.

Physics

Moving away from 'heavy metal' engineering sciences to the natural sciences, the landscape is much less clear. This seems definitely to be the case for the departments of physics, chemistry and mathematics. All three departments have been functioning mainly as a mechanism reproducing teachers for secondary education and for the pre-university exam-oriented tuition centres (*phrondistiria*) which are thriving in Greece. To a great extent this function has conditioned the three departments which are located within the natural sciences schools of five universities (Athens, Thessaloniki, Patras, Ioannina, Crete).

With over 100 faculty members in the physics department of Athens and over 90 in Thessaloniki (MNER 1991), these are two of the largest in the world, with a commensurate share of in-built inflexibility. With

1500 undergraduates in Athens and nearly 2000 in Thessaloniki (see Table 9.2) the physics departments are so overcrowded that laboratories cannot be operated.[4]

At least for the physics departments of Athens and Salonika Universities, which absorb 60 per cent of the students in physics, it seems that most of the forces converge to neutralise all possible developments in this discipline. The sheer arithmetics of populism, according to members of the staff, prevented the running of the laboratories. It also meant that there has been no possibility of radical innovation in course programmes, and no possibility even to discuss necessary adaptations to world developments in the discipline, and to new requirements in the teaching of physics in secondary schools.

There is no structured postgraduate course. Some one-year postgraduate lectures were provided that lead to a Diploma (accepted as equivalent to the MSc) in four areas: Automation, Informatics-computer science, Telecommunications and Meteorology. The most widely attended course, Informatics, broke away creating a new undergraduate department[5] after an intra-academic squabble which had some material implications linked with the realities of heavily financed computer science programmes.

Of the 100 faculty members in the physics department of Athens, some rough estimates suggest that less than 10 per cent are involved in research, and these tend to be the ones involved in international (mainly European) programmes. There has been a comparatively strong tradition in the section of nuclear physics which is largely linked with the nuclear research centre, *Demokritos*. The most prominent of the scientists had a systematic link with the *Geneva Centre de Recherche Nucleaire*. Nevertheless, the core of the curriculum seems to have remained for all intents and purposes unchanged for the past decade.

In the new physics department of the University of Crete, the appointment of certain professors of international standing initially created the preconditions for an alternative functioning of the undergraduate courses linked with research in institutes. But it seems that

4 The level of admissions in Greece is not a prerogative of the departments or the universities but of the government on the basis of criteria of political expediency and not of educational requirements.

5 Which presently seems to have only one member in its teaching staff.

the politics of large student members has undermined to an extent the qualitative presupposition that prevailed during the first stage.

Table 9.2 Physics staff:student ratios academic year 1989–1990

Universities / Schools	Teaching staff:Undergraduates (Ratio)
University of Athens, School of Natural Sciences, Dept. of Physics	1:15
University of Thessaloniki, School of Natural Sciences, Dept. of Physics	1:22
University of Ioannina, School of Natural Sciences, Dept. of Physics	1:20
University of Crete, School of Natural Sciences, Dept. of Physics	1:23
University of Patras, School of Natural Sciences, Dept. of Physics	1:19
Average for physics	1:19
In absolute numbers: Teaching staff	299
Undergraduates	(5762)

Source: Ministry of National Education, Department of Studies and Statistics (MNER 1991)

Note: No comparative data are available on the departmental level since the departmentalisation of the universities began in the mid-1980s. But for an approximate idea see the overall picture emerging from Table 9.5.

Economics as a discipline and business studies as a profession

Economics as a discipline is being taught at six of the seventeen universities. As can be noted (Table 9.3), three of the six universities are institutions linked solely with the Economics and Business University of Athens (ex-Higher School of Economics and Business Studies) and the University of Pireaus (ex-Higher Industrial School of Salonika). In fact, one of the characteristic and most recent developments has been the change in name and hence perceived status from 'Higher School' to 'University'. With no further broadening of the range of disciplines taught, in effect they remain what is internationally known as a 'School' in the broad area of economics and business.

As can be observed when comparing Tables 9.3 and 9.5, the main distinctive feature of the economics schools (and/or universities) and

Table 9.3 Economics staff:student ratios academic year 1989–1990*

Universities/Schools	*Teaching staff: Undergraduates (Ratio)*
University of Athens, School of Law, Economics and Political Science, Dept. of Economic and Political Science	1:227
University of Thessaloniki, School of Law and Economic Science Dept. of Economic Science	1:184
University of Crete, School of Economics, Dept. of Economic Science	1:28
University of Patras, School of Humanities and Social Sciences Dept. of Economic Science	1:48
Economic University of Athens Dept. of Economic Science	1:96
University of Macedonia Dept. of Economic Science	1:142
University of Athens, School of Law, Economics and Political Science	1:183
University of Piraeus Dept. of Economic Science	1:190
Average for economics	1:170
In absolute numbers:	Teaching staff 156 Undergraduates (26,475)

Source: Ministry of National Education, Department of Studies and Statistics (MNER 1991).
* For comparative data see Table 9.5.

faculties is the massive number of undergraduates and the most problematic teacher:student ratio among all Greek universities and departments. From the viewpoint of political populism these schools have been considered the main repository for tens of thousands of youths searching for a place in tertiary education. 200 students per member of the economics faculty is a ratio unheard of in the West despite the worldwide trend in paneconomism. In the extreme cases of the Universities of Macedonia and Piraeus, a total of 87 members of the staff are expected to teach or supervise nearly 20,000 students.

The sheer numbers are so crushing that any discussion of course programmes and content might sound irrelevant. Nevertheless, some general trends and some specific developments are perhaps worthwhile noting:

1. In terms of disciplinary orientation, the Anglo-Saxon hegemony in economics faculties and business schools in the post-war era has been complete. This is reflected in the organisation of the studies, in the bibliography quoted and above all in the instrumental role played in this direction by the staff, 80 per cent of whom have followed postgraduate studies, obtained doctoral theses or taught at American or English universities (Economics University of Athens 1990, p.19). The Anglo-Saxon orientation of the economics faculties is also confirmed by the books and journals available in the corresponding libraries and by the publications of the teaching staff in learned economics, business and statistics journals.

2. On the basis of commonly accepted performance indicators, there seem to arise uneven patterns of quality among the various universities, schools and departments, both as regards the standing of the staff and the exam scores of entering undergraduates.

3. For most departments (but not all) it seems that standard US programmes of the 1960s and 1970s remain essentially unchanged: micro, macro, Philips courve, the theory of money, welfare economics and public finance all figure in today's programmes. Crucial developments in leading American and European universities such as dynamic analysis and income distribution, economic cycles, theory of public choice, evolutionary economics and the most recent formulations of Schumpeterian economics are to a great extent absent from most curricula. What is even more striking is the fact that whole areas are practically non-existent, as for example, methodologies of the social sciences, economic history, history of economic ideas, theory of the State and its economic function and the more recent debate on regulation and deregulation.

4. Underlying the limited interest in theoretical developments and general courses is a tendency for early proliferation and specialisation which are more readily adaptable to employment outlets. In short, economics appears to be a discipline without an associated profession, while business studies appear to be a profession in search of a discipline. The divergencies are reflected in the course programmes. More departments and sections arise in specialisations leading to degrees, e.g. shipping studies (University of Piraeus), accounting (University of Macedonia), statistics and insurance (University of Piraeus) or vegetable production (Agricultural University of Athens). This pre-degree specialisation is linked with the absence of postgraduate studies, on the one hand, and with great pressure for adaptation to employment outlets irrespective of the implications for learning, on the other.

5. A concomitant characteristic is the overemphasis on statistics, econometrics and computer technology, not just as important tools for economic analysis but as disciplines *per se*, as reflected in the existence of departments within economic schools awarding degrees in applied computer science or statistics. One can draw an analogy – albeit within completely different disciplinary environments – with the department of chemical engineering: solid methodological preparation in core courses with emphasis on ways of thinking about engineering and economic systems, as compared with learning in (some) depth a very specific subject matter with insufficient flexibility for wider applications.

6. A sixth characteristic of the economics departments derives from the lack of officially recognised structured postgraduate courses leading to an MA. The Greek university system offers two diplomas: One equivalent to the BA degree and the other to a doctoral degree. There is no other in-between degree legally allowed. This state of affairs has certainly influenced the tendency towards early specialisation in the economics departments as well. Among such departments is the one with orientation in international and European

economic studies of the Economic University of Athens (usually within postgraduate studies in other European countries). It is the only major development among economic schools influenced by the process of European integration. The department was formed in 1989 engaging young economists with links (and publications) in the international network. The emphasis has moved towards more seminars, tutorials in very small groups, with a corresponding reduction in *ex cathedra* teaching. The orientation towards jobs linked with the EC is explicitly stated in the guide to studies (Economics University of Athens 1991, p.20). Additional Jean Monnet University positions on European integration have been institutionalised or financed in other departments such as the Universities of Athens and Crete.

History: a non-discipline

Up to very recently there was no independent-autonomous department of history in Greek universities. As shown in Table 9.4, history is taught at five universities, and at four of them in conjunction with archaeology. Ninety-seven per cent of undergraduates and teaching staff are linked with such departments. The other three per cent are in the sole autonomous department of history at the Ionian University.

Up to 1984, history was one among various other disciplines integrated within the philosophy schools (Kapsomenos 1991; Tsinorema 1991). The latter were split into three departments: philology (literature), history-archaeology, and philosophy-pedagogy-psychology, each one granting a unified degree. The official rationale behind the reorganisation of the studies in the philosophy schools and within the various departments was clearly an adaptation to the requirements of the only realistic employment outlet: secondary education, which theoretically requires professional degrees. According to the same rationale, philosophers, historians, psychologists are just not 'needed', hence they have to adapt and accept existing realities.

Of course, there was a vocal countervailing minority trend, but with no forceful institutions backing it, which supported the organisational autonomy of each discipline (history, psychology, philosophy) as a precondition for research and for raising the overall level of undergraduate and postgraduate studies (Kapsomenos 1991, p.34).

The generalisation reached by Kapsomenos, ex-dean of the Philosophy School of Ioannina, is that in Greece the existing history courses cannot even fulfil their traditional role, i.e. the preparation of competent professional teachers for secondary education, given the blockage of research and postgraduate studies (Kapsomenos 1991). The implications of such statements, subscribed to by most scholars, are far-reaching since they are linked with the preparation of future generations. The alternative approach proposed is to split the departments on the basis of the three major areas of knowledge: the ancient period, from the prehistoric to the Roman period (Greek and Latin literature, history and archaeology); the Byzantine and post-Byzantine period, in conjunction with the Middle Ages in the West; and the modern Greek period, in conjunction with European history (Kapsomenos 1991, p.35).

As for the structure of curriculum in the history and archaeology departments, the relative position of history is reflected by the fact that only 45–48 per cent of the courses (or required modules) correspond to its subject matter. One of the exam requirements for history departments is to pass an obligatory class ancient Greek, not history.

The organisation of teaching in history follows the patterns that have prevailed in the philosophy schools for decades: *ex cathedra* oratory, no seminars which are preliminary or advanced in most cases (Hering 1989). No dissertation is required for the degree.

As for the actual content of the learning process it is to a great extent conditioned by the parrot-like memorising faculties required by the one and only textbook examined and which as a rule defines the limits of lecturing as well (Asdrachas 1988). As an end result according to some, students graduate without knowing how to write a short paper. Disinterest is attributable to all sorts of endogenous institutional factors; rigidity and inertia prevail (Dertilis 1988).

There is one additional element regarding the state of affairs in history studies which seems to be unique to Greece: for the past 15 years, there has been an unprecedented flourishing of historical research and publications outside the official academic institutions. The driving force has been a number of historians who had all been outsiders to the Greek academic world. They have created a new momentum in post-dictatorship Greece having resided in Paris during the dark interim period. They have supervised dissertations in Greek and foreign (mainly French) universities.

Major programmes of historical research have been sponsored by the National Bank of Greece and the Commercial Bank of Greece as well as by the Agricultural Bank, the General Secretariat of Youth and the Centre of Contemporary Hellenism within the National Research Foundation. Conferences, symposiums and round tables have been organised, often at an international level. Finally, historical series were established in leading publishing houses, parallel to the publication of two historical journals *Mnimon* and *Ta Historika*. Pivotal in this scholarly web of activities was what was stated programmatically in the journal, *Ta Historika* (Pesmazoglou 1989): 'Scope of the publication is to meet some fundamental needs for historical studies, such as the renewal of its subject matter and methodology, the revival of interdisciplinary approaches, the relevance of historiography to the present as well as its elevation to the level of cultural demand'. Diverse trends arising from within the *Annales* school are evident.

Two aspects are of relevance in respect to the organisation and content of the history field in Greek universities:

First, the emphasis given to social and economic history thematically suffices by itself to announce the renewal of historical research which with few exceptions have been neglected, if not completely ostracised, in the past, from Greek universities. Academic historiography has been mainly directed as elsewhere in Europe at the causes of nation-building and, later, at nationalistic and ethnocentric tendencies, in the writing and the teaching of history (Historical Archives of Greek Youth 1989; *Synchrona Themata* 1988). Nevertheless, the ideological foundations of the official history programmes do not seem to have been shaken. On the contrary, ethnocentrism and the search of national identity remain pivotal. As stated by George Leontaritis, history professor in the University of Athens, overall institutional reforms affected solely the organisational aspects but not the content and ideology of traditional programmes (Leontaritis 1988).

The second factor is the incapacity of university structures to create the preconditions for the reception of new blood linked with this extra-mural vitality. Teaching in the humanities and the social sciences, without the lively curiosities associated with research, becomes dull. But historical research, as well, without the institutional backing of universities or independent research centres remains at the mercy of party politics and economic cycles. At times of hardship the first to be affected have been research activities: in the year 1990–1991, three of the major research programmes were terminated and the rest considerably cut back.

To conclude this section, the balance between those forces supporting an adaptation of historical studies exclusively to narrowly defined professional needs of the school teaching staff and those forces who believe in history as an area of study that strengthens critical faculties and facilitates understanding of other periods, of other civilisations, or the 'other' in general seems to be shifting decisively against the latter. And this is a period when one would expect the intensification of all historical studies – not just Greek history, but also Balkan, European, Middle Eastern and World history, and not just in autonomous history departments, but also as general courses in all faculties.

Table 9.4 History staff:student ratios academic year 1989–1990

Universities/Schools		*Teaching staff: Undergraduates (Ratio)*
University of Athens, School of Philosophy, Dept. of History and Archaeology		1:42
University of Thessaloniki, School of Philosophy Dept. of History and Archaeology		1:20
University of Ioannina, School of Philosophy Dept. of History and Archaeology		1:24
University of Crete, School of Social Science Dept. of History and Archaeology		1:16
Ionian University, Dept. of History		1:40
Average for history		1:28
In absolute numbers:	Teaching staff Undergraduates	170 (4731)

Source: Ministry of National Education, Department of Studies and Statistics (MNER 1991).

Table 9.5 Greek universities staff:undergraduate ratios

	Academic Year	
	1989–1990	*1979–1980*
University of Athens	1:40	1:16
Technical University of Athens*	1:23	1:9
University of Thessaloniki	1:29	1:10
Economic University of Athens*	1:131	1:43
Athens Agricultural University*	1:25	1:6
Athens School of Fine Arts	1:18	1:10
Panteos University of Political Science*	1:59	1:34
University of Piraeus*	1:109	1:64
University of Macedonia*	1:241	1:82
University of Patras	1:24	1:11
University of Ioannina	1:23	1:8
University of Thrace	1:45	1:9
University of Crete	1:21	–
Technical University of Crete	1:42	1:11
Aegean University**	1:37	–
Ionian University**	1:49	–
University of Thessaly**	1:67	–
Average	1:58	1:14

Source: Ministry of National Education, Department of Studies and Statistics, on the basis of data of the National Statistical Organisation of Greece, July 1990 for the academic year 1989–90 and the volume *Statistics of Education* 1983 for the academic year 1979–80.

* All previously high schools within the university sector, but only renamed as such in the late 1980s.

** The Universities of Aegean, the Ionian and of Thessaly were founded in the 1980s. Total number of students 186,000. Within this total number official estimates speak of 70,000 floating undergraduates of earlier years.

Concluding remarks

If one was to identify summarily preconditions that seem to lie behind tendencies of creative adaptation and innovation on the basis of the previous micro-analysis of the four disciplines they seem to be the following:

1. The existence of a nucleus of teaching staff keen on keeping up course organisation and curriculum content on the basis of epistemological criteria, world developments and national needs.
2. Interest in organising informal structure postgraduate courses and in supervising doctoral theses.
3. Active involvement in research and therefore securing the necessary material, laboratory or library facilities.
4. As a natural outcome of the above characteristics, such pockets of enlightened teaching and research tend to be involved in research programmes, which are usually on a European scale, and occasionally on a world scale.
5. Of obvious interest within a European perspective, is the likelihood that such niches of academic excellence encourage graduates and undergraduates to learn foreign languages, travel and take part in European programmes such as ERASMUS.
6. Finally, the schools, departments or sections that have the open horizons which characterise true learning are those that if they are not perceived within a context of employment outlet may even create them, without implying that such considerations should be their primary ones.

It is not just a matter of chance that a number of the above preconditions even when they exist do not have the continuity and duration so vital for creating permanent islands of excellence. In-built inelasticities, linked to the lack of possibility for interdepartmental cross-fertilisation, reinforce a web of institutional and societal constraints accounting for the uncertainty of such attempts to overcome inertia.

In this respect could one speak of a European catalyst? Greece's entry into the European Community has been running on a parallel track with a decade of populism, and the implementation of the University Reform Act. Can we detect any important impact of the European factor in the functioning of universities and in curriculum content?

The answer is generally no. Nevertheless, after a protracted period of quasi-anti Europeanism linked with the jargon of anti-capitalism and anti-imperialism since the mid-1970s, there are certain minor changes here and there and above all a declared position by some of the most lively forces in the academic world that seem to believe that in conjunction with the existing niches of resistance to inertia the European programmes at undergraduate, graduate and professorial level could play a role of catalyst in the much needed reorganisation of studies and curriculum adaptation.[6]

The ERASMUS programme, although initially blocked by the nature of the radicalisation process, in recent years has begun to give some positive results. Of course, as it is noted in the memorandum on ERASMUS,[7] there is a structural imbalance between outgoing students and ingoing partly due to the language problem.[8]

It has been rightly stated in the objectives of the project that 'attempts to surpass deficiencies in the prevailing literature which is often too narrow in its scope either because of thematic specialisation, or because of nationally oriented perspectives, or because of a lack of theoretical grounding as a result of immediate political expectations are necessary'. At the same time it has been noted that 'existing concepts on basic university functions vary so much within and among European countries ... that an attempt is required to integrate the outcome of national analyses in a broader and systematic European dimension'.

6 Among such adaptations we can include those involving the European factor as such: some courses with a European dimension have been added in various departments (e.g. in the Law Faculty of Athens University a section of European studies has been introduced whereas in the Economic University, a whole department was created).

7 Prepared by its president Pavlos Christodoulides, September 1991.

8 A problem affecting not only Greece but small minority languages in Europe – Holland, Denmark, Portugal, even Italy and Spain.

It is indeed true that no single vocabulary, nowadays, can describe the educational and cultural 'needs' of society. Nevertheless, it seems that amidst a frantically changing Europe, which is once again experiencing an outburst of irrational nationalist, ethnic and religious rivalries, with civil wars raging at our very frontiers and European governments behaving mainly as individual actors, the time has come for the web of European universities to reassert the full meaning of the word. This can be done by drawing from all the humanitarian traditions of each individual European country and recentering the basic courses of all disciplines to include certain general ones: those by the market often despised, but necessary ingredients of a civil society.

I believe it is absolutely essential to reassert in Greece and in Europe, not just in words but in deeds, the *Homo Universalis* principle of a university as a solid context within which 'multi-versities' – to take up an expression used by Richard Lyman, ex-president of Stanford University (Lyman 1991) – will allow for adaptation but not against meditation and against all the faculties linked with the appreciation of all high points of European civilisation and through it the communion with world civilisations.

For the time being at European Community level as well as the national level the logic of a narrowly defined adaptation of education to economic, professional and technological needs seems to be decisively prevailing, against any idea of a *mission civilisatrice* within one's society. The content of such a mission nowadays would be the strengthening of critical faculties and the widening of the horizons in the direction of the understanding of the 'others', of their civilisation, past and present. In a critical period during which one would expect the intensification of all historical and cultural studies and not only in the context of specific departments but as prerequisite general courses in all faculties – professional and technological alike – it is exactly the humanities and the social sciences that are losing on the undergraduate and the research level.

Adaptation and renovation in the Greek case may be essential. But their orientation on a European scale is just of equal or even greater importance. The end of the European twentieth century may well signal a new age of enlightenment but may just as well toll a new period of blind passions and darkness, i.e. a Europe, united but at the same time disjointed, integrating and simultaneously disintegrating. The universities and higher education are called to strenghten unity and integration and to resist – certainly not to adapt – to the perceived regressive societal tendencies of inversion for the weak and hegemony for the strong.

CHAPTER 10

Changing Priorities in Higher Education Programmes in Ireland

Patrick Clancy

Introduction

The major structural changes in the higher education system in Ireland over the past three decades are broadly similar to those which occurred in other Western countries (Clancy 1993). This has been a period of continuous expansion and significant diversification. Enrolments in full-time higher education grew by 242 per cent between 1964 and 1989 while at a structural level the main feature was the development of a large non-university sector. Until the late 1960s the university sector was dominant, accounting for about 80 per cent of full-time enrolments; by the late 1980s this had declined to less than 50 per cent. The choice of a binary strategy and the targeting of the technological sector for more rapid growth reflects an explicit vocationalism and a desire to fashion the higher education system to meet the labour market needs of a rapidly changing economy. The changing distribution of students by sector which has been documented elsewhere (Clancy 1993) reflects the reorientation of higher education. The present chapter seeks to go beyond these sectoral changes and to examine changes in programmes of study in higher education. However, before focusing on higher education, it is appropriate to examine changes in the second level system since the main determinant of increased demand for places in higher education has been the sharp increase in retention rates at second level.

Changes in second level education

There are four separate types of second level schools in Ireland: secondary schools, vocational schools, community and comprehensive schools.

Secondary schools were the first post-primary type to be established and still dominate provision, catering for two-thirds of second level students. Although almost totally financed by the state, these schools are privately owned and managed. The curricular pattern of these schools was firmly established within the humanist grammar school tradition with a heavy emphasis on language and literary studies.

Vocational schools were established following the 1930 Vocational Education Act and represented the first attempt to establish publicly owned schools. These schools were designed to provide a qualitatively different education from that offered by the more academic and mainly middle-class secondary schools. The emphasis was on technical and practical training in preparation for skilled and semi-skilled occupations. While this bipartite structure of post-primary education was not unique to Ireland, the relative size of the two sectors was the inverse of that found in most Western European countries where the grammar-type school catered for the minority of the school population. By the 1960s there was a growing realisation that the structure of post-primary education was unsatisfactory both from the point of view of the needs of the labour force and from the perspective of equality of opportunity. The new policy adopted was designed to erode the academic/technical distinction, to raise the status of the vocational school and to encourage the provision of a more comprehensive-type curriculum in both secondary and vocational schools.

In addition to seeking a reform of existing schools new school types were established, initially comprehensive schools (1963) and subsequently community schools (1970). While these new school types differ in their control and management structure (Coolahan 1981) they are similar in their philosophy since they are both open to pupils of all classes and levels of ability and offer a wide curriculum to match the full range of pupil aptitudes and aspirations.

The post-primary school sector is further differentiated by a distinction between a minority of secondary schools which are fee-paying and the majority which rely exclusively on state support. Fee-paying schools cater for the higher socio-economic groups who can afford to pay fees for their childrens' education. Thus, while the system of second level education in Ireland is highly differentiated with variations in social selectivity, prestige and academic emphasis reflecting the different origin and history of the school types, a formal unity has been achieved by virtue of the fact that all schools prepare students for the same terminal examination, the Leaving Certificate. It is primarily on the basis of performance in this examination that higher education places are allocated.

Recent years have seen a dramatic increase in participation rates at second level and currently about 70 per cent of the age cohort take the Leaving Certificate Examination, preparation for which now dominates second level education. In the senior cycle (last two years) only 18 per cent of total enrolments take programmes other than the Leaving Certificate and many of these students will subsequently follow or have already followed a Leaving Certificate programme.

Second level education in Ireland is normally of five years duration although a small number of schools offer a six-year programme. It is planned to provide a six-year cycle in all schools in the future. The modal number of subjects studied for the Leaving Certificate is seven, with a significant number of students taking six or eight subjects from a total of 32 subjects offered at higher and ordinary level. The majority of students take Mathematics and three languages: Irish, English and French or another modern continental language. There is considerable variability in the additional subjects which students take. One of the trends evident in recent years has been a shift in the pattern of take-up of subjects especially in the senior cycle. This is illustrated in Table 10.1 which shows the percentage of Leaving Certificate students taking selected subjects in 1989 and in 1973, the year from which the range of subjects currently available was first examined.

In languages, French has become the dominant third subject (after Irish and English which almost all students take) and the study of Latin has almost ceased. In the sciences there has been a dramatic increase in the percentage of students taking biology, especially among females, and there has also been a significant increase in the uptake of physics. The percentage of male students taking the three technical subjects has increased threefold while the take-up of two of the subjects from the business studies group has also increased significantly. Much of the increase in technical, business and science subjects had been at the expense of the study of geography and history.

The pattern of take-up illustrated in Table 10.1 reveals distinct gender differences which have become the focus of considerable research interest (Hannan and Breen 1983). It has been found that much of the gender differences can be explained by variation in 'provision', 'allocation' and 'choice'. Differences in provision arise since no school can provide the full range of 32 possible subjects. These differences are greatest between single-sex schools which cater for almost half of all second level students. Some of the gender differences can be accounted for by differences in allocation practices – while a

Table 10.1 Percentage of Leaving Certificate examination students taking selected subjects in 1973 and 1989

	1973		*1989*	
Subject	*Males*	*Females*	*Males*	*Females*
French	33.0	58.6	51.5	78.3
German	1.4	3.1	2.9	7.0
Latin	42.9	27.7	1.9	0.5
History	45.3	42.1	31.1	25.3
Geography	70.0	73.7	41.2	31.8
Art	14.9	29.1	13.7	23.6
Physics	22.3	1.9	31.8	9.3
Chemistry	30.5	7.6	20.9	14.1
Biology	21.1	28.6	37.1	67.9
Economics	21.9	12.3	19.6	9.4
Accounting	17.6	21.0	27.2	30.1
Business organisation	19.1	23.0	36.5	43.0
Technical drawing	8.6	0.0	25.8	0.7
Engineering	5.1	0.001	13.0	0.2
Construction studies	5.5	0.0	15.1	0.2

Source: Department of Education annual reports.

school may teach a subject, not all pupils may have equal access to it; for example, the study of science may be compulsory at junior cycle in boys' schools but not in girls' schools. The third and most crucial determinant of gender differences in subject take-up involves student choices. When a subject is provided in a school and presented as an option it is a pupil's own choice which determines whether or not it will be taken.

Second level – higher education linkages

The curricular patterns at second level are highly relevant for an understanding of developments in higher education as illustrated in Table 10.2 which shows, separately for males and females, the relationship between subject specialisation at second level and third level field of study. As already observed, it is clear that the majority of higher education entrants had three language subjects.

Table 10.2 Average number of science, language, business, technical and 'other' subjects taken at Leaving Certificate by third level field of study and gender

	Science subjects		*Language subjects*		*Business subjects*		*'Other' subjects*		*Technical subjects*	
Field of study	*M*	*F*	*M*	*F*	*M*	*F*	*M*	*F*	*M*	*F*
Humanities	1.10	1.09	3.05	3.15	0.93	0.50	1.39	1.60	0.09	0.00
Art	0.79	0.73	2.33	2.81	0.57	0.42	1.94	2.10	0.46	0.03
Social sci.	1.08	1.17	2.89	3.09	0.94	0.48	1.12	1.45	0.21	0.01
Education	1.15	1.24	2.79	3.05	0.49	0.44	0.87	1.36	0.82	0.01
Law	1.52	1.43	3.18	3.17	0.61	0.43	0.98	1.24	0.11	0.00
Hotel, Catering & Tourism	1.01	0.80	2.87	2.93	1.01	0.89	1.34	1.59	0.08	0.00
Commerce	0.99	0.96	2.76	2.92	1.42	1.00	0.95	1.24	0.12	0.01
Medical sc.	2.65	2.22	2.78	3.10	0.23	0.22	0.53	0.83	0.03	0.00
Science	2.05	1.85	2.84	3.02	0.43	0.37	0.84	1.08	0.19	0.01
Agriculture	1.91	1.83	2.96	3.09	0.57	0.40	0.86	1.11	0.19	0.00
Engineering	1.47	1.41	2.54	2.86	0.56	0.63	0.83	1.23	0.70	0.04
Average	1.41	1.25	2.72	2.99	0.76	0.60	0.95	1.35	0.39	0.01

Source: Clancy 1990.

Also, although not shown in this table, almost all students would have studied mathematics. The main variability in the table reflects the different propensities to choose subjects from the science group, the business group, the technical group and from the heterogeneous 'other subjects' group which includes history, geography, home economics, art and music.

The overall gender differences in the take-up of Leaving Certificate subjects are shown in the final row of this table: males tend to choose more science, business and technical subjects while females tend to take more languages and more from the 'other subjects' group. However, the most interesting feature of this table is the clear pattern revealed in the relationship between subject specialisation at second level and third level field of study. Students who take more science subjects at second level are more likely to study medicine, science and agriculture while those with least science subjects are more likely to study art and design, hotel, catering and tourism, commerce, the humanities and social science. While there is less variability in the take-up of languages, it is clear that those with more languages tend to study law and the humanities while those with fewer languages are more likely to study art and design, technology and commerce. The pattern of choice with respect to the differential take-up of business subjects is more emphatic. Students who entered commerce and hotel, catering and tourism had most Leaving Certificate business subjects, while those who entered medicine had least. The take-up of technical subjects at second level is very low, especially for females, and is associated mainly with those who study technology at third level. The relatively high take-up rate by male education students is accounted for by those who enter Thomond College which educates teachers of technological subjects. Students who study art and design are also more likely to have taken technical subjects. Differential take-up of subjects from the 'other subjects' group is also linked to third level field of study. Those with more subjects from this group are more likely to study art and design, the humanities, hotel, catering and tourism, and social science.

Initially the Leaving Certificate served mainly as a terminal examination and as a selection mechanism for direct entry into employment. However, it currently appears to serve primarily as a selection mechanism for entry into higher education. Since less than 40 per cent of Leaving Certificate students go on to higher education it is felt by many educationalists that the requirements for higher education entry, more particularly the requirements for university entry, have an undue influence on the structure and content of the second level programme. This influence manifests itself both in the choice of subjects studied and in the content of the syllabus within particular subjects. For example, the matriculation requirements for the colleges of the National University of Ireland (NUI) require Irish, English and another language for all faculties and mathematics and a science subject for some faculties. Furthermore, the universities have representatives on the syllabus committees which specify curriculum content and on the standardisation committees which monitor the standards of achievement.

Formerly both the NUI and Trinity College Dublin (TCD) retained their own matriculation examination which could be used as an alternative to or in combination with the Leaving Certificate to select entrants. For a number of years TCD has ceased to offer a special matriculation examination and the NUI suspended its matriculation examination in 1992. Thus, the Leaving Certificate will become the sole vehicle for selecting entrants. The decision by the NUI to abolish the separate matriculation examinations was taken after great controversy. Some academics argued that the universities were surrendering their autonomy and should not have to rely on a state controlled examination system which might not always be influenced by academic criteria. The decision was accepted when the universities were given guarantees about their continuing representation on the appropriate syllabus and monitoring committees, thus ensuring their ongoing influence on the Leaving Certificate.

To secure a university place it is necessary to meet the basic matriculation requirement which varies somewhat for the different universities. For example, in addition to the specific subject requirements noted above, the NUI stipulates that students achieve a minimum of two grade Cs on higher level papers and four grade Ds on ordinary level papers. However, because the number of qualified applicants greatly exceeds the number of available places, entry is highly competitive and requires significantly higher levels of attainment. The universities operate a 'points system' to allocate places in the various faculties. The points system is operated by assigning different numbers of points to different levels of performance in the Leaving Certificate or matriculation examination. Most colleges take into account the sum of points accumulated from the best six subjects and students are then placed in order of merit, those with the highest scores securing the available places. In general, entry into the professional schools is most competitive, thus requiring the highest levels of academic attainment.

Changes in the points requirements to secure entry testify to the growing competition for places at university. Furthermore these changes provide an indicator of the changing popularity of particular programmes of study. This is illustrated in Table 10.3 which shows the median points score and the minimum points necessary to secure entry into eleven different programmes in 1976 and 1990 at University College Dublin, the largest university in the country.

Table 10.3 Level of attainment of entrants to University College Dublin by faculty in 1973 and 1989: median and minimum 'points score'

	1976		*1990*	
Faculty	*Median*	*Minimum*	*Median*	*Minimum*
Medicine	26	24	28	26
Veterinary medicine	24	22	28	27
Physiotherapy	21	20	26	25
Engineering	24	21	25	22
Architecture	23	21	24	22
Commerce	18	14	26	24
Law	19	18	26	25
Agricultural science	17	7	18	16
Science	19	17	21	18
Social science	17	14	19	17
Arts	14	6	19	16

The rise in the level of attainment of entrants is clearly evident from this table. For example, students with a score of six points (the minimum score for any student who meets the basic matriculation requirement) were able to secure a place in the arts faculty in 1976; this had risen to sixteen points by 1990. However, in spite of this general increase in entry standards arts and agriculture remain the faculties in which it is easiest to gain admittance. Over the period medicine and veterinary medicine remain the faculties with the highest level of attainment of entrants, although the 'pecking order' between the two has changed in favour of the latter. The biggest change in the relative ranking of programmes in terms of demand, and thus in terms of difficulty of entry, has been in the case of commerce and law; in the case of commerce, the minimum entry requirement rose by ten points while the median points score rose by eight points. The demand for physiotherapy also rose significantly over the period.

The change in the points requirement for the different faculties reflects change in the pattern of demand. The latter is determined by changes in the perceived desirability of the different occupations available to graduates. Variations in the labour market prospects for graduates are important in influencing student demand. Thus, for example, a buoyant demand for business studies graduates is responsible for the very large increase in the points requirement for entry to commerce programmes. Indeed the high demand for places in all professional courses is partly accounted for by a perception that they prepare graduates for direct labour market entry in contrast to other less vocationally relevant programmes such as arts, science and social science. However, employment prospects are not the only influences operating and status considerations especially those which emanate from the differential prestige of different occupations remain powerful determinants of student demand. The increased popularity of the arts degree in recent years also suggests that students and their parents are taking a broader view and acknowledging that there may be a less close relationship between the content of study programmes and employment prospects.

Programmes of study in higher education

The changes in the distribution of higher education by sector have already been documented (Clancy 1993). This sectoral division is complemented by a differentiation in administrative and coordinating mechanisms. The Higher Education Authority (HEA) exercises an executive role *vis-à-vis* the universities while the Regional Technical Colleges (RTCs), the other Technological Colleges and the Colleges of Education are directly administered by the Department of Education. This division of responsibility is reflected in published statistics which differentiate between the HEA sector and the non-HEA sector.

To delineate the structure of higher education studies it is proposed to examine the level of study, the field of study and the output of academic awards.

Level of study

To differentiate between level of study programmes it is appropriate to start with a threefold distinction between sub-degree level, degree level, and postgraduate level programmes. The duration of sub-degree level programmes ranges from one and two years for certificate courses to three years for diploma programmes. Degree courses vary in duration from three to six years, while postgraduate courses can vary from one year for diploma and some Master's programmes, to three or more years for doctoral programmes.

Table 10.4 shows the distribution of full-time students by level of study programme and by sector. Some three thousand students in a variety of small specialist, mainly non-aided, colleges are excluded from this table because of a lack of data. It is clear that the majority, almost two-thirds, of full-time students are enrolled on degree level courses. Twenty-eight per cent of students are enrolled on sub-degree level courses with a further eight per cent on postgraduate courses.

Most of the sub-degree level awards are conferred by the National Council for Educational Awards (NCEA). The two-year certificate is the most important sub-degree level programme, and for many students this is a terminal qualification. However, recent surveys of destinations of award-holders show an increasing tendency for certificates to proceed to further study. It is estimated that about 43 per cent of certificate holders undertake further study (Department of Education 1989). The NCEA award structure is designed to facilitate student progression such that certificates with a satisfactory level of performance can proceed to earn a diploma after a further years study while diploma holders can proceed to take a degree. Both the NCEA and the Department of Education favour this cumulative award structure, however, at present the majority of diploma students are enrolled on *ab initio* three-year diploma programmes. The number of students transferring from diploma to degree programmes remains small; this involves a further two years of study. This route takes a period of five years to complete a degree involving at least one additional year by comparison with *ab initio* degree students in the same discipline.

It is evident from Table 10.4 that almost all the short cycle, sub-degree level programmes are to be found in the technological sector. However, while this reflects explicit government policy, there is some evidence of 'academic drift' in this sector with more colleges offering diploma level programmes and seeking to offer degree level

Table 10.4 Distribution of students by level of study in higher education programmes 1988–89

Level of study	*HEA sector*	*Technological sector*	*Colleges of Education*	*Total*	*%*
All sub-degree	534	16,187		6721	7.7
One-year certificate	95	846		941	1.6
Two-year certificate		11,508		11,508	19.1
Add on diploma		1398		1398	2.3
Three-year diploma	439[a]	2435		2874	4.8
Degree	31,132	6010[b]	1659	38,801	60.5
All postgraduate	4607	155		4762	7.9
Diploma	1464	55[c]		1519	2.5
Degree	3143	100[c]		3243	5.4
Total	36,273	22,352	1659	60,284	100

(a) different durations in this sector
(b) 2328 students on professional programmes of varying durations have been included in this category
(c) estimate

programmes. This latter pressure is being resisted with a recent report reasserting government policy that provision for degree courses should be made in the RTCs only in exceptional circumstances (Department of Education 1989).

In contrast to the short cycle emphasis in the technological sector the work of the universities is concentrated on offering degree level courses. The duration of these courses varies mainly by discipline. For example all degree courses in medicine take six years while all those in engineering take four years. Honours degrees in science take four years while general degrees take only three years. In contrast with this uniformity within disciplines, there is variability between colleges in the duration of degree courses in arts, commerce, business and social studies; in some colleges these degrees take three years while in others they take four. The colleges of education now offer only degree level courses. Most courses for primary teachers are of three years duration while those offered in the colleges of education, where some secondary teachers are trained, take four years.

Field of study

To examine changes in the distribution of higher education students by field of study it is necessary to examine each sector separately since published statistics use different classification categories. Table 10.5 shows the distribution of full-time students by field of study in the HEA sector for 1987/88, the latest date for which statistics have been published. To monitor change over the past decade this distribution is compared with that which prevailed a decade earlier and the percentage change is calculated. While the largest percentage (40%) of students was still enrolled in the humanities and closely related fields in 1987–88, a clear pattern of change is evident. Over the decade large percentage increases were registered in engineering (77%), commerce (72%) and science (68%), as compared with an overall sector increase of 40 per cent.

Changes in the distribution of students by field of study are also evident in the much faster growing technological sector. Available statistics only allow for a fourfold division by field of study. The distribution of full-time students between these fields in 1988–89 is shown in Table 10.6 together with the pattern of change over the previous decade. Business studies show the most dramatic growth rate recording an increase of 328 per cent in the decade, as compared with an increase of 193 per cent for the entire sector. Currently more than a third of students in this sector are enrolled in business studies, reflecting the large growth in the service sector which characterises all modern societies. However, engineering remains the field of study with the largest enrolment (38.5%) in this sector and recorded an enrolment growth rate of 174 per cent. Enrolment in science increased by 138 per cent, while there was a increase of 114 per cent in the heterogeneous 'other' category which includes art and design, hotel and catering and the humanities.

Table 10.5 Distribution of full-time students by field of study in HEA sector in 1977–78 and 1987–88 and percentage change in decade

Field of study	*1977–78*		*1987–88*		*%*
		%		*%*	*Change*
Humanities	10455	42.1	14034	40.3	+34.2
Commerce	2821	11.4	4852	13.9	+72.0
Law	1027	4.1	858	2.5	+16.5
Science	3349	13.5	5612	16.1	+67.6
Engineering	2618	10.5	4641	13.3	+77.3
Medicine	3643	14.7	3735	10.7	+2.5
Agriculture	940	3.8	1128	3.2	+20.0
Total	24853	100	34860	100	+40.3

Table 10.6 Distribution of full-time students in technological sector by field of study in 1978–79 and 1988–89 and percentage change in decade

Field of study	*1978–79*		*1988–1989*		*%*
		%		*%*	*Change*
Business studies	1708	22.4	7476	33.5	327.7
Science	1274	16.7	3032	13.6	138.0
Engineering	3142	41.1	8599	38.5	173.7
Other	1515	19.8	3242	14.5	114.0
Total	7639	100	22349	100	192.6

In contrast to the spectacular growth in the technological sector and the more modest growth in the HEA sector, there has been a reduction of 15 per cent in enrolment in the colleges of education. This reduction results from an oversupply of teachers and from a sharp decline in the birth rate during the 1980s.

Output of awards

Having examined separately the structure of higher education by level of study programme and by field of study it is now possible to combine these two indicators by focusing on the output of awards from the higher education system. Because of the absence of data this analysis must be confined to the HEA sector and to NCEA awards outside the HEA sector.

Table 10.7 shows the output of primary degrees, postgraduate degrees and postgraduate diplomas in 1987 by field of study in HEA designated colleges. The table also shows the percentage change over the previous decade to enable us to monitor changing trends. Sub-degree awards from this sector are not shown; these totalled only 539 in 1977 and 588 in 1987. The largest percentage of primary degrees awarded were in the humanities, followed by commerce, engineering and science. However, the trend over the decade shows differential growth rates. There was an almost three-fold increase in the output of engineering degrees while the number of primary degrees in commerce and science doubled. These changes over the decade compare with an overall growth of 43 per cent for the sector. There was little change in the output of primary degrees in the humanities while there was a slight reduction in the number of degrees in law and agriculture.

The increase in output of postgraduate degrees over the decade was more impressive. The overall growth rate was 125 per cent, with larger increases in law (from a low base) and commerce. The number of postgraduate degrees awarded in 1987 was highest in the humanities followed by commerce, science and engineering. There was little change in the overall output of postgraduate diplomas although there was considerable variability by field of study. The reduction in the number of diplomas in the humanities is accounted for by a decline in the number of graduates seeking a qualification in education. This reduction is offset by a development of new programmes mainly in commerce but also in science and law and by an expansion of provision in engineering and medicine.

There are no comprehensive data available on the output of academic awards outside the HEA sector. The main validation body, the NCEA, publishes annual statistics and while all the colleges in the technological sector are designated under the NCEA, not all courses in these colleges lead to NCEA awards. The main exclusion from this sector involves some 1077 sub-degree award recipients from the

Table 10.7 Academic awards, by field of study, obtained by students in HEA-sector colleges in 1987 and percentage change in number of awards over the previous decade

	Primary degrees		*Postgraduate degrees*		*Postgraduate diplomas*	
Field of study	*1987*	% *change 1977–87*	*1987*	% *change 1977–87*	*1987*	% *change 1977–87*
Humanities	2748	+5.1	357	+79.4	1299	-23.9
Commerce	1398	+100.9	249	+176.7	200	+*
Law	225	-5.5	76	+230.4	20	+*
Science	1120	+98.9	228	+123.5	59	+*
Engineering	1160	+187.8	150	+123.9	175	+71.6
Medicine	595	+19.0	90	+*	176	+36.4
Agriculture	200	-3.1	43	+16.2	0	??
Total	7446	+43.0	1193	+124.7	1929	-0.6

* percentages not calculated where base was < 20

Dublin Institute of Technology (DIT) which independently certifies some programmes. In addition the DIT, and to a lesser extent some of the RTCs, offer programmes of study where professional bodies provide the appropriate certification.

Notwithstanding these limitations Table 10.8 reveals the overall trends in the output of academic awards in the technological sector. It shows the number of awards conferred by the NCEA in 1988 and the percentage change over the previous decade. To prevent duplication, this table excludes awards gained in the former National Institutes for Higher Education (now University of Limerick and Dublin City University) and Thomond College, since both of these colleges belong to the HEA sector and thus are included in Table 10.7. Degree recipients from the Dublin Institute of Technology, which are certified by Trinity College Dublin are also included in Table 10.7.

Table 10.8 Awards conferred by the National Council for Educational Awards in 1988 and percentage change over previous decade**

	Humanities	*Business*	*Engineering*	*Science*	*Total*
Cert. one-year 1998	356	26	–	48	430
% change	+140	-70		+26	+44
Cert. two-year 1988	201	928	1080	711	2920
% change	+593	+222	+116	+128	+159
Diploma 1988	285	433	529	283	1530
% change	+448	+221	+192	+79	+191
Degree 1988	92	43	35	73	243
% change	+*	+*	+*	+*	+*
Grad. diploma 1988	–	–	–	6	6
% change	–	–	–	+*	+*
Total 1988	934	1430	1644	1121	5129
% change	+308	+165	+141	+121	+162

** awards conferred in the NIHEs and Thomond College which are part of the HEA sector are excluded from this table
* percentages not calculated where base was < 20

Almost three thousand two-year certificates and a little over half that number of diplomas were awarded in 1988. The total number of awards, 5129, represents an increase of 162 per cent over the previous decade. The growth in the number of diplomas awarded was greater than in the case of certificates. In both instances, although starting from a low base in 1977, the humanities was the field of study with the fastest growth rate. However, engineering still continues to be the field of study with the largest number of award recipients. There was only a modest increase in the number of one year certificates awarded over the period and while there were no NCEA degrees awarded in 1977 by these colleges, a total of 243 were awarded in 1988.

Developments in selected disciplines

The following section seeks to examine trends in higher education as reflected by developments in particular disciplines. This examination must necessarily be limited since this topic has not attracted any research or systematic analysis in Ireland. The difficulty arises because of an absence of basic data at the appropriate level of disaggregation. While we have relatively good data on the distribution of students by faculty or school there are no national data available on enrolment in individual subjects. For the purpose of this chapter I have chosen to confine my analysis to the situation in my own college, University College Dublin (UCD). It is felt that, at least for the university sector, this may not be a major limitation, since this is the university with the largest enrolment and the most comprehensive range of faculties.

The enrolment pattern in four subjects, history, economics, physics and engineering is shown in Table 10.9. With the exception of engineering, these subjects are taught in separate departments located within larger faculties. Students are recruited into the faculties and, within limits, are free to choose the subjects they wish to study. In contrast, engineering constitutes a separate faculty within the university. Students seek admission to the faculty with a view to gaining a professional qualification. The first year offers a broadly based programme following which students are admitted to more specialised programmes in each of the engineering specialisations. This pattern of offering a generic first year, after which specialisation commences, is not followed in all Irish universities. Most of the other university departments of engineering recruit students directly from school into each professional specialisation.

Table 10.9 Enrolment of students, by programme level, in history, economics, physics and engineering at University College Dublin in 1980 and 1990

	History		*Economics*		*Physics*		*Engineering*	
	1980	*1990*	*1980*	*1990*	*1980*	*1990*	*1980*	*1990*
First year students								
Faculty total	893	1356	893	1356	265	385	197	275
Subject total	292	332	231	397	240	181		
% of faculty taking subject	32.7	25.5	25.9	29.3	90.6	47.0		
Primary degree level								
Faculty total	565	815	565	815	228	318	174	235
Subject total	172	144	136	306	20	27		
% of faculty taking subject	30.4	17.7	24.1	37.5	8.8	8.5		
Master's degree level								
Faculty total	226	405	226	405	89	97	24	60
Subject total	27	58	19		84	10	16	
% of faculty taking subject	11.9	14.3	8.4	20.7	11.2	16.5		
Doctoral degree level								
Faculty total	41	70	41	70	75	186	10	29
Subject total	3	5	0	1	3	15		
% of faculty taking subject	7.3	7.1	0	1.4	4.0	8.1		

Both history and economics are located within the arts faculty. Economics is also taught within the faculty of commerce as one subject within a more broadly based commerce degree. However, the latter students are not shown in Table 10.9. In 1980, a total of 2198 first-year students were admitted to UCD; this had risen to 3099 by 1990. Enrolments of first-year students in the faculty of arts in the respective years was 893 and 1356. First-year students in the faculty of arts study three subjects selected from a list of 27 subjects on offer. It is evident from Table 10.9 that both history and economics attract large numbers of first-year students, each subject being studied by more than a quarter of the faculty total. However, the trends in enrolments in the two subjects are somewhat different. Between 1980 and 1990 the percentage of first-year students taking history declined from almost a third to just over a quarter, while the percentage taking economics rose over the period to reach 29 per cent in 1990.

Having successfully passed the first-year examination the majority of students proceed to take the BA degree after two further years of study. Most BA students take a two subject degree, either at honours or general level. Some single-subject honours degree programmes are also offered. The differentiation between honours and general programmes is made on the basis of level of performance in the first-year examinations while the choice between one (where available) and two subject honours degree programmes reflects students' preferences.

The differential trends in the take-up of history and economics noted in the case of first-year enrolments is more obvious when we examine the pattern at degree level. The percentage of BA students reading history declined from 30 per cent in 1980 to 18 per cent in 1990, while the percentage reading economics rose from 24 per cent to 37.5 per cent. A trend common to both subjects is the increasing percentage of BA students following honours programmes, rising from about one-third to about three-quarters. However, there are significant differences between the two subjects in the proportion of honours students taking a single-subject degree. The percentage of history students taking a single-subject degree was about 10 per cent while 54 per cent of honours economics students were reading for a single-subject degree.

It is likely that these differences in the propensity to specialise at undergraduate level reflect students' perceptions of labour market demand. It is probable that arts undergraduates perceive economics as a vocationally oriented subject and thus represents a 'safe specialisation'. It should be noted that this client perception is not shared by teaching faculty and is not reflected in course content. In contrast to the position of economics, it is likely that far fewer arts students see the study of history as vocationally oriented. There are few career opportunities for professional historians and few teaching positions at second level which represented the traditional outlet for many BA graduates in history. In this context it may be understandable that many undergraduates eschew specialisation and seek to keep their options open by taking a more broadly based two-subject degree.

Before examining the position of these subjects at postgraduate level it is appropriate to consider briefly the position of economics within the faculty of commerce. The Bachelor of Commerce degree is a broadly based three-year degree which allows for some specialisation from a selection of business studies disciplines, especially in the final year. Economics is one of the required subjects studied during the first two years of the programme and constitutes about a quarter of the student workload. The optional programmes in the BComm degree are grouped into five major areas of specialisations: management, accounting, banking and finance, international, and economics. In this context it is interesting that the choice of economics is very much a minority option attracting only six students annually from a total of about three hundred admitted to the degree programme. Thus, it appears that in contrast to the situation in the arts faculty where the choice of economics may be seen as vocationally relevant, the situation in the more applied and professionally oriented commerce faculty is such that a specialisation in economics is not viewed as a vocationally relevant programme.

The pattern of subject take-up at Master's degree level also reveals some differences. During the past decade the overall number of MA students in the faculty rose by about 80 per cent. While, in the context of this overall expansion, the history department has enhanced its position, increasing its proportion of the faculty total from 12 per cent to 14 per cent, it is clear that economics has contributed disproportionately to the increase in postgraduate numbers, increasing its proportion of the faculty total to 21 per cent.

One of the developments which has occurred concurrently with this increase in the number of MA students has been the increased popularity of the 'taught master's' programme. Traditionally, most degrees at Master's level were by independent research and while this mode is still available it has been superseded by the development of programmes, which consist mainly of course work frequently complemented by minor dissertations. Currently about three-quarters of MA students in history are on taught Master's programmes while all MA students in economics are following such a programme.

Although there has been a significant increase in the number of PhD students over the past decade neither of the disciplines examined here have contributed significantly to this development. The absence of doctoral students, especially in economics, may reflect the strong demand for high calibre graduates in the financial services sector. However, a related factor operative in many disciplines is the long established tradition of students travelling abroad to pursue doctoral studies. North American universities, and Oxford and Cambridge in the UK remain attractive destinations for many of our most able graduates.

The subject physics (designated experimental physics at UCD) is located in the science faculty. While the number of first-year students increased by 45 per cent in the past decade there has been a decline in the number of students taking physics at this level. Less than half of first-year students took physics in 1990 compared to 91 per cent a decade earlier. The changing uptake reflects the changing structure of academic programmes and the greater choice afforded to students. One of the changes over the period was the introduction of computer science, bringing to seven the number of subjects from which students could select their four subjects for the first-year programme. More significant, perhaps, were the changes in the manner in which the choice patterns were structured. In 1980 five programme combinations were offered and experimental physics featured in four of these combinations. By 1990 a total of thirteen programme combinations were available from which students were free to choose; physics featured in seven of these programmes.

The BSc degree programme allows for progressive specialisation; in the second year students take three subjects and this is further reduced to two in the third year and, for honours students, to one in the fourth year. General students graduate after three years; previously they studied three subjects in their final year instead of the present two subjects. The take-up of physics at degree level has changed little over the period, with the percentage enrolment (9%) keeping pace with the growth in the faculty total. The study of physics at undergraduate level is not, of course, confined to those taking a science degree. Students of engineering and medical students are required to take varying amounts of physics as part of their degree programmes.

Postgraduate enrolment in physics has increased at a faster rate than that of the faculty as a whole. Currently, 16.5 per cent of Master's degree students and 8 per cent of PhD students in the faculty are enrolled in experimental physics.

The past decade has shown a sharp rise in participation in engineering studies. First-year student numbers increased by 40 per cent and degree level enrolments by 35 per cent. Postgraduate numbers increased at a faster rate with a 150 per cent increase at the Master's level and an increase of 190 per cent at the PhD level. After the first year of engineering study students are admitted into one of five different programmes: mechanical, civil, chemical, agricultural and food, and electrical and electronic. The latter programme is further differentiated into separate programmes in electronics and electrical in the final year of study. The distribution of students between the different engineering specialisations is determined by the number of places available on each programme and, thus, is supply led. On the demand side electronics is the programme which is most sought after. Furthermore, a higher proportion of its graduates go on to do postgraduate work both at master and doctoral level.

General direction of change

The analysis of developments within the four disciplines reported in the previous section reveals a trend which is consistent with that which was evident from the general review of programme developments. The increase in the study of economics stands in contrast to the decline in the popularity of history as an undergraduate subject. Similarly, the number of students choosing physics as an undergraduate subject has declined, while the study of engineering has increased significantly. In all four disciplines the participation in postgraduate programmes has increased, reflecting the general trend. The growth of a large number of sub-degree programmes in the non-university sector has been compensated for by a large expansion in postgraduate study inside the universities.

Further evidence for these general trends is provided by an analysis of all new course developments in HEA designated colleges over a period of fifteen years. A total of 226 new courses are listed by the HEA (1985) in its *General Report 1974–1984* and in its subsequent annual reports for the period 1974–88. Of these more than half (54%) were at postgraduate level – 58 new postgraduate diplomas and 63 new Master's degree programmes. While almost half of the new undergraduate courses were established in the developing National Institutes for

Higher Education (NIHEs), most of the new initiatives at postgraduate level were established in the longer established universities.

An important aspect of the expansion of postgraduate studies is that it, also, is driven by vocational considerations. Although not evident from the data we have reviewed in respect of the four disciplines, many of the new postgraduate programmes which have been developed, especially at diploma level, are of an applied nature with the objective of preparing graduates for labour market entry. Examples of such programmes include business studies, accounting, journalism, counselling, computer studies and aquaculture. Another feature of the expanded postgraduate sector is the increase in interdisciplinary programmes which include such diverse fields as applied science, women's studies, and regional and urban planning. Disciplinary boundaries are no longer sacrosanct and relevance and the application of knowledge have come to claim a new legitimacy in the academy.

CHAPTER 11

Innovation in Dutch Higher Education

Barriers and Challenges

Peter A.M. Maassen and Egbert de Weert

Introduction

According to Teichler (1989), it can be argued that in a number of respects the Netherlands is the most interesting case in Western Europe for analysing the changing relationships between government and higher education in the 1980s. Not only was the governmental claim for change in the Netherlands larger than in any other Western European country, the intended change also had a clear purpose, i.e. it was expected to bring about (more) innovation in teaching and research and it should lead to an increasing differentiation in higher education. Innovation and differentiation were supposed to be the result of changes taking places within the institutions of higher education. Before the intended changes in the relationship between government and higher education were announced in 1985 a number of structural reforms had been designed and to a large extent implemented. These can be regarded as innovations at the system level. These reforms concerned, among other things, a restructuring of the university educational structure, the introduction of a new, conditional funding system for research, and the upgrading of the higher vocational education sector from secondary education to (non-university) higher education (Maassen and van Vught 1989).

In this paper we will focus on the relationship between higher education and the labour market. We will do so by discussing some intrinsic characteristics of the humanities and the social sciences. We have not focused on the disciplines physics and engineering. On the first, little recent information is available, and the second includes too many separate programmes to allow us to describe and discuss engineering as one discipline. We have described some general characteristics of the disciplines history and economics.

Dutch higher education: input features

Methods of enrolment selection and entrance characteristics

One of the main objectives of higher education policy in the Netherlands is to provide 'higher education for the masses'. As a direct result of this, everyone who meets the formal requirements has the right to enrol in any higher education institution. Contrary to, for example, the United Kingdom, there is no entrance selection and, except for the *numerus clausus,* no limitations on the available student places.

A student can enrol for a university course if he/she:

- holds a pre-university secondary education (VWO) diploma: dependent on the specific course chosen, an institution can require certain subjects to be included in the secondary school matriculation
  - for theology and classical studies: Latin and Greek
  - for medicine, pharmacy and biology: physics and chemistry
  - for other natural sciences, mathematics and engineering: mathematics and physics
  - for economics and social sciences: mathematics
- passed the HBO propaedeutic examination: the same requirements as outlined above are applicable in this case
- holds a HBO or Open University diploma
- has successfully taken a Colloquium Doctum examination: anyone of the age of 21 or over without any of the above qualifications can take an entrance examination.

Anyone who meets one of these conditions has the right to enrol in a university. This right can be limited by the existence of a *numerus clausus,* although this is an exception in the Netherlands. The *numerus clausus* is only enacted after a lengthy procedure and has to be based on either the labour market situation or the teaching capacity of an institution. In the case of a *numerus clausus,* students are selected through a lottery, whereby the draw is weighted in favour of those with the highest secondary education examination qualifications. In the year 1990–1991 the *numerus clausus* was applied to ten courses, among others for business administration, medicine, veterinary science, industrial design and dentistry.

In the non-university sector, the situation is slightly different. Until 1986, when the Higher Vocational Education Act came into force, institutions could select students through additional entrance examinations or intake interviews. Within the new legal framework this formally is no longer possible. In practice, however, these selection procedures can still be operative. Also, the *numerus clausus* can apply to the HBO sector, but only on the basis of labour market considerations.

Regarding higher education participation, for the year 1987–88 the proportion of the 20–24 age group is approximately as follows: university, males 15 per cent, females 9 per cent; HBO, males 12 per cent, females 10 per cent.

Dutch higher education: process features

Length of study programmes

By law, all university first degree courses are limited to a nominal duration of four years. Students are allowed to stay in the university for six years to complete their course. After this, they can still continue their study, albeit at substantially higher costs. The initial four-year period is called the first tier and is followed by a second tier. With respect to the second tier, one can distinguish between the regular PhD programmes, with a duration of four years, and medical training, teacher training courses and design courses with a length of two years.

In the non-university sector, the maximum length of first tier courses is four years. In practice, almost all courses last four years. Second tier courses can be followed in teacher training, healthcare, architecture, music and nautical studies. As in the university sector, students are allowed to stay on for six years in the first tier.

For both sectors a year programme is considered to be the equivalent of 1700 study hours.

Transfer between HBO and university type education is possible in the Dutch system. The vast majority of transfers that occur are from HBO to university courses. In this respect, one has to differentiate between two modes. On the one hand, HBO students can transfer to a university after having obtained their propaedeutic exam. On average,

3 per cent of first-year university students use this route. On the other hand, HBO students can also transfer to a university after graduation. In this case they have the option to either follow one of the specially designed shorter university programmes in a similar field of study, or follow the normal curriculum for which they can obtain a number of exemptions. The number of students using this route has increased over the last couple of years and is at present over 15 per cent of the total university entrance. As an HBO qualification is considered to be a final qualification, this development is regarded as undesirable by the Dutch government. It is perceived to be an 'inefficient' education route.

Organisation of first tier courses: a general description

The university academic year starts in September and ends in late June. The year is divided in either two or three terms, depending on the institution. All regular first degree courses are divided in two stages, i.e. a propaedeutic and a doctoral stage. The propaedeutic stage lasts one year and contains compulsory subjects for all students. It has a two-fold purpose. First, the purpose of orientation: it should offer students the opportunity to get acquainted with the course. Second, the purpose of selection: it should select the students that are suited for the course.

The second stage, lasting three years, is generally divided into distinct parts. First of all there is a compulsory part, in line with the propaedeutic course elements, broadening and deepening the student's knowledge. This is followed by a 'compulsory elective' part, in which the students can select areas to enrich their knowledge further. These two parts can be considered the basic doctoral programme since they are supposed to provide a minimum knowledge base.

After the basic programme, the differentiation and specialisation part follows, in which the following three major types can be discerned:

1. the course without graduation specialisation or variants: freedom of choice is limited to the compulsory and free elective elements
2. the course with a limited number of graduation specialisations: after finishing their basic doctoral programme, the students can choose a certain specialisation, containing compulsory and free elements

3. the course with a wide range of non-specified graduation specialisations: after finishing the basic doctoral programme, students can choose from subjects offered by the faculty and/or can follow 'free' subjects.

Qualification structure

HBO: Graduates of technical and agricultural courses are awarded the title *Ingenieur*, abbreviated *Ing.* All other graduates from four-year HBO study programmes are entitled to the use of the *Baccalaureus* title, abbreviated *Bc.* All graduates can by law also use the English Bachelor title abbreviated B, instead of *Ingenieur* or *Baccalaureus.*

Universities: All first tier graduates are awarded a Dutch academic degree comparable with a *Masters degree. For those graduating in the engineering and agricultural sciences, this is the Ingenieur* title, abbreviated *Ir.* Graduates from law studies are awarded the *Meester in de rechten* title, abbreviated *Mr.*, while all other graduates are awarded the *Doctorandus* title, abbreviated *Drs.*

Nearly all second tier graduates are awarded the *Doctor* degree, abbreviated *Dr.* Students enter the second tier on the basis of competitive selection (faculty criteria), and are employed by the institution. Standard requirement is a university first tier degree (standard situation) or HBO degree (rare exception).

Quality control mechanisms

Until the 1980s quality assessment of teaching was an internal activity. Systematic procedures built into the standard operational procedures of the institutions were scarce; long-term programmes or follow-up were hardly known either. Some external quality control can be discerned in the procedure that existed for *ex ante* approval of curricula in the *Academic Statute*. And there is a procedure for approval by 'sister' faculties for the appointment of professors.

A central role in the quality control process has, since 1988, been taken up by the VSNU (Association of Cooperating Dutch Universities). In the evaluation process designed by the VSNU internal and external evaluation are both used to organise a periodical, ongoing movement towards better quality of education in universities. The VSNU evaluation process has started with a pilot process in 1988 in four disciplines. The process consists of a self-evaluation by each faculty and a visiting committee for all faculties of a certain discipline. The visiting committees were provided by the institutions with the self-study and other data and plans of the institution. Since the STC operation the HBO council has launched two plans for quality assessment in the HBO sector. The first plan was based on institution-wide quality assessment, but somehow that never really got going. In 1989 a new plan was published: the HBO council developed a sectoral procedure remarkably like the VSNU procedure. It is meant to stimulate internal quality care policies; it is based on self-evaluations followed by visiting committees.

Innovation of university programmes

Traditionally for every field of university study in the Netherlands an *Academic Statute* had to be approved by the government. This set, in a relatively broad way, a mandatory frame for corresponding course programmes at each university. If a university wanted to start a new programme the Ministry of Education and Science could approve an experimental phase of five to ten years. After that period the Minister could decide, on the basis of an evaluation, whether a permanent Statute would be enacted.

As a first major change during the 1980s, the Ministry of Education and Science discontinued the traditional practice of universities negotiating with the ministry the provision of corresponding resources when they intended to start a new programme. At most, the ministry was willing to provide limited resources for a short implementation phase. In general the institutions now have to slice the necessary resources out of their lump sum in the expectation that by attracting new students the institution will receive additional resources as part of the general budget allocation in the near future. Second, in 1985 the ministry announced plans to abolish any direct state supervision of programme approval. Instead, teaching should be assessed regularly through a generalised nationwide evaluation scheme, whereby the results of evaluation should inform governmental decisions on budget allocation. These plans are still not yet operational. The current minister has recently suggested that the government should have a role in programme approval. Despite this unclearness, it can be stated that the institutions have at the moment in the transition period from central government regulation to a form of self-regulation (Maassen and van Vught 1989) a large freedom in the development of new programmes.

This freedom poses an important challenge to the institutions. They are expected to react quicker and better to developments in their environment, i.e. especially developments on the labour market. These reactions should result in more relevant curricula.

Tradition and reform of university curricula

During the 1980s the content and organisation of studies in higher education have been the subject of a continuous debate in the Netherlands. The core question is whether the prevailing model based on disciplinary views and standards is adequate in meeting the demands of society and the demands of an increasing heterogeneous student population and whether alternative models of organising knowledge should be further considered.

Broadly speaking, in the traditional model students enrol in a specific discipline and are supposed to follow the programme as required. In fact, the basic requirements of the respective disciplines are stated traditionally by law in the *Academic Statute* which contains degree qualifications for each discipline as well as detailed procedures to approve new programmes. This identification of a specific discipline has the following implications.

First, although there are individual degrees of freedom in choosing certain subjects, students are basically educated in one discipline and the orientation towards an academic research culture is rather strong. The disciplinary views and research methods are the regulating principle on which curricula are organised. Such a model, which is consistent with the internalised theory of knowledge, emphasises the separateness of the disciplines, their internal logic and concerns. Students become part of the academic profession if they develop their professional career towards the researcher/teacher role models.

Second, the traditional model displays a structure in which courses are linked together and curricular changes are mostly discipline-led. As a consequence the student population becomes compartmentalised. For students there is little flexibility to correct earlier course decisions other than to start another field of study from the very beginning. As far as the employment prospects are concerned, the model aims at a relatively small category of students with a strong scientific orientation and eligible for a long and definite study. Not surprisingly, many critics saw this model as an important causal factor of the rather high delay and drop-out rate in higher education.

This traditional model came under severe attack from forces both internal and external to the higher education system. As far as the internal aspects are concerned, the model does not acknowledge theoretical developments which break through traditional boundaries of thought. The increasing proliferation and fragmentation of academic disciplines into smaller distinctive units is a matter of concern to those who believe that such autonomous units hinder the pursuit of promising interdisciplinary perspectives.

The external aspect refers to a need for higher education to become a better preparation for occupational fields outside the teaching and research sectors. Meanwhile, a discussion about the functioning of the *Academic Statute* has resulted in proposals to abolish it, arguing that institutions need more autonomy to adapt curricula to changing external needs and to realise a variety of teaching programmes.

As a result, teaching programmes have changed considerably in content and organisation. Universities have taken numerous initiatives, leading to a broad spectrum of courses, for example, area studies in the humanities, and problem-oriented studies in the social sciences. Several attempts have been made to grasp these developments in curricular concepts. Squires (1990), for example, distinguishes three types of programmes: academic, professional and general. And Teichler (1987), analysing developments in the Federal Republic of Germany, denotes three types of curricular reforms: the breadth of courses, an orientation towards practice and new specialised programmes as an adequate preparation for new occupations.

Taking these kinds of notions as a departure, we will conceptualise curricular developments in the Netherlands in two sets of distinctions. First, the distinction between the traditional disciplinary model and what has come to be known as the convergent model; and second, the theory-practice dichotomy. These two distinctions are not unrelated and we will superimpose them on each other.

The convergent model is the opposite of the traditional model in that it breaks through disciplinary boundaries. Proponents of this model pursue a broadening of programmes, more flexibility and more differentiation in terms of level of teaching, teaching goals, theoretical or practical focus, and duration of studies. Moreover, the relationship between research and education should be decoupled in the sense that not all students are supposed to acquire research skills. Furthermore, a modular course structure is supposed to be the most appropriate organising principle.

In general, the convergent model is less prescriptive than the traditional model and more 'client centred' by encouraging students to select and articulate their interests. This convergent model resembles in many respects the Y-model as developed in the German *Gesamthochschule*.

It has been no accident that the convergent model has gained much acceptance in the humanities and the social sciences (H/SS).[1] It is probably more accurate to say that the development of a convergent model fits in discussions which were held at several faculties and which aimed at cutting through the traditional segregation in disciplines.

Although factors such as the implementation of the two-tier structure, retrenchment policies and funding mechanisms (Maassen and van Vught 1989) may have influenced this process of change, the development itself emerged predominantly from changes with regard to the content of these disciplines and their changing relationship with society. The following explanations can be denoted here:

1. The number of students enrolling in H/SS has increased considerably. Together they constitute one-third of the total student population. Whereas studies in, for example, the natural sciences were more selective in admittance requirements as a crude guarantee of quality and other studies, such as the medical sciences, had a *numerus fixus*, it can reasonably be stated that H/SS were obliged to accept anyone who wanted to enrol and who met the minimal entrance requirements. As a consequence, the student population of H/SS became more heterogeneous in motivation, interests and quality of students. A convergent model may be better equipped to deal with this heterogeneity.

1 The humanities and the social sciences correspond largely to two sectors that are distinguished in most statistical data published on Dutch higher education, i.e. the sector 'language and culture' and the sector 'behaviour and society'. Language and culture encompasses a broad spectrum of disciplines and fields of study: several languages and their respective literary traditions (Western and non-Western), philosophy, history, theology, history of art and archaeology. Behaviour and society includes disciplines such as psychology, anthropology, sociology, geography, educational sciences, public administration. Economics and business studies, classified according to the International Standard Classific- ation of Education (ISCED) in the social sciences, are in Dutch statistics categ- orised as a separate 'economics' sector.

2. The job market for H/SS graduates in particular has become more uncertain and diffuse. Graduates increasingly enter a potentially open employment market with broad occupational fields. The opportunities for teaching jobs have decreased especially whereas, for example, a language study still may reflect the language as taught in secondary education.

   In other words, the concept and content of studies are constrained by professional requirements deriving from clearly defined ends and means related to teacher training. It can be added that this is a mutually reinforcing process as university teachers are involved in developing these requirements.

3. A trend towards convergence cannot be understood without taking into account the internal structure and developments of disciplines. In the field of languages, for example, the focus of interest shifted gradually from differences between languages to features they have in common. As a consequence, research occupied itself more and more with structural phenomena underlying all languages which in its turn paved the way to convergent tendencies in theory development. This development is pronounced particularly in structural linguistics, literary theory and philology, although in other fields these convergent tendencies can be delineated as well. The essential point is that these developments make the traditional boundaries between autonomous basic units around a particular language obsolete in many ways while these boundaries may impede other, more promising combinations of studies. Most research extends into the whole field of linguistics which subsequently leads towards new diversifications regarding fundamental questions. Likewise, historical research of various phenomena belonging to the same period resulted in a need to cross disciplinary boundaries and to incorporate viewpoints drawn from the social sciences and economics.

A convergent model does not necessarily imply that compared with a traditional, disciplinary model a closer link is achieved between education and employment. Disciplines can possess many pragmatic and

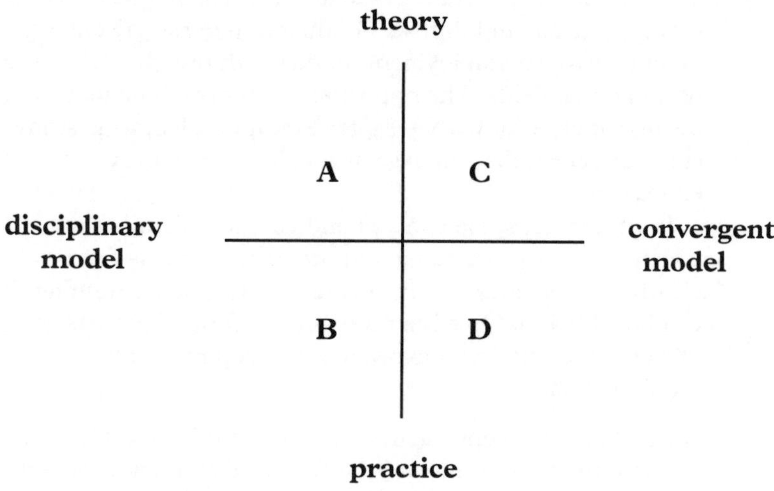

Figure 11.1 Classification of teaching programmes

utilitarian values, whereas students in a convergent model may after a broad basic training specialise in a field which has no immediate practical value. Therefore, a second distinction will be used here, namely between theory and practice. If these two kinds of distinctions are superimposed on each other, the picture shown in Figure 11.1 appears. This schema generates four types of programmes. Although in reality the boundaries are much less clearly demarcated, these types are represented here in an ideal form.

Cell A of the scheme contains programmes based upon clear disciplinary approaches. Adherents of this type of programme argue that the best way of ensuring employment perspectives is to provide students with a solid scientific background. Examples are several specialisms in psychology, history, sociology and non-Western languages. A concern for quality functions as an argument for justifying the traditional scholarly approach. A study of a non-Western language, for example, needs four years of intensive study and adding more 'marketable' elements to the curriculum may – as is argued – violate its central purposes.

In Cell B disciplines can be classified which are practical or problem-oriented. Curriculum content is in most cases strongly influenced by occupational practice. Examples are language studies as a preparation for the teaching profession or for a translating job, and interdisciplinary programmes such as public administration.

The current trend is to merely add courses with 'marketable' options; for example, 'language and management' belong to this category as long as the language is the dominant disciplinary focus.

Programmes on the right-hand side of the scheme are less clearly defined. In a convergent model the theory–practice dimension depends on the kind of options students choose and the intended purposes of individual programmes. Cell C contains programmes which offer a broad range of knowledge and experience, so that students' employment chances are enhanced for a wider variety of employment. Liberal arts belong to this section, but in its strict sense does not occur in the Netherlands. Quite recently, new programmes are in the process of development in which a theoretical and intellectual focus is stressed (e.g. cultural studies in Rotterdam and Maastricht).

More pronounced in Cell D is the current trend to select courses from various disciplines and combine these into a new setting with an explicitly vocational perspective.

The usefulness of a particular course is considered in the context of the overall purpose of a new programme. The proliferation of these kinds of programmes has increased considerably in the last few years: area-studies (Russian, Japanese, European) and problem-oriented studies (environmental studies, business studies). Some programmes offer a four-year degree, others are short cycle (two or three years) in which students can enrol after finishing a propaedeutic year in some basic discipline.

In most area-studies, language proficiency skills are an important purpose around which practical, economic, and cultural elements are built. In European studies at the University of Amsterdam, for example, students mostly take a language from a country belonging to the European Community as a major and add courses in economics, law, political science. The programme has been developed as a preparation for jobs in international organisations.

An exception is Japanese studies at Rotterdam, a two-year course in which understanding of management and economics is the main purpose and courses in Japanese language and culture are means to that end. It is expected that graduates from this programme will arrive in middle-management jobs of firms trading with Japan.

Problem-oriented studies take a specific societal field as an area for specialisation. For example, programmes on 'management of the arts' emerged at several universities, combining general business economics and specific art business with courses on cultural phenomena (arts, music).

Programmes in Cells B and D are particularly developed to improve the employment perspectives of graduates. The aims are to lay a foundation for work, to transmit knowledge and develop skills which are transferable within certain occupational fields. In recalling the theoretical perspective as outlined above, we might say that there is an attempt, especially within H/SS, to move from an 'open market and non-relevant education' to an 'open market and employment-relevant educational base'. Although graduates will enter the first type of market, the designers of such programmes hope that they will be particularly well-equipped with knowledge, skills and disposition to compete in the second one.

The boundaries between Cells B and D cannot clearly be drawn. For example, a certain shift can be noticed regarding the general social sciences programmes in Utrecht and Tilburg into the direction from D to B, whereby Utrecht adheres still more to the convergent model than Tilburg.

Generally speaking, it might be stated that programmes in Cell B are more founded on a few basic and related disciplines than those in Cell C where parts of disciplines are more loosely connected. Programmes in Cell B are more subjected to pressures in developing an integrative perspective and consequently in establishing distinctive institutional units than in Cell C where courses, to a lesser extent, are taught in relation to each other.

Before going into some characteristics of the disciplines history and economics, we will discuss briefly some aspects of the potential relationship between H/SS and science and engineering.

H/SS and the training of scientists and engineers

In assessing the potential of the H/SS disciplines in the training of scientists and engineers, the word 'potential', may refer both to current developments in this field and to the presumed contribution of H/SS to science programmes. The latter is beyond the scope of this paper as it concerns an intrinsic quality assessment of H/SS disciplines. Here we concentrate on the former and distinguish three main trends:

1. curricular programmes in the tradition of science, technology and society
2. the need to develop non-technical skills in science and technology curricula
3. tendencies towards the development of interdisciplinary science programmes of which H/SS subjects form a part.

Each of these will be touched upon briefly.

Science, technology and society programmes (STS)

STS programmes emerged in the 1970s from a growing concern about the social responsibility of scientists. Programmes were developed to foster an understanding of the ethical, social and economic considerations in professional practice. First in chemistry, and subsequently in other disciplines in science and technology, STS became a rather familiar subject. An essential element in STS programmes is to create an awareness among students of the impact and consequences of science and technology in society. As the cognitive aspect is not the main focus, students participate in projects in which they learn how to judge the pertinence of a variety of components in situations where science and technology play a dominant role. They learn how to assess the interconnected economic and sociological implications of any technological discussion, while participating in such projects which may also enhance social and communicative skills.

STS, conceived as service-education on behalf of science faculties, has evolved in different ways at Dutch universities. Some programmes are merely optional, whereas others belong to the compulsory part of a science or technology curriculum. In other cases the content of STS programmes is especially geared to students' major subjects. For example, in Utrecht different programmes have been developed for physics, chemistry and biology students.

Finally, STS in its most institutionalised form has existed since 1983 at the University of Twente, where students can enrol in a four-year programme after having passed a propaedeutic examination in a science or technology subject. At the same time, service education to other faculties is provided.

The orientation of STS programmes also varies. Some deal with the effects of technological innovations: for example, environmental impact assessment, technology assessment and risk analysis. Other programmes are more oriented towards the way social factors and scientific developments are intertwined (science dynamics). In these areas the research component has become an important part of STS activities.

Not surprisingly, the development of STS has experienced inherent tensions. Its importance has continuously to be shown to students and to many science and technology faculty members who are primarily interested in technical issues. When these people are confronted with social and philosophical aspects of science, they tend to be merely marginally interested as soon as they do not see the immediate relevance of the information provided for their own situation. STS courses, therefore, will be more effective if the relationship with the major programme of students becomes manifest.

Originally started as a group of enthusiastic individuals, STS staff at most universities now consist of professionals who have become scholars in their own field. Some of them are in science studies and others in the field of impact assessment studies. In the last few years STS staff have played an important role in expanding new interdisciplinary programmes.

The need for non-technical skills

Discussions about required skills and qualifications for scientists and engineers often boil down to the generalist versus specialist or theory versus practice dimension. Rather than dealing with these issues, we will briefly indicate what kind of non-technical qualifications are mostly stressed from the viewpoint of employment. Qualifications mostly stressed by employers refer to the changing occupational field. Enterprises are developing increasingly complex networks which require a variety of expertise. An understanding of the context in which professionals function and a readiness to collaborate in research projects have become indispensable requirements.

In this connection skills most frequently mentioned are:

- social communication skills; interpersonal and affective abilities
- organisational and management skills

- project management skills; marketing and cost-benefit analysis
- language proficiency, both in Dutch and in one or more foreign languages.

The possibility to incorporate courses which are intended to provide those skills meets much resistance, particularly in the technology curriculum. Engineers feel much under pressure to accomplish a four-year programme in which the basic technological knowledge is taught. Hardly any room seems to be left for other subjects. However, a solution to leave courses in the technical sciences to continuing education, which in one way will be effective because these courses will always be attractive to industry, is seldom considered.

Interdisciplinary programmes

Interdisciplinary programmes in technology have some tradition in Dutch higher education. Industrial engineering for example, taught at the three technical universities, contains social science subjects. The programme focuses on the analysis, design, control and improvement of operational processes in organisations. In that connection attention is paid to management, marketing and organisational aspects.

Although the emphasis is on the 'engineer character', the curriculum includes compulsory courses such as economics (10%), management and organisation (10%) and industrial sociology and psychology (together 10%). Civil engineering at the University of Twente is another example of achieving an integration between technical subjects and aspects of public administration. At present, other universities are aiming to acquire a more technical profile in their business studies.

Mentioning these examples is not to say that at other universities no developments with respect to the relationship between H/SS and sciences would occur. Generally stated, the tendencies to infuse insights from H/SS in science and technology can increasingly be notified. Recalling Figure 11.1, we can say that of these insights some are more instrumental (Cell D) and others more reflective (Cell C) in nature. In both cases, however, the reciprocal connections between a variety of subjects become more obvious.

Disciplinary perspective: history

In the general programmes in H/SS in the Dutch universities the visibility of separate disciplines has declined in favour of an interdisciplinary educational concept. Compared with these programmes it is often believed that disciplines are an unchanging entity, led by internally based problems and issues and that in disciplines the balance between instrumental and academic objectives swings to the latter. The nature of problems is not supposed to be determined by practical problems, but rather by disciplinary based problems.

This general picture needs some corrections as in these respects many differences between disciplines exist. Contemporary research in the sociology of science actually focuses on these differences, for example in the extent to which the disciplinary boundaries are permeable for external practical issues. Hereafter, we deal with the question how from the point of view of the discipline the relationship with employment can be conceived and how responsive the discipline is or can be to external needs. The discipline reviewed here will be history. Although reference will occasionally be made to specific departments, the main purpose is to make generalisations about history in the Netherlands, ignoring some of the subtler institutional variations.

History: general characteristic

History as an academic discipline is currently taught at seven Dutch universities. With some exceptions it is organisationally subsumed in the faculty of letters as a more or less autonomous sub-unit. This sub-unit is responsible for teaching and research, course evaluation, student advice and tutoring.

History grew in a period of rapid educational expansion resulting in a high demand for teachers. Actually, most history graduates went back into the education system in one way or another and other employment outlets were hardly considered. The number of entrants in the decade 1970–1980 nearly quadrupled. One major reason for this increase may be the change of entrance requirements. Originally, only those who had finished grammar school were eligible to take history. In the 1970s it became a general rule that for history there are no special requirements as to the subjects which are taken at secondary school. Not surprisingly, the committee which in 1988 reviewed all history sub-units complained in their report about deficient knowledge and reading skills of history students.

Despite the deterioration of employment possibilities in the teaching sector, the interest of first-year students to take history as a main subject does not decrease substantially. As a consequence, faculty members, students and graduates have joined hands to explore new employment outlets for history graduates and discuss changes regarding content and organisation of curricula, practical training and so on. In addition, historians are eagerly searching to improve their image, particularly in the private sector. Employers too often express persistent notions about historians as stuffy bookworms dealing with historical data. To date, much effort has been made to increase an awareness among employers of the knowledge and potential abilities of history graduates.

Curriculum content and organisation

The curriculum is organised along the traditional pattern of historical periods: ancient history, medieval history, new history, contemporary history and, in addition, economic and social history.

Starting from a broad, structured base in the first two years, students gradually take specialist options, concentrating almost wholly on one period. Other subjects are compulsory for all students: theory, methodology, philosophy and didactical training. In the 1980s other specialisms emerged in which historical issues are treated in a more thematic way, such as regional and local studies and women's history. Presently, contemporary history and economic and social history attract many students.

Characteristic for the history curriculum in general is the great amount of individual choice in taking course options. Specific study routes are offered, but those students who want to deviate from this are free to do so. Thus, curriculum development is strongly influenced by student demand as students can influence the directions and content of courses through choices. There are some pressures from students to specialise earlier in their programme, with a minimum of courses belonging to other historical periods. This pressure is opposed by staff, arguing that essential parts of any history programme may be violated if there is too much concentration on one historical period.

The concern about job prospects of history graduates has led towards three distinctive types of employment orientation, namely teaching, research and general education. The latter, which attracts by far the most students, functions as a general-purpose education for a wide variety of jobs. Students are given a maximum amount of freedom in choosing their courses according to their own preferences. The underlying assumption is that students will improve their chances on the labour market if they are able to develop their own profile. Yet a very fundamental problem arises for students, i.e. how to collect their courses to increase their chances on a very diffuse labour market if very little is known about the relation between a particular profile and its employment prospects.

A rather distinctive history programme which should be mentioned here is 'history of societies', established in 1978 at the Erasmus University in Rotterdam. Instead of departing from a chronological division, the programme starts from a typology of societies within the broad categories of industrial and pre-industrial societies in which again more refined typologies are distinguished. In developing this field of study much attention is paid to social sciences (economics included) and social research methods. As insights from these sciences are considered important for the analysis of historical processes and structures, it is generally acknowledged that history actually is a social science.

With respect to graduate employment, students can take courses which together cover two occupational fields, i.e. communication/public relations (including journalism) and policy/administration. Besides, students can take more general options.

In each of the years between 1985 and 1990, around 130 first-year students entered the Rotterdam programme. Women were slightly over-represented. The number of graduates increased from 19 in 1985 to 121 in 1988. From these 121 graduates 59 were women.

Graduate employability

In 1988 the unemployment rate of history graduates was 23 per cent. As can be expected, the proportion of graduates that goes back into the education system (teaching and research) has decreased in the 1980s to about a third of the total group of graduates. Their position, however, has deteriorated. Many of them have no full-time position and have temporary contracts. According to the principle 'last in, first out', their position has become very vulnerable.

In the late 1980s several surveys were held among history graduates to determine their labour market position. The data showed evidence that graduates did find employment outside the educational sector to quite some extent. From a survey among graduates of the Free University at Amsterdam it appeared that the percentage of graduates employed in the private sector increased from 4 per cent in 1980 to 24 per cent in 1985 and 40 per cent in 1986. In 1987 it declined to 20 per cent (Veeneman 1988). However, there were differences with respect to the labour market position in terms of level of job, utilisation of degree qualifications and stability of the job.

At one extreme, graduates were able to acquire jobs in the sphere of general management and policy-making, jobs in which qualifications history graduates possess are presumably useful. Others pursued a career in journalism. At the other extreme, graduates were employed in lower-level occupations, such as secretaries and service workers, occupations that have little correspondence to their educational qualifications. Sub-utilisation, low wages and short-term contracts are the rule rather than the exception (Wielers 1986).

In searching for characteristics which may influence the employment opportunities of history graduates, conclusions from the data available are very tentative. It appears that those graduates who have specialised in contemporary history and economic and social history tend to have better chances for jobs in the private sector than other history graduates. The differences, however, are too small to draw any straightforward conclusions. The importance of other additional courses outside history are difficult to assess as well, as most of these courses have been clustered in the survey. More evidence is available concerning the effect of extracurricular activities on the chances of finding a job corresponding to their educational level. Those who during their studies were involved in other activities, such as being on an educational board, found better jobs than other graduates. Also, a practical training period turns out to have a positive effect. In general, it may be stated that those who are active during their studies are also prepared to accept jobs beyond the traditional teaching sector. Finally, no relationship was found between duration of study, sex and employment. For staff and management jobs it appeared that the 25–30 age group was relatively over-represented.

From the foregoing it can be concluded that employment opportunities for history graduates have increased. Whereas most of them used to become teachers or researchers and occasionally archivists or librarians, the scope has broadened. Historians do penetrate in other types of jobs. Although some have acquired a job corresponding to their qualifications, most graduates have no solid employment prospects.

At present, the problem of graduate employability is of a major concern in virtually all history departments. Other than decreasing the number of first-year students, the proposals for solutions are related to the way historians are to be perceived – either as specialists or as generalists. Adherents of the specialist view propose to develop specialist course structures oriented to specific occupational fields and designed primarily in relation to employment needs. They aim at a closer connection between content of studies and job requirements. Others oppose this view strongly, arguing that this may limit the employability and flexibility of graduates in a broad spectrum of jobs. According to these critics, employers do not specify the subject or content of a degree as they are screening for general abilities, capacities and attitudes.

There are no clear answers to these questions on the basis of the empirical data available. Probably the truth lies somewhere in between. Graduates may increase their employment by taking additional courses or acquiring skills and competencies which make them better equipped for effective employment. Most historians are convinced that a practical training period for their students is very useful. Students become familiar with professional practice and are compelled to investigate for themselves the potentiality of a history degree in professional practice.

Perspectives

The current employment situation of history graduates puts quite some pressure on the curriculum. If history tends to be converted into elements of non-disciplinary and applied courses what is then the place of history? To what extent can a graduate from such a programme be labelled a historian? For the main part, Becher states, the historian is an individual, lonely scholar, whose prime concern is with 'understanding how things came about' rather than 'with producing solutions to problems' (Becher 1989, p.265). Whether this image is disappearing or not, Dutch historians have organised themselves to improve their image and show what historians can mean to employers. They stress the ability of historians to handle complex and diverse materials and information and to make sense of it. Through these organisations projects are attracted, for example, to investigate the history of a particular firm, or to prepare books of commemoration, jubilee volumes and so on. At the same time historians are in the process of examining what employers precisely expect of a general historian. It is expected that contacts with employers may contribute to an understanding of the general image.

Economics: general characteristics

Course offerings

Within the economic discipline in universities, courses are offered in, for example, actuarial sciences, business administration, administrative information sciences as well as in the traditional fields of economics and econometrics. Numerous specialisations are offered within traditional economics, such as general economics, business economics, quantitative economics, international management, administrative information sciences, financial economics, regional economics, fiscal economics and political economics. It should be noted that econometrics is offered as a distinct course, with a full four-year programme.

Each university course consists of an initial phase (*propaedeutic*) and a secondary phase (*doctoraalfase*). In describing the separate study programmes, three faculties have been selected that are supposed to give a reliable picture of what is offered at Dutch universities in terms of economic programmes. The three universities are:

- the State University of Groningen (RUG)
- the Catholic University Brabant (KUB)
- the Erasmus University of Rotterdam (EUR)

Each of the three offers three courses: economics, fiscal economics and econometrics. All have the standard Dutch nominal length of four years. For fiscal economics, the propaedeutic phase is the same as for economics. In this section the information is primarily focused on (general) economics.

During the propaedeutic the following subjects are offered:

- introduction to general economics
- introduction to business economics
- introduction to quantitative methods (mathematics, statistics and bookkeeping).

After the propaedeutic phase, at the beginning of the doctoral phase, students choose either a general economics or a business economics programme. The first year of both doctoral programmes consists of a number of compulsory subjects. At the beginning or during the third study year (second year of the doctoral phase) students can compose, within certain limits, their own study programme. At the three universities a great number of specialisations exist out of which students can make their choice.

Differences in content/objectives between university and HBO 'economics'

One of the major differences between economics in university and HBO is that the former type of education is more applied in nature (e.g., the application of fiscal law), while the latter accentuates explanation. Second, within HBO hardly any emphasis is put on economics in relation to mathematics. Solving problems of an economic nature through the use of formal equations, definitions and formulas hardly occurs in this type of education. Third, several courses within HBO (hotel management, tourism and recreational sciences) do not have a counterpart in the university economics discipline.

Student enrolment

In 1988–89, 22,276 students were enrolled in the university economic discipline. Of these, approximately 5.7 per cent were part-time students. The spread over the various courses was: 77.4 per cent economics, 9.4 per cent econometrics or actuarial sciences, 12.8 per cent business administration and 0.4 per cent Japanology (no separate data available for administrative information sciences). Table 11.1 gives an indication of the enrolment development for the various courses.

Table 11.1 Student enrolment for the economic university courses by year

	1980	*1985*	*1988*
Economics	10,414	13,882	17,246
Econometrics/act.	923	1354	2104
Business administration	729	2006	2858
Japanology	–	37	68

Admission requirements

The same admission requirements operate for the three faculties: a pre-university secondary degree with mathematics I and/or II, or a similar qualification with sufficient mathematical input. This requirement is determined by law. Two of the three faculties indicate that mathematics II is an almost necessary requirement for the econometric propaedeutic phase, if this programme is to be completed successfully.

There are no legal or faculty requirements regarding the knowledge of one or more modern foreign languages for entering students. One faculty (RUG) argues that first-year students have a deficit in terms of oral capability for French, German and English.

Entering students: some facts and figures

In the following tables some quantitative data are presented on entering students for the three economic faculties.

1. The gender of entering students

Table 11.2 Student entry by gender

	KUB		*RUG*		*EUR*	
Year	*male*	*female*	*male*	*female*	*male*	*female*
1982	86%	14%	89%	11%	87%	13%
1985	83	17	83	17	82	18
1988	74	16	79	21	81	19
1989	74	26	79	21	81	19

Source: Self-study reports economic faculties KUB/RUG/EUR 1990.

The Table 11.2 shows an increase in female students over the years. However, male students are still dominant in the three faculties.

2. Previous education of entering students

Table 11.3 Previous education of enrolling students, in economics and econometrics

	KUB				*RUG*				*EUR**	
	1982	*1985*	*1988*	*1989*	*1982*	*1985*	*1988*	*1989*	*1982*	*1985*
VWO	86%	89%	92%	90%	82%	87%	94%	94%	87%	80%
HBO	8	5	3	3	10	6	3	2	5	11
Other	6	6	5		78	7	3	4	7	9

Source: KUB and RUG Self-study reports, 1990 EUR, Bureau of Education and Examinations, 1990.

* For the EUR, no more detailed information is available.

3. Number of entering students per cohort

Table 11.4 number of first-year students per cohort

	KUB		*RUG**		*EUR*	
Cohort	*Economics*	*Econometrics*	*Economics*	*Econometrics*	*Economics*	*Econometrics*
1984–85	404	81	363	51	1043	138
1985–86	448	96	572	81	1179	181
1986–87	529	102	–	–	1403	194
1987–88	720	157	–	–	1388	323

Source: Education reports, KUB, RUG, EUR 1989.
* No distinction is made between full-time and part-time students. For other cohorts, detailed information is not available. The average number of students for the last six cohorts is 417 in economics and 56 in econometrics.

Table 11.4 shows a strong increase in the number of first-year students for all three faculties. The explanation for this increase provided by the faculties has largely to do with the good labour market perspective for the graduates.

CHAPTER 12

Change Under Exogenous Pressure

Belgian Higher Education after Thirty Years

Johan L. Vanderhoeven

Introduction

Education policy in Belgium has been affected dramatically by the process of state reform. From 1989 on almost all aspects of education policy making have been transferred to the autonomous authority of the three language-related communities: the Flemish community, the French-speaking community and the German-speaking community. With respect to higher education policy, only the largest communities are involved: the Flemish and French-speaking communities. This evolution complicates the structure of this contribution.

When discussing the internal functioning and the organisational patterns of teaching and learning in higher education in Belgium (universities and other institutions), one is quickly confronted with a paradox. On the one hand the evolution of the role and function of higher education, as in other countries, has been subject to dramatic changes over the last three decades, while on the other hand the organisation of teaching and learning has remained rather traditional. For about twenty years real 'in-depth' change seemed to be hampered by the framework set out in a law which was once called 'epoch-making'. Only recently have exogenous pressures become important and strong enough to lead to decisive steps being taken towards change. Analysing those trends towards change in the near future is therefore linked to the analysis of the external developments themselves.

Higher education in Belgium

Higher education was first organised within a comprehensive legal framework by the Act of 7 July 1970 covering the general structure of higher education (Wielemans and Vanderhoeven 1993). The 1970 Act grouped and brought together nearly *all* forms of education following secondary school. Teacher training was integrated in this framework shortly afterwards. The Act classified all educational forms according to the organisation of studies and their ultimate qualification. At the start of the 1960s only three types of higher education were to be found in Belgium: (a) universities; (b) higher technical (mainly training programmes for graduate engineers and interpreters/translators), higher economical and higher arts education (including architecture); and (c) teacher training. A fundamental change of policy was undertaken based on two main principles. First, there was a strong commitment to the *democratisation* of education, especially higher education. Second, major shifts *in labour market requirements* became apparent. In fact, both principles reinforced each other. From a structural viewpoint higher education was integrated into a three-fold framework: university education (at least four or five years of study), higher education outside the universities long term (four years of study) and higher education outside the universities short term (three years of study).

Democratisation

Access to all forms of higher education was made entirely free of any restrictions thanks to a deliberate policy on the part of the authorities, who are seeking, by means of the *Omnivalence Act* of 1964, to promote real democratisation of higher education. As a consequence of this Act all secondary school leavers had in principle free entrance to virtually all forms of higher education. Admission to short-term higher education required a Certificate of Higher Secondary Education, which is awarded on completion of a full cycle of secondary education or, since 1984, of a seventh year of vocational education (on a full-time basis). Entry into long-term higher education or university requires the Higher Education Admission Diploma, which came to be awarded almost automatically in the same examination period as the Certificate of Higher Secondary Education (with the exception of vocational education). Precisely because of the fact that this awarding procedure had become almost a formality, the Flemish community decided, after the transformation of Belgium into a federal state in 1989, to abolish this

Admission Diploma. At the same time the Certificate of Higher Secondary Education was changed into Diploma of Secondary Education.

Only in a few limited cases was access to higher studies subject to an entrance examination (the Faculty of Applied Science – civil engineering training – and the Royal Military School). Recently, officials of the Flemish Department of Education have been calling for access to higher education (especially the university) to be governed by stricter conditions and for 'suitable selection procedures' to be introduced, especially for medicine and dentistry. It is expected that new rules on entrance procedures in these two cases will become operational from the academic year 1997–98, following a Flemish community Decree dated 24 July 1996. This entrance exam will be organised on an inter-university basis. It will be split up into two parts: the first testing actual knowledge of physics, biology, chemistry and mathematics at the level of the third stage of general academic secondary education; the second testing the learning ability of the candidate. Every year two sessions of the exam will be organised (July–September). Every student has two chances to pass the exam. Further policy proposals are under consideration. The French-speaking community has not so far echoed this call.

Although studies that have been carried out indicate a lower level of concern about offering equal educational opportunities and democratising university education in the Flemish community (Deleeck and Storms 1989; Lammertyn 1987, 1992), there is still a high number of 18-year-olds who choose to go on to higher education. In 1994 in Belgium, enrolment of 18-year-old students reached 12.2 per cent in higher education outside the university and 18.9 per cent at the universities. For 19-year-olds these figures rise to 20.6 per cent and 20.3 per cent. At the age of 20 statistics show environment figures of 23.4 per cent and 18.4 per cent (CERI 1996).

For the majority of disciplines there still is no requirement for a *numerus clausus* in the strict sense of the term, and no constraints on taking up or dropping studies. Information campaigns to guide young people, particularly girls, towards disciplines offering good future prospects (chiefly at the level of secondary education) enable certain imbalances to be corrected. Even the new Flemish entrance exams for medicine and dentistry do not imply a *numerus clausus* or *fixus*.

Labour market requirements

On 1 January 1994 Belgium had 10.1 million inhabitants. The 'active' population (20–64 years old) represented approximately 60.26 per cent of the population (or 6.1 million people) at the end of 1993. Overall, 3.2 million people were employed in the labour market in 1993.

Table 12.1 Distribution between economic sectors in 1970, 1988 and 1994

	1970	*1988*	*1994*
Primary sector	174000 (4.7%)	98000 (2.6%)	16000 (0.5%)
Secondary sector	1537000 (41.6%)	1045000 (27.8%)	910000 (29.0%)
Tertiary sector	1987000 (53.7%)	2614000 (69.6%)	2230000 (70.5%)
Total	3698000 (100%)	3757000 (100%)	3200000 (100%)

Source: National Institute for Statistics.

As in all other western industrialised countries, the tertiary sector has continued to grow in importance to the detriment of other sectors. In Belgium 70 per cent of the working population is currently employed in the tertiary sector, the highest figure in Europe. A high enrolment rate in higher education is therefore of vital importance (see Table 12.1). By way of comparison, the corresponding figure for France is 63 per cent and for West Germany 56 per cent.

Structural consequences

As a consequence of this policy of integrating all kinds of programmes as far as possible into the three-fold system of higher education, the full-time, post-secondary sector for school-leavers aged 18 (the end of a 12-year period of compulsory education in Belgium) became very small. The school attendance figures for the 1990–91 academic year are shown in Table 12.2. Since then the Flemish community adopted legislation aiming at further integration of higher education as a whole (cf. infra). At the same time the so-called 'post-secondary' sector has been moved away from tertiary education and integrated into secondary education as its non-compulsory fourth stage. Similar proposals are being discussed in the French-speaking community.

Table 12.2 School attendance in Belgian higher education (1990–91)

Type	*Enrolment*	*% of enrolment*	*% of 18–22 age group*
University	111845	44	16
Outside university	135758	54	54
Post-secondary	5955	2	0.8
Total	253558	100	35.9

Source: *Nationaal Instituut voor de Statistiek, Departement Onderwijs, Ministère de l'Education, de la Formation et de la Recherche.*
Note: The percentage of the 18–22 age group (total age group = 705507) is a slight over-estimate due to the fact that a number of higher education programmes consist of five or, in one case, seven years of study.

The trail-blazing integration of nearly all full-time education starting at age 18 goes some way to explaining why Belgium chose not to adopt a *multipurpose* or *binary* structure for its higher education system but – in common with France and West Germany – a *specialist* model (Neave 1992). This typology is based on two criteria: the structure of the educational programmes and the organisational structure and management of the higher education institutes. In a recent study Jallade (1992) developed a different framework for classification (binary, unitary and fragmented systems) based only on the general structures of the educational programmes. In this classification Belgium belongs to the binary systems. For the argument to be developed in this article we include however the organisational aspects as well (cf. infra on the relation of secondary and higher education). The option for a specialist model implied the creation of a type of higher education organised quite independently from the university. Its organised courses tend on balance to be vocational and finite in nature. The range of programmes is relatively limited, specialising in a few generically or occupationally related sectors (teacher training, lower engineering, nursery work, social work, accountancy, secretarial work, etc.). All these 'short-term' higher education programmes adopted a three-year structure in accordance with the definitions in the European Directive of 21 December 1988 relating to the equivalence of higher education diplomas.

Most of the above 'traditional forms' of higher technical, economical and arts education were integrated in an intermediate structure, the 'long-term' higher education system with programmes lasting at least four years. Under Belgian law short- and long-term higher education was originally termed 'non-university higher education'; later this was changed to 'higher education outside the university'. In both cases however the distinction between the two sectors was rather negative ('non' or 'outside'). Contrary to what happened in England or the Netherlands the system did not, at the time, achieve a real binary or multipurpose status, although transitions from one type to another were *de facto* possible. In general, however, distinctions remained (and remain) rather important in different ways. On the other hand this three-fold structure is slightly confusing. OECD statistics, for example, are based on the number of study years in a programme. Consequently, they always integrate the long-term type into the university figures.

Different roots in the history of education policy

As explained elsewhere (Wielemans and Vanderhoeven 1993) the universities have always been treated separately in Belgian education policy. Higher education outside the university literally grew out of secondary education. Even today the links between secondary schools and higher (especially short-term) education institutes remain striking. In many cases the latter are monotechnical sections located in the same building as a secondary school and often even structured under the same school head. They are subject to the same regulations and organisational principles. Class norms, inspection procedures, curriculum development – all these were closely related to the habits and traditions of a secondary school. The 1995 reform in the Flemish community (cf. infra) definitely wants to change this tradition. The transfer of the post-secondary sector, as indicated, is but one element of this new policy. Nevertheless, deeply rooted traditions do not change easily.

In addition to this the 1970 Act did not contain a clearly defined and strategic rationalisation and/or programmation plan. The number of schools is far too high and student:school ratio far too low to provide a solid basis for the organisation of real higher education at an appropriate level.

Table 12.3 illustrates this problem of scale in the Flemish community in 1991.

Table 12.3 Number and size of higher education institutes in the Flemish Community (1 February 1991)

Short-Term Higher Education

	Number of schools	*Number of students*	*Average number*	*Smallest number*	*Largest number*
Community	25	9441	377	92	1932
Off. GR.A.	24	9188	383	85	1824
Free GR.A.	88	35398	408	129	1476
Total	137	54567	398		

Long-Term Higher Education

	Number of schools	*Number of students*	*Average number*	*Smallest number*	*Largest number*
Community	8	5451	681	173	1128
Off. GR.A.	6	3070	511	275	909
Free GR.A.	14	18172	1298	235	2880
Total	28	26693	953		

Higher Arts Education
(fully integrated in the long-term type from 1 September 1992 onwards)

	Number of schools	*Number of students*	*Average number*	*Smallest number*	*Largest number*
Community	5	1961	392	65	538
Off. GR.A.	3	899	299	212	405
Free GR.A.	5	1827	365	114	526
Total	13	4687	360		

Source: Departement Onderwijs.
Note: Schools in Belgium (not the universities) are grouped into three major networks based on the kind of organising board for each of them: the Community Network (former state schools), the Official Grant-aided Network (Provincial or Municipal Schools) and the Free Grant-aided Network ('private' – mainly Catholic schools, but fully funded from public means).

These figures have to be compared with those of the universities in the Flemish community: nine universities containing 64,530 students.

A similar situation could be found in the French-speaking community. In 1990 they had 90 'short-term higher education' institutions for 47,457 students and 20 'long-term higher education' institutions for 15,346 students. Only three institutes offered both. Eight institutions organised university education for 59,167 students.

In the Flemish community from 1 September 1995, the distinction between short-term and long-term higher education disappeared as a consequence of the decree dated 13 July 1994 on higher tertiary education as a whole. Instead the newly established higher education institutes offer single cycle studies (three years of study, with only one exception in paramedical short term, *viz.* midwife requires four years) and two cycle studies (at least 2x2 or four years of study). At the same time nearly 160 'independent' higher education institutes offering either short-term courses or long-term courses or, exceptionally, both, have been merged into 29 new higher education institutes with generally at least 2000 students and offering all types of higher education outside the university. At the same time, following earlier preparatory legislation, all rules on staffing, programmes, teaching, research and so on have been integrated into one uniform framework. Within this unified framework the specialist option has been reinforced. Courses offered by single cycle higher education programmes prepare students for various occupations in sectors such as industry, commerce, transport, agriculture, medical auxiliary and social work, teaching, translation, interpreting, the hotel trade, fashion, information technology, applied arts, the media, etc. Study focuses on practical aspects and provides direct access to employment. Courses offered by two cycle higher education programmes prepare students for various occupations in more or less the same sectors as the single cycle programmes. Those courses, however, train technical staff who will carry out and be responsible for executive tasks of a highly scientific and technical nature. The decree thus introduced a clear distinction between two cycle higher education and university education. The universities provide education based on scientific research, whereas higher education institutes provide education based on scientific knowledge. The Flemish authorities dictated that the higher education institutes cannot conduct scientific research autonomously (though this is possible in collaboration with the universities), and neither can they award doctoral (PhD) degrees.

The French-speaking community is expected to adopt a similar approach over the next period. To that end proposals have already been presented and are being discussed.

Effects on teaching and learning

In terms of its dominant curriculum tradition, Belgium belongs to what McLean (1990) calls *The Encyclopaedic Heartlands*. Characteristic of this curriculum tradition is the idea that all students must acquire as much knowledge as possible about valid (rational) subjects. All students will follow more or less the same curriculum, organised in accordance with fairly strong ideas about the hierarchy of topics and disciplines. But it must be clear that this tradition has a strong practical orientation. All human activities are supposed to become more efficient through the application of rational procedures. Therefore even vocational studies, at whatever level, should begin with rational scientific ideas. The power of this ideology lies in its capacity to survive the continuous pressures for differentiation which have been brought about by the democratisation of lower-secondary schooling and the diversification of upper-secondary education or by the ever-changing demands of the labour market.

As a consequence, in all forms of higher education there is still a strong tendency to organise all programmes according to the same principles. Every year there is a more or less fixed programme starting with a broad, general and theory-oriented introduction to a certain discipline. Later this general knowledge will be applied to more concrete problems. Every year each student has to pass a fixed number of formal examinations. This largely explains the continuing resistance in higher education to modular or credit systems. The same goes for programmes based on only one subject or on learning by practice. In teacher training, for example, a considerable number of teacher trainers still adhere firmly to the idea of teaching practice being the application of principles learned in theoretical courses. The same approach can also be found in other disciplines. As a consequence the interaction between the labour market and education programmes (initial training and in-service training) is not always optimal – though it has to be said that labour market requirements are sometimes rather unstable or poorly defined.

The new 1995 legislation in the Flemish community implemented also the introduction of a course credit system. This system makes it possible to determine the study load objectively. One year is said to be equivalent to 60 study points or 1500 to 1800 hours of study activities (including classes, personal work and exams). This credit system also enables students to apply credits from courses successfully completed to other disciplines. The implementation of this new strategy is still going on. But the former encyclopaedic tradition has not yet completely disappeared.

Change under pressure

Until recently the teaching and learning climate in higher education, especially in the short-term programmes, was still closely linked to the traditional patterns of schooling at primary and secondary schools. Although universities have traditionally operated under a different 'cultural' climate, there is still a very strong sense of the encyclopaedic tradition (formal curricula, examinations, broad spectrum programmes, etc.). The long-term type of higher education occupied a more or less intermediate position, though came closer to the university.

Up to 1989 the authorities had not yet taken any explicit measures either to improve the internal effectiveness of the educational establishments or to bring them more into line with the actual needs of the labour market. They had tried only to influence the funding of higher education in general and of scientific research in particular (Wielemans and Vanderhoeven 1991). Some statements issuing from academic and political circles do give the impression that marketability and economic competitiveness have gained in importance in the criteria used for assessing the quality of research and education. However, the Belgian authorities did not regard it as their task to take measures to exert a direct influence on developments in this area. They were forced to refer to experiences in other countries when evaluating the quality of establishments – for example through accreditation procedures, inspection etc. – since Belgium has no yardsticks for measuring the performance of higher education establishments as a basis for determining and awarding financial resources.

It could be said that Belgium used to be a perfect example of *demand-led* policy (Neave 1984). At a certain point in the mid-80s, higher education policy itself became a victim of the demand-led ideas. We agree with Neave's thesis that the erosion of demand-led policies in higher education can be seen as symptomatic of the departure from the stance that governed the expansion of higher education from the early 1960s onwards (Neave 1984, p.114). In the Flemish community at least, this tendency – and the replacement of a demand-led policy by a more *expenditure-driven* one – became gradually apparent after 1989 (the federalisation of the Belgian State). Although certain tendencies can also be observed in Belgium's French- and German-speaking communities, it is only in the Flemish community that a real shift in policy strategy has been launched. In this community it is becoming possible to overcome the obstacles standing in the way of the government's ability to move over to a more expenditure-driven policy. The old restraints – being partly a function of the highly segmented nature of Belgian society and also of the political power that various segments can wield against the government – are still more influential in the field of education policy in the French-speaking community (Hecquet 1984).

The pressures for change are three-fold: the consequences of a demand-led policy; shifts in the labour market; the internationalisation of higher education. It should be borne in mind that the first and second factor correspond perfectly to the two leading principles of the expansion of higher education in the 1960s.

School attendance levels

As stated earlier, there is no educational planning policy in Belgium, nor any *numerus clausus* or *fixus*. The lump-sum cost per student still remains the basis for financing or grant-aiding higher education, hence the importance of changes in the number of students per establishment and per discipline. In the Flemish community the universities have a slightly different funding formula. The number of students only partially counts; financial means also take into account the importance of scientific research in every university. For the new Flemish higher education institutes a complicated set of parameters is introduced to compensate for the merger costs. However, all institutions now have lump-sum financing, but the student numbers remain important. The two factors determining changes in student numbers are population trends and school attendance levels in full-time education.

Various statistics show that in terms of birth rate, 1980 was a peak year for the 18–20 age group, and was followed by a continuous decline over the next ten years. The evaluations and predictions that have been made forecasted a decline of 14.8 per cent by 1990 and of 27.5 per cent by the year 2000. The falling birth rate, which first began in 1965, therefore heralds a smaller base from which to recruit higher education students. This does not, however, imply that the higher education sector will never grow again in the future.

The second major factor determining actual demand is the school attendance level in full-time education, or the number of young people wishing to go on to higher education. In view of the freedom of choice for studies in Belgium and taking into account the influence of the market mechanism, an ever-increasing number of young people are opting for higher non-university education. The actual demand for university places has reached saturation point in the Flemish community, while the French-speaking community has in recent years seen an annual growth rate of 5 per cent in the non-university sector and 2 per cent in the university sector.

The decision in 1984 to extend the statutory school-leaving age to 18 and the increase in the number of female students have had a positive influence on the number of enrolments in higher education. In the early 1980s female students accounted for no more than 40 per cent of the total university population. In 1989–90 for the first time their number amounted to more than 50 per cent of Flemish first-year students and represented roughly half of the total in the French-speaking community. Other possible, but not quantifiable, reasons for an increasing number of young people choosing non-university forms of higher education may be: a fear of university studies; financial considerations (university education is more costly to the student); greater employment opportunities for holders of non-university higher education diplomas; and the overly theoretical nature of university education. There is also the possibility that the social and economic background of the students may act as either a stimulus or an obstacle to higher education.

Attendance in full-time higher education in the Flemish community

As regards school attendance, the Flemish community differs from its French-speaking counterpart in that it has a proportionally higher number of students participating in higher non-university education and a lower proportion involved in university education. In addition to this, two other factors need to be taken into account: (a) the French-speaking community has more than twice as many foreign students in its universities as the Flemish community; and (b) the percentage of non-university students is on the increase in both the Flemish and

French-speaking communities. It has been argued that the trend towards a stagnation or even a decline in the number of university students is neither fortuitous nor influenced by the overall economic situation, and should be seen as a lasting development (Baeck 1987). This assumption needs to be qualified, however. The number of first-year students in the Flemish community's universities dropped by 8 per cent between 1982–83 and 1987–88, but rose again by 5 per cent in 1988–89. As stated earlier, the Flemish Department of Education is expecting a limited rise in the number of university students in the coming years (1988/89: -0.3%; 1989/90: +0.3%; 1990/91: +0.7%). A similar and even more pronounced development is expected in Flemish higher non-university education (1988/89: +3.2%; 1989/90: +1.5%; 1990/91: +2.2%). As Table 12.4 shows this tendency is persisting.

Attendance in full-time higher education in the French- and German-speaking communities

On the side of the French- and German-speaking communities, the increase in the number of first-year university students stood at 12 per cent over the same period. The overall number of university students rose by some 7 per cent between 1983 and 1989 and a rise of about 3 per cent was expected for 1990–91. There is an even higher rate of growth in higher non-university education. As Table 12.4 clearly shows this tendency is persisting.

Sectorial shifts and the labour market

Significant sectorial shifts have occurred in university education and higher non-university education in both the French-speaking and Flemish communities. Particularly in the short-term type of higher non-university education, there has been a large shift towards higher economic education. In the case of higher technical education, the student population rose slowly but consistently from the early 1980s in the Flemish community, but rather more sporadically in the French-speaking community. The other sectors of short-term higher non-university education are in a state of balance with first-year students accounting for more than 60 per cent of the total enrolments. Further, in the case of disciplines offering less promising opportunities on the labour market enrolments are declining, but a greater proportion of females are seen to be taking up these disciplines. Holders of short-

Table 12.4 Changes in the number of higher education enrolments, broken down according to the type of education (university or non-university). Absolute numbers and percentages for each community

	*Flemish community**					*French-and German-language community***				
Year	*University*		*Total*	*Non-univ.*		*University*		*Total*	*Non-univ.*	
	N	*%*	*N*	*N*	*%*	*N*	*%*	*N*	*N*	*%*
1984/85	53756	43.65	123158	69402	56.35	50387	56.20	89618	39231	43.80
1985/86	54159	43.54	124401	70242	56.46	50472	55.80	90505	40033	44.20
1986/87	53838	41.87	128597	74759	58.13	50702	55.20	91772	41070	44.80
1987/88	54275	41.27	131522	77247	58.73	50111	55.10	90983	40872	44.90
1989/90	55452	40.40	137259	81807	59.60	53845	54.80	98365	44520	45.20
1992/93	61231	41.90	146089	84858	58.10	59167	48.50	121970	62803	51.50

Source: (*) Statistisch Jaarboek van het Onderwijs.
(**) Y. Ylieff (1990)

term higher non-university education diplomas are facing ever-increasing competition on the labour market from those who have qualified in long-term higher non-university education disciplines and from university students who enrol in related disciplines.

Major sectorial shifts have also occurred in the universities. The level of employment in the secondary sector (the processing industry in particular) is on the decline (providing jobs for almost 38% of the Belgian working population in 1960 (this figure is now down to roughly 25%)), whereas in the tertiary (services) sector, it is on the increase: from about 46 per cent in 1960 to more than 65 per cent now. Belgium, like so many other countries, is undergoing a *third industrial revolution*, a new form of industrialisation focused on the manufacture of hi-tech goods. But this highly innovative industry is not proving to be a huge source of employment either. That being the case, the industry will be offering university graduates relatively few career opportunities in the future.

Alongside the private sector, the grant-aided tertiary sector has until only very recently offered wide employment opportunities for university graduates. Belgium has the most highly developed social security system in the European Community after the Netherlands. University faculties supplying graduates to the generously funded tertiary sector underwent a huge expansion in the period between 1960 and 1980. But as a result of the thorough reorganisation of finances in the social welfare sector in 1983 and the *Val Duchesse* plan for economic cutbacks in 1986, the upward trend in the number of people employed in the sector went into reverse. This reversal (resulting from the interplay of political and market forces) led to a sharp decline in the demand for people qualified in psycho-pedagogic, socio-cultural, medical and paramedical disciplines and the pattern of demand on the labour market came to be reflected in the distribution of the student population among the various faculties. The reform of the welfare state system primarily affected those faculties and disciplines where most of the graduates would go on to find jobs in the grant-aided social sector: dental science, pharmacy, physical education, philosophy and letters, psychology and the educational sciences. In the Flemish community, a comparison of the number of first-year students enrolled in certain disciplines in the 1982–83 school year with the number following the same disciplines in 1988–89 shows the following changes: economic sciences +72%, oriental philology +60%, social sciences +18%, engineering +18%, law +12, medicine +2%, pharmacy -0.3%, Germanic philology -35%, psychology and educational sciences -36%, mathematics/information technology -46%, physical education -69%, classical philology -82%. Table 12.5 presents a comparison between the French-speaking and the Flemish communities over a period of nearly a decade. Since then, the figures for the Flemish community at least have shown overall persistent tendencies.

Table 12.5 Changes (in percentage) in the number of students in higher education

	Flemish community[1]			*French/German-speaking communities*[2]		
	*1981/82**	*1988/89*	*Index*	*1981/82**	*1988/89*	*Index*
Short-term						
technology	4306	6824	158.5	2025	2669	131.8
economics	11,814	22,586	191.2	6440	12,805	198.8
paramedic	11,464	9481	82.7	8363	7769	92.9
social work	4072	3687	90.5	3113	3001	96.4
artistry	849	855	100.7	1029	1523	148.0
agriculture	469	842	179.5	457	729	159.5
education	15,042	10,549	70.1	10,251	7108	69.3
Total ST	**48,016**	**54,824**	**114.2**	**31,678**	**35,604**	**112.4**
Long-term						
economics	4298	990.9	230.5	4086	5965	146.0
technology	8035	12849	159.9	4812	5270	109.5
artistry	un-known	1183	–	2057	1453	70.6
maritime sc.	un-known	142	–	–	–	–
	1981/82	*1988/89*	*Index*	*1981/82*	*1988/89*	*Index*
social work	–	–	–	268	465	173.5
agriculture	–	–	–	328	356	108.5
Total LT	**12,333**	**24,083**	**195.3**	**11,551**	**13,509**	**117.0**
University						
Relig. science	526	441	83.8	184	117	63.6
Philosophy	65	72	110.8	42	181	431.0
Philol./ Letters	7728	5753	74.4	5320	4589	86.3
Law	5988	8112	135.5	4647	5589	120.3

Table 12.5 continued

Sciences	4354	4442	102.0	4137	4115	99.5
Medic./ Dentist.	7825	6149	78.6	8013	5869	73.2
Pharmacy	1152	1610	139.8	981	1516	154.5
Physical ed.	2060	1488	72.2	1497	900	60.1
Veterinary medicine	902	781	86.6	1272	855	67.2
Applied sciences	3256	4611	141.6	3022	4232	140.0
Agronomy	1362	1914	140.5	1167	1487	127.4
Soc. pol. econ. sc.	3025	4742	156.8	3261	5494	168.5
Appl. econ. sc. and commerce	3245	6904	2212.8	1756	4429	252.2
Psych. Pedag.	3100	2643	85.3	2166	2110	97.4
Total univ.	**44,588**	**49,662**	**113.8**	**37,465**	**41,483**	**110.7**

For university education, the reference year is 1980–81 rather than 1981–82
Students entitled to funding *and* students not entitled to funding.
Source: Statistische Jaarboeken van het Onderwijs/Vlaamse Interuniversitaire Raad
Long and short-term types: Ministère de l'Education, de la Recherche et de la Formation/University: Fondation Universitaire.

The upward trend in the social sciences is attributed, among other things, to the increasing popularity of the communication sciences and the employment opportunities they offer. The declining interest in mathematics/computer technology is said to be caused by the growing attraction of engineering disciplines. A growing trend is perceived for female students to be in the majority in the final year of disciplines for which the employment prospects are poor. The same tendency is reported in the French-speaking community, but in proportions which are less pronounced.

All this goes to show that for university graduates the labour market has undergone a fundamental change. The market's reduced capacity to absorb certain categories of graduates has created a glut of diplomas. There is still a strong demand for students who qualify in subjects such as economics, applied economics, law and science. Furthermore, a division seems to have occurred in the humanities: disciplines which are more concrete and useful in labour market terms, such as economics and certain branches of sociology and psychology, are highly rated for their usefulness in the social sphere. They are held in high esteem because of their contribution to the developments in social engineering. Disciplines of a more abstract and philosophical nature have far less potential for producing a workforce with a sufficient level of adequate and applicable skills.

Those most likely to find themselves ill-equipped in this way are graduates from the so-called cultural sciences or the disciplines provided by the Faculty of Philosophy and Letters. This trend could well lead to a marginalisation of the cultural sciences at universities and induce an ever-increasing number of students to enrol for disciplines offering better employment prospects. And in the long run, this can only mean cultural impoverishment for the whole of society.

Another factor which needs to be considered is that of *underemployment*. Recent studies carried out at the universities of Gent and Leuven point to a significant level of underemployment: between approximately 15 per cent (social sciences) and 30 per cent (criminology and philosophy and letters (Bossiers 1989; Schodts, Smedts and Hoornaert 1989–1990; Smedts 1993)). Disciplines which have an extremely low ratio of underemployment are those in which economics, law and applied sciences are taught (between approximately 1.5% and 5%). The figures do indeed reflect the trends already noted, but one surprising fact needs to be considered. In the study carried out at the University of Gent, the social sciences clearly emerge as one of the most all-round disciplines (alongside others such as economics, science, law and agronomy). The social sciences seemingly offer wider employment opportunities, although the jobs on offer do not match up to the level of academic achievement. Similar developments are seen in the French-speaking community.

The figures in Table 12.6 are an indication of changing employment patterns. The topic of underemployment remains open for discussion due to the lack of clear definition. In a recent study Smedts (1993) proposes to use the criterion of *underpayment*. If a graduate earns less than 25–30 per cent of an average salary he or she is considered to be underpaid. For university graduates 25 per cent are underpaid six months after graduation, but this figures falls to 15 per cent after 18 months.

Table 12.6 Changes in the job patterns of university graduates in the Flemish community (in %)

sector	*diploma obtained in*			
	1964–70	*1971–73*	*1976–78*	*1982–86*
Secondary or high. non-univ. ed.	34.1	29.8	26.0	16.5
University and scientific research	17.9	15.3	13.9	12.3
Civil service	9.7	10.3	9.0	12.6
Private sector	22.1	24.4	26.7	39.9
Liberal professions	16.2	20.2	24.4	18.7
Total	100.0	100.0	100.0	100.0
Absolute numbers	3875	2517	1889	4093

Source: Bossiers 1989.

However, men earn more than women, which is partly attributable to course choices and to the proportion of women holding part-time jobs.

Overall, graduates from tertiary education have a far better chance on the labour market compared to other population categories. Breaking into the market is, however, not easy. Compared with the graduates from higher education institutes, this problem is even more acute for university graduates.

The same is true when comparing the long-term, two cycle programmes to the short-term, single cycle programmes, the latter having better access opportunities to the labour market. Nevertheless, the proportion of higher education graduates among the unemployed remains rather low.

To conclude, as a result of the developments seen on the labour market for diploma-holders and in the study choices of first-year students, there has been a major change in the way politicians, teachers and students see their role in higher non-university and university education. Two consequences of this development are now clearly visible: first, confidence in higher non-university and university education as a guarantee of obtaining a satisfying and well-paid job has declined quite considerably among young people; and second, higher education is becoming increasingly out of step with the world of employment and with the changing economic, social and cultural requirements. In both cases growing pressure is noticeable. Students are urging for more flexible and labour market-oriented training schemes at all levels of higher education. The public authorities and industry are looking to the academic and other higher education circles to make a serious attempt to use resources in a more effective way, based on future requirements for training and research.

The need for a broader basic training – without premature specialisation – allowing for a smoother transition to continuing professional training (including for people with practical experience) has already been recognised but not yet followed up in all fields of higher education.

Internationalisation

In fact, on the topic of internationalisation we can be very brief. All statements and policy papers (e.g. Humblet 1991; Ambtelijke Commissie 1992), as well as the daily experiences of all those involved in higher education, reflect the same influence of the ongoing internationalisation. The mutual exchange between incompatible systems and traditions, stimulated by EC programmes such as the ERASMUS scheme, is leading to a growing awareness of the need for greater flexibility (Neave 1988). Recent legislation in the Flemish community has brought higher education into line with European Directives. These remove all restrictions to the free movement of persons within the European Community, and even include a translation of the university teaching and learning programmes into a newly developed credit system. At present two systems are operated at the same time, which inevitably leads to confusion. However, a path towards the future has been laid.

New principles for teaching and learning in the Flemish community

After several attempts to change the legislation on higher education under the former national regime prior to 1989, the Flemish community took up the challenge of realising this change immediately after gaining autonomy on educational matters. Modifications of the higher education system induced a new discussion about the triple structure of higher education.

In June 1991 two Acts were passed aimed at bringing about a fundamental reorganisation of academic education (i.e. university education). First of all, new relations were established between the universities and the authorities, based on greater autonomy and local financial responsibility (Wielemans and Vanderhoeven 1991). From now on, universities will receive 50 per cent of their funding according to the number of students on 1 February of the previous academic year. The other 50 per cent is fixed and varies depending on the index of consumer prices and wage costs. This way, spending is more stable and long-term planning easier. No perfect solution for rationalising the educational programmes offered by the different universities has yet been found. Rationalisation and programming standards were set up for financing reasons only (a shift towards an expenditure-driven policy). This policy has been confirmed in the 1994 legislation (Decree dated 13 July 1994) stating the large scale merger in higher education outside the universities.

The old system of *ex ante* supervision by the authorities has been replaced by an *ex post* system. It is based on the idea that universities and higher education institutes are capable of independent management. However, in view of their responsibility towards society, a general form of quality control and supervision of the educational content have been introduced via 'visitation committees' for peer review. Despite this the inspectorate still has a more intensive involvement in the quality control of the single cycle courses. This may be only a relic from the old times with their strong links between secondary education and the short-term system, as indicated. An attempt to replace the traditional inspection functions in the field of tertiary education has failed.

The academic education map was redrawn in 18 branches of study, including an overall number of about 80 acknowledged study programmes (academic degrees and diplomas). Postgraduate programmes are also structured: complementary training, specialisation, doctoral training and academic teacher training. Students can follow courses on a full-time or part-time basis, which may be of either the face-to-face or open university type. For the time being, training remains divided into cycles and years. But each year (four to a maximum of seven, depending on the branch of study) consists of between 1500 to 1800 periods and other activities. Together, they provide 60 'study points'.

In October 1991 another Decree was passed relating to the long-term higher education, confirmed in the 1994 Decree. Although it will not be integrated into the universities, it provides education of an 'academic level'. In general, two cycle education observes the same rules as academic education. The main new element is the much greater autonomy of two cycle institutions, backed up – first and foremost – by overall package financing.

The new rules also introduce a more flexible system for transitions between the different levels of training. Apart from a number of very general principles, the actual responsibility is in the hands of the institutions themselves. The 1994 Decree opened up the possibility for doctoral training at the universities for students who have completed their studies in a two cycle higher education institute.

The 1994 legislation aimed for the reorganisation of higher education 'outside the university'. The financing mechanism will be adapted to encourage institutes to create larger multitechnical 'high schools', integrating both types within the same institute. In any case the authorities want to decouple short-term, single cycle higher education completely from secondary schooling. At the same time it is hoped that economies of scale will help to reinforce the basis for quality development in teaching and learning, as well as keeping the higher education budget under control in the future.

Conclusion

Teaching and learning in Belgian higher education have undergone virtually no dramatic changes over the last thirty years. An 'epoch-making' law on integrating the higher education system was not efficient enough to revitalise the system in relation to its environment. The successful expansion of the system and the demand-led policy sustaining it ultimately contributed to the replacement of traditional policies by expenditure-driven decisions (at least in the Flemish community; the French-speaking community is expected to echo similar trends).

CHAPTER 13

Changes in Danish Higher Education in the 1980s

Poul Bache

Higher education in Denmark: general features

In Danish post-secondary education there are study programmes at three different levels:

- shorter programmes of one to two years, very often including practical vocational training
- medium-level programmes of three to four years, for example teacher training, engineering, social work or business studies
- long programmes of normally six years leading to the *kandidat* degree. Graduates with the *kandidat* degree can go on with postgraduate programmes leading to the PhD degree.

Post-secondary education is offered at a variety of educational institutions, which can be divided into three main sectors: the university sector, the college sector and vocational schools.

The university sector

This sector consists of the five Danish universities and 13 other university-level institutions (*højere læreanstalter*) concentrated in the larger Danish towns, in particular in the Copenhagen and Århus areas. These institutions are the only institutions which are entitled to offer courses for the *kandidat* and PhD degrees, and they undertake research as well as teaching.

Traditionally, the *kandidat* degree has been the first degree at Danish universities, and until recently the university sector did not – with a very few exceptions – offer courses shorter than the (minimum) five-year courses for the *kandidat* degree.

As a rule a university course now consists of a three-year Bachelor's degree course, followed by a two-year course leading to a Master's degree. In most cases, a degree subject is a self-contained structure which students choose at the start of their studies.

The college sector

Higher educational programmes shorter than the long degree courses in the university sector have traditionally been reserved for institutions which were specialised in middle-level educational programmes.

There are 90 of these institutions, which are almost all very small compared with universities, and which only offer education within a very narrow range of subjects. The institutions are spread over the whole country. Typical examples of such colleges are colleges of engineering, teacher training colleges, pre-school teacher colleges, colleges of social work and colleges of physiotherapy and ergonomics.

Vocational schools

Schools for vocational training have as their main task vocational training and education at upper-secondary level. In addition, these institutions offer courses at tertiary level. Many of the tertiary-level courses are primarily used as further training for persons with a basic vocational training, but in recent years courses of this type have received an increasing number of school leavers from the upper-secondary schools.

Changes in higher education study programmes

It has often been argued that higher education institutions are conservative by nature and that innovation in higher education is a difficult process (van Vught 1989).

In Denmark, the need for educational reforms in higher education has regularly been stressed in reports commissioned by the Minister for Education (Christensen 1983; Larsen-Udvalget 1985) during the 1970s and 1980s. The similarity of the recommendations of these reports suggests that educational innovation is a slow process.

But innovation does occur in Danish higher education. Many new higher education courses have been set up in Denmark throughout the 1980s, and many of the existing courses have undergone more or less substantial changes. Observers have even talked about sweeping reforms and of turbulence and confusion in higher education institutions (Conrad 1990). How many changes have actually been brought about and how radical have they been? Who took the initiative in bringing about these changes? What was the aim and what was the result? In this paper, we will try to give an answer to these questions.

In the first section of the paper we will try to give a general overview of the most important changes in study programmes in the university and colleges sectors. We will focus on:

- the establishment of new study programmes
- the discontinuation of existing programmes
- major changes in the structure and contents of existing programmes.

In the second section we will present four cases as illustrations of the more general trends in Danish higher education.

The legal framework

The legislative basis of study programmes offered at higher education institutions of the university sector is the University Administration Act, which empowers the Minister for Education to lay down regulations for individual study programmes. The Act does not comprise any provisions about the structure and contents of the programmes. Framework provisions of a similar nature can be found in the Act on engineering colleges and the Act on business schools. In some areas, primarily in the area of teacher training, legislation does, however, contain provisions about the structure and content of courses. Educational changes are thus only in exceptional cases a legislative matter.

The Ministry of Education and Research lays down overall guidelines for individual courses in ministerial orders or regulations which contain provisions about aims, duration, structure, main contents, examinations and so on.

In the case of some courses, ministerial orders contain rather detailed provisions about the organisation of programmes, but a great and ever-growing part of the orders are framework orders which lay down the overall framework of the programmes without containing any more detailed provisions about their organisation.

Within the framework of the orders, the individual educational institution as a main rule draws up a curriculum which describes contents and structure of the programme. In a number of cases, quite considerable changes have been implemented through changes in curricula within the framework of the orders. A survey of major implemented educational measures can thus not be based solely on a stocktaking of adopted changes to acts and orders.

A survey of educational change

Drawing up a list of adopted changes to curricula would be a very substantial task which would only be of limited interest in the context of this paper, as a great number of changes are adjustments of a more routine nature.

The following survey has instead been based on information about educational changes found in two official publications during the period 1980 to 1990. The publications, which provide information to applicants for higher education courses, are *Vejledningsavisen*, issued by the Ministry of Education, and *Studie- og Erhvervsvalget*, issued by the Council for Education and Vocational Guidance. The latter contains information on all higher education study programmes in Denmark, while the former gives information on recent changes and developments in higher education study programmes and admission rules.

It may be reasonably supposed that all substantial educational changes are described in these publications. More than 90 changes were registered for the period 1980–1990, the distribution of which over disciplines and institutional sectors is shown in Table 13.1.

By far the majority of changes – approximately 75 per cent – took place within the university sector, and a considerable part of these changes affected social sciences programmes. There were a relatively high number of changes within the humanities, natural sciences and technical sciences courses, but considerably fewer changes in the areas of health education and teacher training.

The formal basis for changes

As mentioned earlier, changes in the higher education sector normally do not require any legislation. Only three cases have been registered which have involved the passing of legislation. A great number of the

Table 13.1 Registered educational changes in the period 1980–1990 distributed on educational area and institutional sector

	University sector	*College sector*
General	1	0
Humanities	10	2
Social sciences	34	3
Natural sciences	19	1
Technical sciences	4	10
Health education	3	2
Education	0	2
Total	71	20

Source: Undervisningsministeriet 1980–1990.

changes were brought about by the Ministry of Education issuing new orders or revising already existing orders. Furthermore, there were a number of cases where an educational change required the approval of the Ministry, although changes in the educational orders were not necessary.

A total of 54 cases were registered where the formal decision about the change of a course has been made in the Ministry of Education.

In 37 cases, changes were implemented in the form of the establishment of a new curriculum or changes in already existing curricula. Such changes could normally be carried out by the institutions themselves without the formal approval of the Ministry. It is however possible for the Ministry to exert an influence on such changes through its control of the intake to the programmes and the distribution of grants. The institutions therefore often discussed these changes with the Ministry or its advisory bodies, although this was not a formal requirement.

The total number of changes in curricula made in the period in question is much greater than the cases registered here. Changes in ministerial orders will always require changes in the affected curricula. For example, the change in the order on humanities courses of the universities in 1985 in itself led to changes in approximately 130 curricula at humanities faculties.

To this should be added the frequent current adjustments of curricula which are carried out by the institutions but which do not lead to any fundamental changes in courses.

The formal basis for the changes may be summarised as follows:

Legislation	3
Changes in ministerial orders etc.	54
Changes in curricula	37
Total	94

Scope of the changes

Educational changes can be carried through as major educational reforms which comprise a significant part of the education system or they can be limited to one single or a few courses in one single or a few institutions.

General educational reforms

During the period in question, two educational reforms were carried through which led to changes for many of the higher education institutions.

One was the introduction of a system of open education which was introduced by statute in 1990. Open education concerns part-time education programmes organised for adults in full-time employment. These courses may be existing courses offered as part-time courses or courses specifically developed for this purpose. Institutions which offer open education courses are allocated a grant by the Ministry of Education with a fixed amount per registered student. But, as opposed to what is the general rule in the higher education sector in Denmark, there is also a certain contribution required from the students themselves, typically amounting to around 20 per cent of the costs involved.

Today, by and large all institutions in the university sector and a great part of the other higher education institutions offer open education courses. As the Act on open education implies that open education shall be organised, administered and financed in a different way from the ordinary courses, the Act has resulted in considerable educational innovations at the institutions involved. The institutions' development of new study programmes under the auspices of the open education system is not registered in this survey.

The second general reform was the introduction of the Bachelor's degree which was established by ministerial order in 1988. This reform, which ended many years of debate about the need for such a degree in Denmark, led to the introduction of a Bachelor's degree awarded on completion of three years of studies in all courses in the university sector which usually are of five years duration.

All students who complete the first three years of a university course are awarded the Bachelor's degree, and therefore, the reform did not imply a direct change in the individual courses. But it was the aim of the Ministry that the first three years of the courses were gradually to be organised as regular bachelor degree programmes as the individual curricula were being revised. This was the case in the humanities and natural sciences faculties of the universities as well as with a number of other courses. Some of the changes in existing courses which were registered in the survey comprised, among other things, the establishment of an actual Bachelor's degree programme as the first part of an already existing long cycle university degree programme.

Specific educational reforms

In a number of cases, there was a change to the general framework of a course or a type of course existing at several institutions. As a rule, such changes are brought about through changes of the education orders.

Sixteen specific educational reforms of this kind were registered. Of these, 13 were changes to existing programmes, two were the establishment of new programmes and one the discontinuation of a programme.

Two reforms were brought about by legislation, whereas the remainder were brought about as amendments to orders and regulations.

Other changes

In 11 cases, changes were registered which affected several but not all institutions offering a certain programme. Four of these cases concerned the establishment of new programmes in a cooperation between two institutions, each of which are responsible for a part of the programme. Finally, 66 per cent of the registered changes only concern one educational institution.

Different types of change

The registered changes can be distributed as follows:

The establishment of a new programme	57
Change to an existing programme	27
The discontinuation of a programme	8
General reforms	2
Total	94

As shown above, eight cases were registered by which a course was discontinued. In six cases, the initiative was taken by the Ministry in the form of a decision to the effect that there would no longer be any intake of new students to the course in question. In one of these cases, the reason for the decision of closing down the course was criticism of the quality of the course in question. In the remaining five cases, the background has been a wish to concentrate a certain subject area in fewer educational institutions. In two cases, an educational institution has taken the initiative for the discontinuation of a course.

Changes in existing programmes

Twenty-seven cases were registered where an existing programme was changed. These cases were typically changes in the duration of a programme or more substantial changes in the structure or content of the programme. Twenty-one of them took place in the university sector; 12 of them were specific educational reforms which concerned a certain type of course at all institutions where it was offered.

As previously mentioned, the structural reform of the humanities university courses in 1985 led to a change in approximately 130 curricula at the humanities faculties of four universities. The introduction of the Bachelor's degree in 1990 led to a similar number of changes in the curricula, and in the same way, the reform of the university natural sciences programmes led to a change in approximately 50 curricula of five universities.

As a consequence of the specific educational reforms, programmes in the university sector, with very few exceptions, changed considerably at least once in the period from 1980 to 1990.

These reforms reflect the policies of the Ministry. In particular, it has had the following objectives:

- a better adaptation to the labour market through greater flexibility in curricula
- a reduction of expenses through a reduction of the duration of the programmes (in a few cases there has, however, been an increase in the duration) or through a reduction of particularly cost-demanding parts of the courses
- a harmonisation of the educational structure.

As a result of these reforms, almost all programmes in the university sector have the same structure. In general they consist of five-year *kandidat* programmes (Master's programmes), divided into three-year Bachelor's degree programmes and two-year postgraduate programmes. (Cases illustrating this development are found in the last section of this paper.) There are, however, still a few *kandidat* programmes which last longer than five years, and there are still courses where Bachelor's degree programmes have not been created.

New programmes

In the period from 1980 to 1990, 57 new programmes were registered. As Table 13.2 shows, these were not distributed evenly over all disciplines.

Table 13.2 Number of new programmes per discipline

	Number of programmes existing in 1980	*Number of new programmes*	*Increase in %*
Humanities	177	11	6
Social sciences	36	18	50
Natural sciences	38	17	45
Technical sciences	22	6	23
Health education	17	0	0
Education	5	0	0
Total	295	52	18

By far the majority of the new programmes were set up in the university sector. These courses are – with a few exceptions – organised as five-year programmes culminating in the award of the *kandidat* degree. In a number of cases, the Ministry required that the programmes were divided into a three-year Bachelor's degree programme and a two-year postgraduate programme leading to the *kandidat* degree. Since 1988, this has been compulsory. The new programmes which were set up in the medium-cycle higher education sector are of three years' duration.

A great part of the new programmes are combination programmes, i.e. programmes which combine elements from two and sometimes more university subjects in a new way. By doing this, these combination programmes aim to provide new skills, based on the assumption that there is a need on the labour market for qualifications which cut across the traditional disciplines. According to their contents, the new programmes have distributed themselves on the following main groups:

A number of programmes were set up with a special emphasis placed on computer science. These are typically combination courses where computer science is combined with another natural sciences or social sciences subject.

These programmes were established in the first half of the 1980s when there was a shortage of computer scientists on the labour market. The computer science departments of the universities had a very lim-

Computer science combinations	11
Biotechnology	5
Internationalisation	12
Economics combinations	9
Other	15
Total	52

ited capacity and so, during this period, the Ministry and its advisers urged the institutions to set up courses with a computer science content.

In the last half of the 1980s, the government initiated a major biotechnological research programme. In order to ensure recruitment of researchers for the programme, the Ministry of Education stimulated the establishment of a corresponding education programme which aimed to increase the number of graduates in biotechnology. During this period, several institutions set up new programmes in related subjects.

Twelve new programmes were registered with, in different ways, an international orientation, and which seek to take into account the increasing internationalisation of the labour market. Most of these programmes are combinations which combine language and culture studies with, for instance, economics or technology. In several cases, study periods abroad constitute a compulsory part of the course, and a major or minor part of the teaching may take place in a foreign language. In addition to these computer science and international relations-based combination courses nine new combination programmes were also set up combining economics and business studies with another discipline, such as mathematics or law.

Of the 52 new courses which were registered as having been established during the period from 1980 to 1990, five have been discontinued, and one has changed considerably. The reason for this has in all of the cases been a falling influx of students.

In Denmark, there is no systematic evaluation of new courses, but some have been evaluated – in some cases on the Ministry's initiative and in others on the initiative of the institution in question. In no case has a new course been discontinued as a result of an evaluation.

The initiative for changes

The implementation of educational changes is a process in which several actors take part. The most important actors are politicians, the Ministry of Education, the advisers of the Ministry, the labour market and the institutions of higher education.

Politicians

The government and Parliament were involved in a small number of cases where it was necessary to pass legislation. Apart from these cases, parliamentarians have only very rarely taken any initiatives for or in any other way occupied themselves with bringing about changes in higher education. Local politicians have just as rarely committed themselves to questions relating to changes in courses offered by local educational institutions.

The Ministry of Education

A significant number of the changes, as mentioned, required the Ministry's approval. The Ministry has also often taken the initiative in bringing about changes in courses.

Advisers of the Ministry

During the period in question, the Ministry had advisory boards (until 1989 the advisory committees to the Ministry of Education) of the higher education courses as advisers in questions relating to higher education. There were five such advisory boards, one for each of the following areas: the humanities, the social sciences, the natural sciences, the technical sciences and health education. The members of the boards were experts in the field of education and labour market relations, and came from educational institutions and businesses and organisations outside the education sector. These advisory boards often played a significant role in changes which were brought about on the initiative of the Ministry, and the advisory boards themselves also often took initiatives for changes.

Besides the advisory boards, the Ministry also in some cases looked for advice from *ad hoc* committees or individual experts.

The labour market

As mentioned, there were labour market representatives on the advisory boards. Beyond this, businesses, labour market organisations, professional bodies, authorities and individuals outside the education sector played a role of varying importance in connection with changes; a role which was often of an informal nature. The Ministry often insisted that the proposals of the institutions for the setting up of new courses be submitted to the users so that the approval of the Ministry could depend on the result of this consultation, but this procedure was used in all cases.

Institutions of higher education

The higher education institutions in the university sector enjoy considerable autonomy when it comes to contents and organisation of courses. Curricula are drawn up by the institutions and do not normally have to be approved by the Ministry. According to the 1990 Administration of the Institutions of Higher Education Act, the universities shall consider proposals for new or amended education orders and, accordingly, proposals for amendments to education orders often originate from the institutions (Administrations of Personaledepartementet 1990).

Origins of new programmes

The initiative for the establishment of new programmes most frequently came from the educational institutions themselves. In the 52 cases mentioned above, the initiative was distributed as follows:

Institutions	34
Institutions and the Ministry	6
The Ministry	7
The labour market	3
Total	52

It is remarkable that the labour market only in three instances was registered as the originator – especially in view of the fact that many new programmes aimed to respond to presumed new needs of the market.

Whereas employers are represented on the boards of the majority of the institutions in the medium cycle higher education sector, they do not have any formalised influence on programmes of the university sector. The many new programmes must therefore to a large extent be regarded as an attempt by institutions to adapt to an anticipated development in the labour market and the Ministry's demand for labour market-oriented programmes.

Background for change in higher education

Institutions in the university sector enjoy a rather high degree of autonomy when it comes to the organisation of study programmes, and this is part of the background for the relatively many innovations which have taken place in the university sector. In the medium cycle higher education sector, where the number of changes has been fewer, the degree of freedom of institutions is also less significant.

The limited number of changes within the areas of health education and teacher training correspondingly reflect the fact that institutions in these areas are bound by rather detailed ministerial orders for courses.

The relatively high number of new programmes and changes in the university sector can be seen as an element of the universities' adaptation to new requirements from the surrounding world, primarily the labour market, the students and the political system.

Economic factors

Higher education in Denmark is 100 per cent government funded. In the last half of the 1980s the Government made an annual general 2 per cent cut in expenditure.

The Ministry's funding of higher education institutions has depended mainly on the number of active students. Therefore, if institutions wanted to avoid decreasing funds, they had to increase the number of students. The Ministry has furthermore allocated earmarked grants to institutions for the development of new education programmes. Thus, institutions have had a financial incentive for educational changes which could attract more students.

Adaptation to the labour market and the choices of students

Some of the new programmes are an expression of attempts to offer programmes which are more adapted to the labour market. At the beginning of the 1980s, a relatively large and increasing unemployment problem affected many types of university graduates, and as a result the Ministry of Education reduced the number of study places in those programmes where the employment prospects were most unfavourable. In addition, the choices of students did to some extent favour the courses with better employment prospects. In order to counteract this development, a number of new courses of education were developed by the institutions and a number of changes were brought about in already existing courses, in particular in the humanities and social sciences faculties of the universities.

Some faculties – particularly the technical/natural sciences faculties of universities and engineering colleges – have had difficulties in attracting a sufficient number of qualified students. In order to increase the intake universities and engineering colleges have set up a number of new courses, aiming to make the technical/natural sciences courses more attractive and to extend the recruitment basis by creating courses which appeal to females.

Conclusion

As we have seen, changes in Danish higher education have only in very few cases been subject to legislation. The actors of the labour market – the employers and various organisations – have played an important but mostly very indirect role. The main actors in the process of change have been the institutions and the Ministry of Education.

Many of the changes can be seen as results of ministerial policies. From the point of view of the institutions, frequent changes in higher education have often been described as a result of an increasingly centralised steering from the Ministry (Administrations- og Personaledepartementet 1990; Hansen 1991). Seen from the Ministry, on the other hand, the last half of the 1980s was characterised by increased autonomy of institutions in educational matters (Undervisningsministeriet 1990b).

Ministerial regulation of the framework of the study programmes was much less detailed in 1990 than it was in 1980. So in this respect a real decentralisation had, at least formally, taken place. But, on the other hand, frequent budget cuts and the Ministry's tendency to detailed financial steering, especially in the mid-1980s, explain why institutions tend to see many educational innovations as a result of pressure from above, giving little choice to the institution.

However, the steering by the Ministry must not be exaggerated. Ministerial policies have been an important force behind educational changes, but not all policies have succeeded. For instance, the attempts to establish medium cycle programmes at universities, which have had high priority in the Ministry's policies since the mid-1970s, have not found any substantial success. In this, as in other cases, universities have been able to withstand the pressure for change.

Important traditional values and attitudes concerning the essential mission of the university have been preserved. For instance, the view that university education must be based on research and must be of long duration (five years at least) is still predominant. But at the same time university attitudes to the relationship with the outside world have obviously changed considerably. The many institutional career guidance services, employer-contact programmes, PR-activities and so on which have been introduced by universities in the 1980s, illustrate this.

This paper has not dealt with the internal institutional decision-making processes behind educational changes. Such an analysis would probably have shown a shift towards 'market-orientation' and a growing emphasis on effective management. A running debate on university leadership and decision-making procedures (Administrations- og Personaledepartementet 1990; Uddannelse 1991), shows that within universities there is a growing demand for more efficient institutional management. Universities have since the early 1970s been governed by representative bodies, elected by staff and students. This system is now under criticism for being inadequate to manage the complex relationships between universities and the outside world.

The Contributors

Inés Alberdi
Complutense University, Madrid

Poul Bache
Ministry of Education, Copenhagen

Ronald Barnett
Institute of Education, University of London

Tony Becher
Department of Education, University of Sussex

Ewald Berning
Bavarian State Institute for Research on Higher Education, Munich

Patrick Clancy
Department of Sociology, University College Dublin

Claudius Gellert
Faculty of Education, University of Reading

Eduardo Marçal Grilo
Calouste Gulbenkian Foundation, Lisbon

Mary Henkel
Department of Government, Brunel University, London

Maurice Kogan
Department of Government, Brunel University, London

Emilio Lamo de Espinosa
Complutense University, Madrid

Peter A.M. Maassen
Centre for Higher Education Policy Studies, University of Twente, Enschede

Roberto Moscati
Department of Sociology, University of Trieste

Guy Neave
International Association of Universities, Paris

Stefanos Pesmazoglou
University of Social and Political Sciences, Athens

Einhard Rau
Faculty of Education, Free University of Berlin

Johan L. Vanderhoeven
Centre for Comparative Education, Catholic University, Leuven

Egbert de Weert
Centre for Higher Education Policy Studies, University of Twente, Enschede

References

Administrations- og Personaledepartementet (1990) *Modernisering af universiteternes ledelse – en turnusundersøgelse*. København: Undervisningsministeriet.

Ambtelijke Commissie (1992) *Eindrapport hoger onderwijs buiten de universiteit*. Brussels: Departement Onderwijs.

Arbeitsgemeinschaft für Hochschuldidaktik (1990) *Bielefelder Memorandum zur Stärkung der Qualität der Lehre in den Hochschulen*. Bielefeld: AFH.

Asdrachas, S. (1988) 'From the need of history, to the need of forming historians.' *Synchrona Themata*, special issue, 96–97.

Augusti, G. (1991) 'Il Caso Ingegneria.' In *Universitas 39*, Gennaio-Marzo, 26–30.

Baeck, L. (1987) *Universitaire opleiding en arbeidsmarkt*. Brussels: Universitaire Stichting.

Baldridge, J.V., Curtis, D.V. Ecker, G. and Riley, G.L. (1978) *Policy Making and Effective Leadership*. London: Jossey-Bass.

Barnett, R. (1992) *Improving Higher Education: Total Quality Control*. Buckingham: Open University Press.

Becher, T. (1989a) *Academic Tribes and Territories*. Milton Keynes: Open University Press.

Becher, T. (1989b) 'Historians on history.' *Studies in Higher Education 14*, 3, 263–279.

Becher, T. (1990) 'Physicists on physics.' *Studies in Higher Education 15*, 1, 3–20.

Becher, T. (1992) 'Graduate education in Britain: the view from the ground.' In B.R. Clark. (ed) *The Research Foundations of Graduate Education*. Berkeley: University of California Press.

Becher, T. and Kogan, M. (1991) *Process and Structure in Higher Education*. London: Routledge.

Becker, K. (1934) *The Heavenly City of the Eighteenth Century Philosophers*. New York.

Berning, E. (1992) *Corsi post laurea e post diploma nelle universitàe Fachhochschulen in Germania*. Milano: Fondazione Rui.

Bernstein, B. (1971) 'On the classification of educational knowledge.' In M.F.D. Young (ed) *Knowledge and Control*. New York: Collier- Macmillan.

Bossiers, G. (1989) 'RUG-Enquête over tewerkstelling bij ruim 4000 universitair afgestudeerden.' *Intermediar 20*, 43, 1–4.

Boys, C.J., Brennan, J., Henkel, M., Kirkland, J., Kogan, M. and Youll, P. (1988) *Higher Education and the Preparation for Work*. London: Jessica Kingsley Publishers. Summarised under the same title in CNAA Development Services Project Report 23.

Brennan, J. (1991) *Graduate Experiences in the United Kingdom Labour Market.* London: Council for National Academic Awards (mimeo). Paper given at a joint seminar held at Sigtuna, Sweden, June 1991 by the Department of Education, Uppsala University and the Centre for the Evaluation of Public Policy, Brunel University.

Brennan, J. and Henkel, M. (1988) 'Economics.' In C.J. Boys *et al. Higher Education and the Preparation for Work.* London: Jessica Kingsley Publishers.

Bundesminister für Bildung und Wissenschaft (1992) *Grund- und Strukturdaten (1991/92)*. Bonn: BMBW.

Butler, R. (1983) 'The control and management of higher education in Great Britain, with special reference to the role of the University Grants Committee and the Committee of Vice-Chancellors and Principals.' *Oxford Review of Education 8*, 3.

CERI (1996) *Education at a Glance. OECD Indicators.* Paris: OECD.

Christensen, J.P. (1983) *De Højere Uddannelser som Politisk Problem.* København.

CIHE (Council for Industry and Higher Education) (1987) *Towards a Partnership, Higher Education-Government-Industry.* London: CIHE.

CIHE (Council for Industry and Higher Education) (1990) *Collaborative Courses in Higher Education*. London: CIHE.

Clancy, P. (1990) 'Selection for college: some implications for second level.' *Compass: Journal for the Irish Association for Curriculum Development 19*, 1, 7–23.

Clancy, P. (1993) 'Goal Enlargement and Differentiation: The Evolution of the Binary System in Ireland.' In C. Gellert (ed) *Higher Education in Europe*. London: Jessica Kingsley Publishers, 122–134.

Clark, B.R. (1983) *The Higher Education System: Academic Organisation in Cross-National Perspective*. Berkeley: University of California Press.

Clark, B.R. (ed) (1993) *The Research Foundations of Graduate Education: Germany, Britain, France, United States, Japan*. Berkeley: University of California Press.

CNAA (Council for National Academic Awards) (1990) *CNAA Annual Report 1989–90.* London: CNAA.

Conrad, J. (1990) 'Prospects for the 1990s: necessary renewal or alarming change in the Danish higher education system.' *European Journal of Education 25*, 2.

Consejo de Universidades (1986) *Las Enseñanzas Universitarias en España y en la Comunidad Economica Europea*. Madrid: Ministerio de Educación.

Consejo de Universidades (1987) *El Mercado de Trabajo de los Titulados Universitarios en España*. Madrid: Ministerio de Educación.

Consejo de Universidades (1990) *Titulaciones Universitarias Directrices Generales Propias*. Madrid: Ministerio de Educación.

Consejo de Universidades (1991) *Anuario de Estadistica Universitaria 1990*. Madrid: Ministerio de Educación.

Coolahan, J. (1981) *Irish Education: Its History and Structure*. Dublin: Institute of Public Administration.

Courtois, G. (1991) 'Le Plan Jospin: simplification des filières, renforcement de l'orientation et modules capitalisables en premier cycle.' *Le Monde*, 26 June.

Croham Report (1987) *Review of the University Grants Committee*, Report of the Committee Under the Chairmanship of Lord Croham, Cm 81. London: HMSO.

Dahrendorf, R. (1965) *Bildung ist Bürgerrecht*. Hamburg: Nannen.

Dallinger, P., Bode, C. and Gieseke, L. (1978) *Kommentar zum Hochschulrahmengesetz*. Tübingen: Mohr.

Davies, J. (1985) 'The agenda for university management in the next decade.' In G. Lockwood and J. Davies *Universities: The Management Challenge*. Windsor: Society for Research in Higher Education and NFER-Nelson.

Deleeck, H. and Storms, B. (1989) 'Blijvende ongelijkheid in het onderwijs: tien jaar later.' *De Gids op maatschappelijk gebied*, 80, 1119–1138.

Department of Education (1989) *Full Time Courses in VEC Colleges: Report of a Committee Established to Examine Third-Level Courses Which Lead to Awards By NCEA and Other Bodies Outside the Universities*. Unpublished.

Department of Employment, White Paper (1991) *Enterprise in Higher Education. Key Features in Enterprise in Higher Education. 1990–1991*. (This report, collated by the Employment Department, is based in part on reports of independent evaluations made by the Tavistock Institute of Human Relations (1989) and the National Foundation for Educational Research (1990). It is difficult, however, to see which parts of the document derive from these independent studies, or from other academic works which are inadequately referenced in the text.)

Der Bundesminister für Bildung und Wissenschaft (1988) *Grund- und Strukturdaten*. Ausgabe 1988/89. Bonn: BMBW.

Dertilis, G. (1988) 'University teaching of history.' *Synchrona Themata*, special issue.

DES (Department of Education and Science), White Paper (1987) *Higher Education, Meeting the Challenge*, Cm 114, London: HMSO.

DES (Department of Education and Science), White Paper (1991) *Higher Education: A New Framework*, Cmd 1541. London: HMSO.

Deutscher Akademischer Austauschdienst (1992) *Studying in Germany*. Bonn: DAAD.

Diakoulakis, N. (1991) 'Introduction.' In *The Education of the Chemical Engineer in Greece*. Athens: TUA.

Doumenc, M. and Gilly, J.P. (1977) *Les IUTs: Idéologie et Ouverture*. Paris: Editions du Cerf.

Dusch, M. and Müllner, W. (1989) *Diplomarbeiten als Instrument des Wissens- und Technologietransfers zwischen Fachhochschulen und Unternehmen,* Studien zu Bildung und Wissenschaft 75, Bonn.

Economics University of Athens (1990) *The Faculty Staff of our University.* Athens: Economics University of Athens.

Economics University of Athens (1991) *Brief Guide to Studies.* (mimeo). Athens: Economics University of Athens.

Ellwein, T. (1985) *Die Deutsche Universität vom Mittelater bis zur Gegenwart.* München: Athenäum.

Etzold, S. (1992) 'Miwirtschaft an der Uni.' *Die Zeit,* 29.05.1992, 37.

Fachhochschulführer (1989) *Ständige Konferenz der Rektoren und Präsidenten der staatl. Fachhochschulen der Länder in der Bundesrepublik Deutschland.* Frankfurt/New York: Campus.

Fragniere, G. (1978) 'Changes in the structure and contents of courses.' *Paedagogica Europaea, xiii,* 1, 107–120.

Fulton, O. 'Equality and higher education.' In B.R. Clark and G. Neave (eds) *Encylopedia of Higher Education, Vol.ii.* Oxford: Pergamon Press.

Furth, D. (ed) (1973) *Short Cycle Higher Education: Identity and Crisis.* Paris: OECD.

Garin, C. (1989) 'Renforcer l'autonomie des établissements.' *Le Monde de l'Education,* No.144, October, 20–22.

Gellert, C. (1988) *Vergleich des Studiums an Englischen und Deutschen Universitäten.* Frankfurt: Peter Lang.

Gellert, C. (1991a) 'Andersartig, aber gleichwertig. Anmerkungen zur Funktionsbestimmung der Fachhochschulen.' *Beiträge zur Hochschulforschung* 1/1991, 1–26.

Gellert, C. (1991b) 'Higher education: changing tasks and definitions.' *Higher Education in Europe XVI,* 3, 28–45.

Gellert, C. *The Changing Functions of the European Universities.* Florence: Mimeo.

Goguel, F. (1946) *La Politique des Partis sous la 11Iè, Republique.* Paris: Armand Colin.

Guin, J. (1990) 'The re-awakening of higher education in France.' *European Journal of Education 25,* 2, 123–146.

Hannan, D.F. *et al.* (1983) *Schooling and Sex Roles.* Dublin: Economic and Social Research Institute.

Hansen, H.F. (1991) *Danske FoU-institutioners organisering.* Handelshøjskolen i København, COS.

Hecquet, I. (1984) 'Prospects for revitalising the Belgian University system.' *European Journal of Education 19*, 2, 131–149.

Henkel, M. (1990) 'Higher education and the preparation for work.' *Higher Education Policy 3*, 4.

Henkel, M. and Kogan, M. (1992) 'Research training and graduate education: the British macrostructure.' In B.R. Clark (ed) *The Research Foundations of Graduate Education.* Berkeley: University of California Press.

Hering, G. (1989) 'Teaching history in the German-speaking zone: some comparisons with the Greek university.' *Synchrona Themata,* (in Greek).

Higher Education Authority (1985) *General Report 1974–1984.* Dublin: Higher Education Authority.

HIS Hochschul-Informations System (1990) *Hochschulstudium in der DDR, Statistischer Überblick.* Hannover: HIS.

Historical Archives of Greek Youth (1989) *Didaktiki kai Historia* (teaching and history). Proceedings of the International Conference, Panepistimio: Ideologia kai Paideia (University, Ideology and Education), second volume. Athens, 605–640.

Humblet, J. *et al.* (1991) 'Het hoger onderwijs, harmonisering en differentiëring.' *Persoon en Gemeenschap 43*, 9, 325–342.

Instituto Superior de Economia e Gestao (1991) *Guia 1991–92 Instituto Superior de Economia e Gestao.* Lisboa: Instituto Superior de Economia e Gestao.

Instituto Superior Technico (1991) *Planos de Estudo dos Cursos Ministrados.* Lisboa: Diá ro da República, II Série.

Jallade, J.P. (1992) 'Undergraduate Higher Education in Europe: towards a comparative perspective.' *European Journal of Education 17*, 1/2, 121–144.

Jarratt Report (1985) *Report of the Steering Committee for Efficiency Studies in Universities.* London: CVCP.

Jilek, L. (ed) (1984) *Repertoire Historique des Universités Européennes.* Genéve: Conférence des Recteurs Européens.

Jones, S. (1991) *The Enterprise in Higher Education Initiative* (mimeo). Sigtuna Conference.

Kalogirou, Y., Paöayiannaki, L. and Sacharides, G. (1980) 'The Greek chemical industry on the verge of the 1980s.' *Politis 36*, (in Greek).

Kapsomenos, E. (1991) 'About the reorganisation of the philosophy schools in the university.' *Politis*, July.

Kerr, C. (1982) *The Uses of the University.* Cambridge, Mass: Harvard University Press.

Kessler, M.C. (1978) *La Politique de la Haute Fonction Publique*. Paris: Presses de la Fondation Nationale des Sciences Politiques.

Kirkland, J. (1988) 'Electrical engineering.' In C.J. Boys *et al. Higher Education and the Preparation for Work*. London: Jessica Kingsley Publishers.

Kogan, M. (1988) 'History.' In C.J. Boys *et al. Higher Education and the Preparation for Work*. London: Jessica Kingsley Publishers.

König, R. (1970) *Vom Wesen der deutschen Universität*. Darmstadt: Wiss. Buchgesellschaft.

Lammertyn, F. (1987) 'Sociale ongelijkheid en universiteit.' *Leuvense Perspectieven*. Onze Alma Mater, 14(3), 151–185.

Lammertyn, F. (1992) *De democratisering van het hoger onderwijs buiten de universiteit* (2 Vols). Leuven: Departement Sociologie.

Lamo de Espinosa, E. (1989) 'Educación y Universidad en el horizonte del año 2000.' *Revista de Occidente 97*, 134–156.

Lamo de Espinosa, E. (1993) 'The Spanish university in transition.' In C. Gellert (ed) *Higher Education in Europe*. London: Jessica Kingsley Publishers, 84–96.

Larsen-Udvalget, K. (1985) *Handlingsplan for bedre balance de langvarigt uddannedes arbejdsmarked*. Undervisningsministeriet, Jan. 1985.

Leontaritis, G.B. (1988) 'The permanent – and perhaps insurmountable – crisis of historical studies in Greece.' *Synchrona Themata*, special issue, 122.

Lockwood, G. and Davies, J. (1985) *Universities: The Management Challenge*. Windsor: Society for Research in Higher Education and NFER-Nelson.

Lullies, S. and Berning, E. (1991) *Country Report of the Federal Republic of Germany on Further Education*. Paris: OECD.

Lyman, R. (1991) *The American University: Past, Present and Future*. (mimeo).

Lynton, E.A. and Elman, S.E. (1987) *New Priorities for the University*. London/San Francisco: Jossey-Bass Publishers.

Maassen, P.A.M. and van Vught, F.A. (1989) *Dutch Higher Education in Transition*. Utrecht: LEMMA.

Marçal Grilo, E. (1993) 'The transformation of higher education in Portugal.' In C. Gellert (ed) *Higher Education in Europe*. London: Jessica Kingsley Publishers. 99–108.

Marinos-Kouris, D. (1980) *The Pathology and the Dynamics of Chemical Engineering* (mimeo).

McLean, M. (1990) *Britain and a Single Market Europe. Prospects for a Common School Curriculum*. London: Kogan Page.

Meier, T. (1982) 'Grundsätzliche Dissense. Bundesweite Studienreform am Ende?' *Mitteilungen des Hochschulverbandes 4*, 173–175.

Ministère de l'Education Nationale (1990) *Repères et Références Statistique*. Paris: Ministry of Education.

Ministèrio da Educaçao (1992) *Sistema Educativo Português – Situaçao e Tendências 1990*. Lisboa: Minist,rio da Eduçacao, Gabinete de Estudos e Planeamento.

Moodie, G.C. and Eustace, R. (1974) *Power and Authority in British Universities*. London: Allen and Unwin.

MURST (Ministero dell'Università e della Ricerca Scientifica) (1990) *La Formazione in Ingegneria*. Proceedings of the National Committee, Rome.

National Advisory Board (1987) *Management for a Purpose, The Report of the Good Management Practice Group*. London: NAB.

Neave, G. (1984) 'Démographie de l'enseignement supérieur: Le monis est-il correlaire du mieux?' In CRE, *Dossier du viii, Assemblée Générale de la Conférence Permanente des Recteurs Européens*. Genéve: CRE.

Neave, G. (1984) 'On the road to Silicon Valley? The changing relationship between higher education and government in Western Europe.' *European Journal of Education 19*, 2, 111–129.

Neave, G. (1985) 'France.' In B.R. Clark (ed) *The School and the University: An International Perspective*. Berkeley/Los Angeles/London: University of California Press.

Neave, G. (1988) 'Cross-national collaboration in higher education: new initiatives in European Community Policy.' *Compare 18*, 1, 53–61.

Neave, G. (1990a) 'On preparing for markets: trends in higher education in Western Europe 1988–1990.' *European Journal of Education 25*, 1, 115.

Neave, G. (1990b) 'On preparing for markets.' *European Journal of Education 25*, 2, 114–116.

Neave, G. (1992) 'Into the charmed circle, or the expansion of the nonuniversity sector of higher education in Europe.' *European Education 23*, 4, 45–61.

Neave, G. (1993) 'Séparation de corps. The training of advanced students and the organisation of research in France.' In B.R. Clark (ed) *The Research Foundations of Graduate Education*. Berkeley: University of California Press.

Neave, G. and Rhoades, G. (1987) 'The academic estate in Western Europe.' In B.R. Clark (ed) *The Academic Profession: National, Disciplinary and Institutional Settings*. Berkeley/Los Angeles/London: University of California Press.

Neave, G. and van Vught, F. (eds) (1991) 'Introduction.' In *Prometheus Bound: The Changing Relationship Between Government and Higher Education in Western Europe*. Oxford: Pergamon Press.

OECD (1986) *France: Innovation Policy*. Paris: OECD.

ONISEP (1991) *L'Université Pour Quelles Études*? Paris: ONISEP.

Panhellenic Association of Chemical Engineers and the Technical University of Athens (1991) *The Education of the Chemical Engineer in Greece*, April 1991.

Pesmazoglou, S. (1989) 'Current trends in Greek historiography.' *Modern Greek Studies Yearbook*, University of Minnesota, 493–512.

Picht, G. (1965) *Die Deutsche Bildungskatastrophe*. München: Deutscher Taschenbuchverlag.

Popper, K. (1970) *Die Offene Gesellschaft und Ihre Feinde*. Bern: Francke.

Pratt, J. and Silverman, S. (1986) 'Responses to constraint in higher education: the 1984–85 NAB planning exercise in the English public sector.' *International Journal of Institutional Management in Higher Education, 10,* 3.

Premfors, R. (1980) *The Politics of Higher Education in a Comparative Perspective*. Studies in Politics No.15. Stockholm: University of Stockholm.

Prinborgne, C.D. (1992) 'France.' In B.R. Clark and G. Neave (eds) *Encyclopedia of Higher Education, Vol.i. Countries*. Oxford: Pergamon Press.

Rau, Einhard (1993) 'Inertia and resistance to change of the Humboldtian university.' In C. Gellert (ed) *Higher Education in Europe*. London: Jessica Kingsley Publishers, 37–46.

Roizen, J. and Jepson, M. (1983) *Expectations of Higher Education: An Employer's Perspective*. (mimeo). London: Brunel University.

Schmidt, S. and Schindler, B. (1988) *Beschäftigungschancen für Magisterabsolventen*. München: Bayerische Hochschulforschung Monographien Neue Folge 22.

Schodts, L., Smedts, D. and Hoornaert, J. (1989–1990) *Arbeidsmarkt voor universitairen* (Series). Leuven: Dienst voor Studieadvies K.U.Leuven.

Schramm, Jürgen (1991) 'Hochschulreform und hochschulplanung.' In *FU – Info*, 5/91, Berlin.

Scotford Archer, M. (1978) *The Social Origins of Education Systems*. Beverley Hills/London: Sage.

Scott, P. (1986) 'Efficiency studies in the British universities.' *International Journal of Institutional Management in Higher Education, 10,* 1.

Silver, H. and Brennan, J. (1988) *A Liberal Vocationalism*. London: Methuen.

Sizer, J. (1987) *Institutional Responses to Financial Reductions in the University Sector, Final Report*. London: DES.

Skoulikidis, Th. (1991) 'Modifications in the programme of undergraduate studies in the Department of Chemical Engineers between 1987–1990.' *The Education of the Chemical Engineer in Greece*.

Smedts, D. (1993) *Arbeidsmarkt voor universitairen. 8. Follow-up van K.U.Leuven-afgestudeerden na 5 jaar*. Leuven: Dienst voor Studieadvies K.U.Leuven.

Squires, G. (1987) *The Curriculum Beyond School*. London: Hodder and Stoughton.

Squires, G. (1990) *First Degree: the Undergraduate Curriculum*. Bristol: The Society for Research into Higher Education.

Squires, G. (1990) *First Degree*. Milton Keynes: Open University Press.

Statistisch Jaarboek van het Vlaams Onderwijs. Schooljaar 1994–95 (1996) Brussel: Ministerie van de Vlaamse Gemeenschap – Departement Onderwijs.

Statistisches Bundesamt (1975) *Fachserie 11 Bildung und Kultur, Reihe 4.1 Studenten an Hochschulen*. Stuttgart: W. Kohlhammer.

Synchrona Themata (1988) special issue on contemporary Greek historiography, December 1988, 84–130.

Teichler, U. (1987) ' Higher education and new challenges of the occupation system.' In H. Roehers (ed) *Tradition and Reform of the University Under an International Perspective*. Frankfurt a.M.: Lang, 293–307.

Teichler, U. (1989), 'Government and curriculum innovation in the Netherlands.' In F.A. van Vught (ed) *Governmental Strategies and Innovation in Higher Education*. London: Jessica Kingsley Publishers.

Trow, M. (1973) 'From élite to mass higher education.' In OECD, *Equality of Educational Opportunity*. Paris: OECD.

Tsinorema, V. (1991) 'Social and institutional aspects of the crisis in the universities.' *Politis*, June 1991.

Uddannelse (1991) *En generation af ledelsesmœssige eunukker*. Undervisningsministeriets tidsskrift, 6 1991, Temanummer.

Undervisningsministeriet (1980–1990) *Vejledningsavisen*, issued yearly 1980–90, Copenhagen.

Undervisningsministeriet (1990b) *Det nye mønster i Dansk Uddannelses- og forskningspolitik*. 1990–91, Copenhagen.

Université d'Avignon et des Pays de Vaucluse (1991) *Guide des Etudes*. Avignon: Universit, d'Avignon.

Université de Nancy II (1986) *Guide de l'Etudiant 1986–87*. Nancy: Facult, de Droit, Sciences ,conomiques et gestion, (mineo).

Université de Sciences Sociales Grenoble II (1989) *Guide de l'Etudiant*, (xerox). Grenoble: UER de sciences ,conomiques.

Université Grenbole I (1988) *Livret de l'Étudiant: Guide des Formations Condusiant à un Diplôme d'Etat*. Grenbole: Université Grenoble I.

Ushiogi, M. (1977) *The Changing Industrial Society and Employment of University Graduates*. (Mimeo) Institute for Democratic Education.

USR (1990) *USR Ann Report Students 1989–90*.

van Vught, F.A. (1989) 'Innovations and reforms in higher education.' In van Vught, F.A. (ed) *Governmental Strategies and Innovation in Higher Education*. London: Jessica Kingsley Publishers.

Veeneman, S. (1988) *De historicus aan het werk*. Een onderzoek naar de positie op de arbeidsmarkt van aan de Vrije Universiteit van 1980 tot 1987 afgestudeerde historici, Amsterdam.

VVAA (1988) *La Educación Postsecundaria*. Madrid: Fundación Santillana.

VVAA (1989) *Las Situaciones y Perfil del Desempleo y Subempleo de los Totulados Universitarios*. Madrid: Consejo de Universidades, Ministerio de Educación.

Webler, W.D. (1983) *Geschichte der Hochschule seit 1945*. Enzyklopädie Erziehungswissenschaften Bd. 10. Stuttgart: Klett-Cotta.

Westdeutsche Rektorenkonferenz (1989) *Bildungspolitische Daten*. Bonn: WRK.

Wielemans, W. and Vanderhoeven J.L. (1991) 'Market impact and policy drift: Belgian higher education.' In G. Neave and F. Van Vught (eds) *Prometheus Bound. The Changing Relationship Between Government and Higher Education in Western Europe*. Oxford: Pergamon Press.

Wielemans, W. and Vanderhoeven, J.L. (1993) 'New tasks and roles for higher education in Belgium and Luxembourg.' In C. Gellert (ed) *Higher Education in Europe*. London: Jessica Kingsley Publishers, 152–167.

Wielers, R. (1986) *Historici en Arbeidsmarkt*. Groningen.

Wissenschaftsrat (1988) *Empfehlungen des Wissenschaftsrates zu den Perspektiven der Hochschulen in den 90er Jahren*. Cologne: Wissenschaftsrat.

Wissenschaftsrat (1988) *Higher Education Perspectives in the Nineties*. Cologne: Wissenschaftsrat.

Wissenschaftsrat (1990) *Perspektiven für Wissenschaft und Forschung auf dem Weg zur deutschen Einheit. Zwölf Empfehlungen*. Cologne: Wissenschaftsrat.

Wissenschaftsrat (1991a) *Empfehlungen zur Entwicklung der Fachhochschulen in den 90er Jahren*. Cologne: Wissenschaftsrat.

Wissenschaftsrat (1991b) *Stellungnahmen zu den auáeruniversitären Forschungseinrichtungen in den neuen Ländern und in Berlin*. Cologne: Wissenschaftsrat.

Ylieff, Y. (1990) *L'enseignement de l'An II*. Bruxelles.

Youll, P. (1988) 'Physics.' Chapter 4 in C.J. Boys *et al.* (eds.) *Higher Education and the Preparation for Work*. London: Jessica Kingsley Publishers.

Zentralinstitut für Hochschulbildung (1990) *Hochschulatlas Übersichten zu Ostberliner Hochschulen*. Berlin: ZFH.

Zentralinstitut für Hochschulbildung (1990) *Hochschullandschaft Berlin Leistungs- und Ressourcenentwicklung Ost-Berliner Hoch- und Fachschulen*. Berlin: ZFH.

Further Reading

Andersen, N.O., Olesen, D. and Nielsen, S.E. (1987) *Kandidater i matematik-, fysik- og kemifagene: Hvor gik de hen?* Århus Universitet.

Carabaña, J. (1988) 'Comprehensive educational reforms in Spain: past and present.' *European Journal of Education 23*, 3–213.

Censis, (1986) 'I Nuovi Ingegneri: Percorsi Formativi e Professionali.' *Università Progetto 16*, Novembre, 42–45.

CIDE (1985) *The Spanish Educational System. Report of Spain*. Madrid: CIDE, Ministerio de Educación.

Consejo de Universidades (1989) *La Financiación de la Enseñanza Superior.* Madrid: Ministerio de Educación.

Faculdade de Economia da Universidade (1992) *Guia 1992–93 Universidade Nova, Economia*. Nova de Lisboa: Faculdade de Economia da Universidade.

Garcia de Cortazar, M.L. (1987) *Educación Superior y Empleo en España*. Madrid: Ministerio de Trabajo.

Giner, S. (1972) 'Spain.' In M.S. Archer (ed) *Students, University and Society.* London: Heinemann.

Greco, G. (1986) 'Ingegneria: Storia di una Mancata Riforma.' *Università Progetto 8/9*, Gennaio-Febbraio, 16–26.

International Council for Educational Development (1987) *The Spanish University Reform. An Assessment Report*. Madrid: Consejo de Universidades.

Jallade, J.P. (1991) *L'Enseignement Superieur en Europe*. Paris: La Documentation Française.

Jannaccono-Pazzi, R. and Ribolzi, L. (eds) (1991) *Università Flessibile: Percorsi Universitari Alternativi e Domanda delle Imprese*. Milano: Etas Libri.

Lamo de Espinosa, E. (1986) 'Oferta de Empleo y Planes de Estudio.' *Enseñanza Universitaria y Mercado de Trabajo: el Primer Empleo de los Titulados Universitarios*. Madrid: Fundación Universidad-Empresa, 51–71.

Lloyd Braga, C. (1991) *A Razao Alunos/Docente e a Escolaridade Semanal no Ensino Universitá rio*. Lisboa: Secretaria de Estado do Ensino Superior.

Lygeros, B. (1991) 'Security in the chemical industry and the education of the chemical engineer.' *The Education of the Chemical Engineer in Greece*, April.

Markatos, N. and Rigas, P. (1991) 'Security-hygiene-environment: the last (perhaps) hope for (part) application of the profession of the chemical engineer in Greece.' *The Education of the Chemical Engineer in Greece*, April.

Onida, F. (1986) 'Economia: per una Cultura Generalistica.' In *Università Progetto* No. 14/15, Giugno-Luglio 1986, 42–45.

Perez Vera, E. (1990) 'La Reforma de las Enseñanzas Universitarias.' In *Politica Cientjfica 25*, 6–8.

Sdralevich, A. (1985) 'Le proposte per la Facoltà di Economia.' In *Università Progetto* No. 3/4, Giugno-Luglio 1985, 20–24.

Secretaria de Estado do Ensino Superior (1991) *O Ensino Superior no XI Governo.* Lisboa: Secretaria de Estado do Ensino Superior.

Wielemans, W., Vanderhoeven, J.L., Delmelle, R. and Phillipart, A. (1991) 'Higher education and scientific research.' In J.L. Vanderhoeven (ed) (1991) *Education in Belgium: The Diverging Paths.* (OECD: Review of National Policies for Education). Brussel-Bruxelles-Eupen: Ministerie van de Vlaamse Gemeenschap, Departement Onderwijs-Ministères de l'Education, de la Recherche et de la formation-Verwaltung der Deutschsprachigen Gemeinschaft, Abteilung Unterricht.

Subject Index

Name Index